67

WALES IN HISTORY

BOOK III, 1485-1760

SIR HUGH MYDDELTON (1560-1631)

A typical Tudor-Stuart 'adventurer', industrialist and man of affairs in his native Wales, and goldsmith, merchant and public benefactor in his adopted London.

WALES IN HISTORY · BOOK III · 1485–1760

THE ADVENTURERS

BY

DAVID FRASER

UNIVERSITY OF WALES PRESS
CARDIFF
1976

© UNIVERSITY OF WALES PRESS 1976
ISBN 0 7083 0610 1

WALES IN HISTORY

Earlier volumes by David Fraser:

Book I, *The Invaders:* to 1066, Second Edition 1965.

Book II, *The Defenders:* 1066–1485, 1967, Reprinted 1975.

In Welsh:

Cyf I: *Y Goresgynwyr* (translation by T. H. Parry-Williams) 1966, Reprinted 1975.

Cyf II: *Yr Amddiffynwyr* (translation by Bedwyr Lewis Jones) 1967.

Printed by CSP Printing of Cardiff

TO
A. AND K.

PREFACE

This third book in the series is intended for both the upper forms of secondary schools (including 'O' and 'A' level examination classes) and the general reader. The suggested Exercises are accordingly set apart as an Appendix. The main aim is still the same: to present the story of Wales in the wider context of British, European and World History.

The writers to whom I owe an obvious and enormous debt are a host too numerous to name. Grateful tribute, albeit too small, is paid to them in the Extracts appended to each chapter and in the References.

To some, however, I owe special thanks: to Professor David Williams, whose classic 'Modern Wales' inspired the work; to Professor Glanmor Williams, the outstanding contributor on the sixteenth century, for his most helpful reading of the typescript; to my colleague Mr. D. Aneurin Thomas who kindly read the first draft; to Dr. Margaret Davies for her attractive execution of the maps and diagrams; to Dr. R. Brinley Jones of the University Press for his unfailing encouragement and sure guidance over long years; to Miss Lowri Morgan, also of the University Press, for her care in marshalling the illustrative material; to CSP Printing of Cardiff for their immaculate work; and to Mrs. Doreen Hughes of Menai Bridge for her speedy and careful typing. To them all I am sincerely grateful.

1976   *DAVID FRASER*

CONTENTS

LIST OF ILLUSTRATIONS, MAPS AND CHARTS

CHAPTER I

INTRODUCTION

Th is book covers almost three centuries of Welsh History. At the outset, a fugitive from Wales returns to win the crown of England. Fifty years later his son officially unites the two countries. Wales still keeps much of her identity in her law-courts, her literature and of course her language, but in general her destiny tends to be swallowed up in that of England. Her story must therefore be studied in the context of English history, and both in turn against a European and even a world-wide background. Inevitably we shall often be describing Welshmen who adventured outside Wales. For, as Professor A. H. Dodd reminds us, these 'London Welsh . . . played a vital part in the evolution of Wales'.*

During Tudor and Stuart times there is an air of apparent inertia, certainly of compliance about the people of Wales. They fall in—more perhaps than the English—with the establishment, with, that is, Crown and Church in England. Here in Wales there is no rebellion of any size, for Reformation or Counter Reformation, against poverty, or in support of a Jacobite; no national movement or upsurge of national feeling until the Revival of the eighteenth century. It is true that Welshmen figure largely in the Civil War 1642–48, but only out of personal loyalty to local gentry, to king or, rarely, to parliament, and not for any Welsh national reason and certainly not on any nation-wide plan of campaign.

Yet it is a period rich in prominent individuals. It is this which gives the story its obviously biographical approach. Almost all its characters are of the class of gentry. If the history of Wales in the

---

* A. H. Dodd: *Studies in Stuart Wales*, p. 46.

Middle Ages centred on its castles, in this early Modern Period
it focuses on its country houses. This book might well be called
The Gentry. Such a title, however, would be misleading in imply-
ing that our concern is with this more evident, more assertive
class alone. Nor does it suggest the variety, colour and excitement of the very active life of the period.

It seemed more appropriate to title the story *The Adventurers*.
For it tells of men, and women, who dare to venture, be it to
fight for fame and freedom like Sir Roger Williams, to buccaneer
in the Spanish Main like Thomas Prys, to open a lead-mine like
a Myddelton or a Mackworth, to translate the whole Bible single-
handed like William Morgan, to promote a nation-wide system
of reading it like Griffith Jones, or simply to amass a family-
empire by marriage like Katheryn of Berain. They are all adventurers in the sense that they undertake tasks with a high risk
of failure; indeed they often do fail, like martyred Richard Gwyn
or John Penry in the sixteenth century, eccentric William
Vaughan who pioneered a Welsh colony in Newfoundland in
the seventeenth, or loyal David Morgan who died for the Young
Pretender in the eighteenth. There are 'adventurers' too in the
less reputable sense of the word—knights like John Perrot, the
master-mind of smugglers, or John Wynn the wily squire of
Gwydir, and pirates like Henry Morgan and Black Barty Roberts.

Geography must as ever be kept in mind in the study. It is
the fundamental factor in such features as the altered global position of Wales, the overwhelming difficulties of communication,
the fact that the Civil War was fought around the perimeter of
Wales and only rarely at its centre, and the phenomenon of both
Catholic and Puritan extremists worshipping in pockets along the
Welsh border, 'a land', says Dr. Thomas Richards, 'where persecution was paralysed by geography' *Constant reference should
accordingly be made to the many maps given here, and always
with the underlying physical features in mind.

The Original Extracts at the end of each chapter also deserve
detailed study. Like the Illustrations they should be not only of

---

* Thomas Richards: *Wales under the Penal Code*, p. *107*.

interest in themselves, but serve to fill out references in the text, and provide material for the Exercises which are appended. Most important of all, they pay tribute to the chief researches from which the material of the book is taken, and so, with the brief Bibliography, provide further lines of study.

Our story begins with the accession of Harry Tudor and ends with the death of Griffith Jones in 1761. So when, as ancient legend foretold, the Welsh nation emerged from some dark cave after its long sleep, it was led not by a soldier with a drawn sword—an Arthur, an Owain Lawgoch or a Glyndŵr—but by a preacher/teacher with a Bible in his hand. His was an enterprise designed specifically for the common people of Wales and not for her gentry alone. With him we stride into the period of The Democrats.

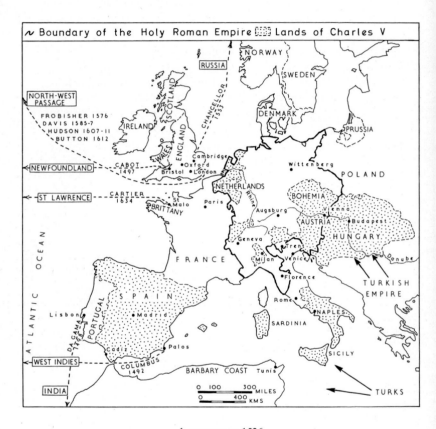

1. EUROPE IN 1526

CHAPTER II

THE MODERN PERIOD: RENAISSANCE AND REFORMATION

WHEN Henry VII won this throne at Bosworth in 1485, Wales stood on the fringe of a world that was changing. In seven years' time Columbus would land in the West Indies and Wales would thereafter be at the centre of the western world.

Henry's world, however, was changing in much more than in this physical sense. In 1450 the average European was still a "medieval" with his whole outlook conditioned by the dictates of the universal Church. By 1550 his attitude to culture, to politics, to religion, even to every day life and work is more akin to our own. He has become a 'modern'. This chapter will review the main features of Modern times which appeared in this very active century of change which is called broadly the Renaissance period.

'Renaissance' means 'rebirth' and was originally applied to the revival of the classical culture of Greece and Rome, particularly in the rich cities of Italy. This, however, was but one aspect of a new outlook, the keyword of which is Humanism. Simply, this means an interest in man as man. The medieval Church had thought of man in relation to the world to come; the Humanist would think of him as a creature of worth in the "here and now". This new attitude would make the artist and sculptor present the nobility and beauty of his body as it is; the man of science to accept only the facts of life as they are; the geographer to fashion his maps by accurate survey and not by hearsay; the politician and man of affairs, alas, to consider only his own personal good or that of his own country.

In short, Humanism permeated every aspect of life and the word 'Renaissance' takes on a broader meaning covering the new learning, new 'nation-states', new beliefs, new lands and new economy.

NEW LEARNING

The 'High' Renaissance reached its peak in roughly the period 1490-1536. With it we connect the outstanding work in architecture, painting, sculpture and science of Leonardo da Vinci, Raphael and Michelangelo. This exciting fashion was essentially the product of wealth, of leisure and of town life: it flourished particularly in Rome, under the patronage of popes like Julius II and Leo X, in Florence and later in Venice.

The spread of the Renaissance was, of course, dependent upon easy communication. Geographically, the old trade routes, particularly those across the Alps and down the great artery of the Rhineland, facilitated its movements northwards, until it reached the narrow seas and was carried eventually to England and even Wales.* As it went, the movement seemed to react to the colder climate. It became less visual and more verbal, less concerned with architecture, painting and sculpture and more with words and books, less colourful but more thoughtful. Here the tremendous factor in communication was the printing-press.[1] Thanks to the easy multiplication of copies, the new learning became more broad-based, less aristocratic and more democratic, appealing now to all ranks of men who could read. In particular there came a demand in all countries for the printed word in the native tongue or vernacular.[2] The importance of this to the wider reading of the Scriptures is obvious.

NEW 'NATION-STATES'

The political feature of the Modern Period is the rise of nation states. These, however, were centred as yet not so much

---

* We must remember that the traffic of the Renaissance was not altogether one-way. Painting in oils originated in the Netherlands, and the printing press in Germany, though it is true that the type we now generally use was designed in Italy.

NOTE: The references numbered in the text are not to footnotes but to relevant Extracts at the end of each chapter.

on the will of the nation as on the strength of the monarch or dynasty. They had appeared in the western countries long before the Italian Renaissance and owe little to Italy. But it was now, contemporary with the Italian (High) Renaissance, that England, France and Spain in particular finally became strong, separate national states under Henry VIII, Francis I and Charles V, respectively. Kings were no longer merely the first among their baronial equals, but distinct autocrats ruling alone, and, they claimed, by divine right. Their kingdoms now acquired most of the characteristics of a present-day state: national boundaries, often established at the expense of smaller neighbours (Brittany annexed by France and Wales by England, for example); a distinct national language (though Switzerland happily accepted three); a national army and navy, though not permanent at first; a nation-wide system of regular taxation; a diplomatic service concerned with maintaining the national interest in "balanced" relations with neighbours; and a national policy for regulating the country's wealth and work. These features were not of course as evident in the sixteenth century as they are today; nor were they all present in every country. Even so they stood in marked contrast to the characteristics of the Middle Ages.

By 1520 these national units had taken their place on the map of Europe (see page 4). In England Henry VIII ruled as an autocrat though, like all his family, he was aware of the will of his people. Wales he united to England in 1536, but Scotland under its Stuart kings and Ireland under its tribal chiefs remained restless and independent.

Charles V now ruled not only Spain but also southern Italy, Sicily and Sardinia, the Netherlands and Austria and vast uncharted tracts in the New World. Not since Charlemagne had one man held so much of Europe; the pity was that the several parts of his empire were so diverse in race and so scattered. In 1519 too he was elected Holy Roman Emperor. Not that the title of Holy Roman Emperor was altogether a blessing. The Empire was a loose federation of some 350 states and cities of varying sizes and different nationalities, including Austria,

Switzerland and northern Italy. Nominally ruled by the Emperor and his Diet or representative council, it had little unity, all its princes, bishops, knights and cities pursuing their own ends.

France, by contrast, was already much the same square block of country that she is today. Francis I (1515–47) succeeded to this strongest monarchy in Europe, ruling all-powerful with the aid of a well-organized civil service.

Italy alone had no single ruler. It was divided by the jealousies of its enormously rich city-states of Milan, Venice, Florence, Rome (the Papacy) and Naples, and lay at the mercy of its powerful neighbours, all of whom claimed parts of it.

It seems to us that these rich, powerful states now had a grand opportunity to pool their resources and unite for the common good, perhaps to develop the vast New World in the west or defeat the ever-encroaching Turks in the east. Alas, the pursuit of national interest tended to fragment rather than to unite Europe. National pride and national power made for international conflict rather than concord.

The rivalry of France and Spain was the main factor in the conflict. For more than sixty years, 1494–1559 they fought for land and loot in Italy. An event of importance which did stem from the Italian Renaissance was the publication in 1513 of The Prince by an Italian political thinker, Machiavelli. In it he declared boldly that the ruthless 'power-politics' of the warring princes was justified in the national interest.[3] Another significant event was the sack of Rome in 1527 when the Pope was made a prisoner by Charles V of Spain. Finally, exhausted, the combatants agreed to the Treaty of Cateau Cambrésis of 1559. Italy, her lands and cities devasted, became a colony of Spain for a century and a half, with her national unity delayed for three centuries.

Henry VII managed by careful diplomacy to keep England out of the ding-dong struggle. Henry VIII however, aided by his chancellor Thomas Wolsey, joined in, lining up first with Spain and then in 1527 against her, a step which proved disastrous in view of his attempt to divorce his Spanish wife. Thereafter Henry and his successors, Edward VI and Mary were occupied to the exclusion of all else with the 'ups-and-downs' of the Reformation—the struggle between Catholic and Protestant.

NEW BELIEFS

The High Renaissance in Italy in one direct sense brought about the Reformation. The vast sums needed to build palaces and to adorn them with paintings and sculptures by the masters emptied the purses of pope after pope and notably that of Leo X (1513–21), the great Renaissance patron who was challenged by Luther and Zwingli.

The church was certainly in need of reform. We shall detail its state in Wales in Chapter III. Here it is enough to say that the hierarchy of pope, cardinal, bishop, abbot, monk and friar was generally lazy, and often criminal, guilty of selling offices in the church (simony), of holding too many of them by one individual (pluralism), or of giving them to family relations (nepotism). But there had been spendthrift popes before, and protests too

By permission of the National Portrait Gallery, London
2. TWO REFORMING HUMANIST FRIENDS
(a) Erasmus   (b) Sir Thomas More.

from honest men like St. Francis. But they had all been silenced. Three factors made the situation in the Europe of Erasmus and Luther wholly new and different: the critical power of humanist thought; the strength of national feeling; and, perhaps above all, the propaganda value of printing.

The early Reformation was the work mainly of two monks, Erasmus and Luther. Erasmus (1466–1536) is *the* great humanist and cosmopolitan. Born a Dutchman, he was really a man for all Europe. He journeyed extensively in it discussing and corresponding with thinkers and rulers everywhere. He visited England in 1499 and made his home there during 1509–14. In many books such as his *Praise of Folly* he poured scorn on the priests and monks of his day for their loose-living and neglect of the simple essentials of Christian teaching. More constructively, he edited afresh the works of the ancient Christian fathers, and published in 1516 a revised Greek text and Latin translation of the New Testament, believing all too hopefully that once men could read Christ's teaching for themselves they would follow it and unite to restore the church. For Erasmus, in spite of all his criticism, remained a good Catholic.[4a]

In the following year a German monk, Martin Luther (1483–1546) nailed to the church door of Wittenberg a list of ninety-five arguments condemning indulgences.[4b] These were documents sold by the Pope's agents; in popular belief, the purchaser was assured everything from the forgiveness of past sin to a guarantee of heaven in the future. Luther's protest caused an outcry, but he refused to retract. He was excommunicated by the pope and banned by the emperor Charles V and went into hiding. He backed his protest with a translation of the New Testament into German and by composing hymns for congregational singing. His popular appeal as a result was enormous. Suddenly this emotional, self-searching monk found himself riding on the crest of a wave of national as well as religious feeling. Many princes now jumped on this 'band-waggon' and used the Lutheran protest for their own political and commercial gain. When the downtrodden peasants, however, saw in it salvation from their

3. AN INDULGENCE: THE OLDEST PRINTED SHEET FROM WALES

From Strata Marcella Abbey, 1528-9. Curiously enough the first known printed
sheet relating to England also is an Indulgence from the Abbey of Abingdon,
dated 1476. Extract 1, page 37 gives a translation of the illustrated Indulgence.

misery and revolted in 1525, Luther, fearing anarchy, condemned
them. Thus quickly Protestantism had become a political force
dividing the princes. The Emperor, distracted by the wars in
Italy and the Turkish menace, was helpless to interfere on behalf
of Catholicism. Gradually the opposing rulers formed two military camps and war broke out in 1547. Finally, at Augsburg in
1555 it was agreed that each prince should decide whether his
state should be Catholic or Lutheran. No other belief would be
recognized. The Peace of Augsburg was unsatisfactory, but it
lasted for sixty-three years until in 1618 there broke out the
Thirty Years' War, the most savage religious conflict of all time.
Erasmus's scorn and Luther's protest had irrevocably split the
Church and destroyed the Empire.

Meanwhile in Switzerland, still nominally a part of the Empire, two humanists and followers of Erasmus had in turn derived from the Scriptures a faith even more advanced than Lutheranism and, ultimately, far wider in its world-wide extent. Contemporary with Luther, Zwingli attacked not only indulgences and the authority of the Pope but also some of the deep-seated beliefs of Catholicism such as transubstantiation,* celibacy and purgatory. Soon the cantons of Switzerland were divided like the states of Germany between the old religion and the new. Here again came a brief war ending with an agreement that each canton should democratically decide its creed for itself. Zwingli was killed in the fighting, but what he had begun was later taken up and vastly extended by John Calvin (1509–64) a humanist lawyer who had been driven out of France by Francis I's persecution of non-Catholics and had settled in Geneva. In the year of Erasmus's death, 1536, Calvin wrote his *Institutes of the Christian Religion*, the greatest of his many works. In it his interpretation of the Scriptures was even more logical, severe and far reaching. All men are by nature damned, he declared, but God in his infinite goodness has elected to save some.[4c] This iron doctrine of Predestination and the Elect became an essential canon in the Calvinist faith the world over, including of course the Calvinistic Methodism which by the nineteenth century had become a major creed of Wales.

The great surge of the Reformation inevitably brought its own reaction. Good Catholics like Erasmus had long seen the need to put their church in order. About 1530 a movement gathered momentum to reform the old church from within, to marshal its defences, and then to attack Protestantism at its heart. This we call the Counter Reformation.

The lead came, not unnaturally, from the popes. Paul III and Paul IV in the period 1534–59 abandoned much of their own wordly ambitions, set up commissions to inquire into abuses, and

---

* *Transubstantiation*—the conversion of the bread and wine at Holy Communion (Eucharist) into the body and blood of Christ.
Celibacy—remaining unmarried.
Purgatory—state or place of spiritual cleansing between dying and attaining paradise.

called a general council of the church to put them right. For eighteen years (1545–63) this Council of Trent, on the border of Italy and Austria, argued out questions of dogma and reform, bedevilled by the bickering of Protestant and Catholic in the early meetings, and of the different national groups at all times. Finally, the 'hard-liners' won, and Catholic doctrine was re-stated clearly and without compromise.

Meanwhile, a new Catholic army had been recruited by Ignatius Loyola, a remarkable Spanish soldier turned saint. His Society of Jesus was approved by Paul III in 1540. The Jesuits were 'plain-clothes priests' sworn to poverty and chastity and to obedience to their General and the Pope in whatever field, how-ever far-flung, to which they might be sent.[4d] Intelligent, dedicated, resourceful, and often ruthless, they pursued the aims of re-formed Catholicism relentlessly. In so doing, however, they achieved much for the arts and for education.

Catholicism also found a new weapon in the Inquisition. This was a sort of secret police, revived by Paul IV in 1542 and governed by a group of cardinals, which was empowered to deal with heretics by imprisonment, torture and even death if neces-sary. In its attempt to check all 'dangerous' thought the In-quisition realized significantly the need to restrict the power of the printing press. In 1559 was issued the first 'Index' or list of censored books. An approved book, even today, bears the stamp of the censor with the words *Nihil Obstat*—'nothing stands in the way'. This might well be the motto of the whole Counter-Reformation.

By 1559 then, the Catholic Church was ready to move to the attack, its dignity restored in the reformed papacy, its authority reaffirmed in the Council of Trent, its soldiers enlisted in the Jesuits, and its sword sharpened in the Inquisition.

Thus by the middle of the sixteenth century the Reformation had spread a patchwork of belief over the map of once-Catholic Europe. In the south, in Italy, Spain and Portugal, Catholicism and the authority of the Pope remained unchallenged. In Scandinavia and northern Germany the Lutheranism of the

princes was equally predominant. In the middle the Netherlands,
Switzerland and Bohemia were divided between Catholicism and
Calvinism. France remained Catholic under the control of its
monarchs, but it had a growing Calvinist minority in the industrious Huguenots of the south west. Ireland in the misty west
remained firmly Catholic, but Scotland was becoming rapidly
Calvinist under John Knox. Chapter V will tell how England
and Wales broke with the pope, and swung from the Catholicism
of Henry VIII to the Lutheranism of Edward VI and back again
to the Catholicism of Mary.

NEW LANDS

The Modern Period is most clearly distinguished from the
Medieval by the 'Oceanic Revolution' brought about by the
voyages of discovery at the end of the fifteenth century. The
Renaissance revived interest in Greek scientists like Ptolemy.
Scholars now accepted that the world was round. But it was the
voyages of Columbus to the west in 1492 and of Vasco da Gama
to the east in 1498 that turned the legends of the Viking voyagers
and of Madog the Welshman* into fact. The world of here-and-
now would increasingly become a much vaster place with
almost unlimited possibilities for enterprise and exploitation.
Hereafter Humanist man must think world-wide.

The voyages had a marked effect upon every other aspect of
the Renaissance. Politically, it brought a weighty factor into the
rivalry of the nation-states of the west, resembling that between
the U.S.A. and Russia over Space in our own day. Columbus had
sailed for Spain and Vasco da Gama for Portugal, and by 1500
these two countries, with the Pope's blessing, had divided the
whole new world between them. Magellan's ship in circum-
navigating the globe in 1520 laid the seal upon their monopoly.
The other princes of the west, however, resented being made
interlopers if they ventured into the oceans. Henry VII had
already in 1497 employed an Italian captain, John Cabot, and a
Bristol crew to sail west and discover Newfoundland. Francis I

* See *The Invaders* p. 152.

By permission of the National Museum of Wales

4. A COIN OF CHARLES V

A German silver coin, a 'thaler' (from which derives our English word 'dollar') from Kempten, Bavaria, dated 1541; in the name of the Holy Roman Emperor, Charles V. Found on a beach in South Wales in 1972. The Latin on the obverse reads KAROLVS-V-ROMA(norum) : IMP(erator) : SEMP(er) : AVGV(stus).

sent Jacques Cartier on much the same route in 1534 to plant the Cross and the French flag at the mouth of the St. Lawrence, the gateway to Canada. Thus the English and French challenged the right of the Spaniards to North America, and early in the seventeenth century the Dutch ousted the Portuguese in the Far East.

The new lands, secondly played their part in the religious changes. America in particular became the receptacle for the spill-over from the turmoil of the Reformation. When the Counter-reformation failed in Europe, Catholic priest and Jesuit found consolation and a new empire in Central and South America. And in the next century the faithful of every creed, men like John Miles and his Welsh Baptists in 1663,* rejected in their homeland, sailed to the west to find new homes and establish the United States.

The voyagers and colonists took with them, thirdly, much of the new culture and outlook of the Renaissance. In Central America and Peru, conversely, they found ancient civilizations of great wealth and magnificence. Much of these, alas, they

* See below, p. 239.

merely robbed and destroyed, leaving the remnants to be fully
appreciated at last by our own twentieth century.

NEW ECONOMY

It was in the field of trade and industry and national wealth,
fourthly, that the discoveries had the greatest effect, for they
revealed enormous possibilities for raw materials, new markets
and precious metals. The new lands offered escape from poverty
in Old Europe to many like William Vaughan, the scholarly
Carmarthenshire squire who in 1617 founded the ill-fated Welsh
colony of Cambriol in Newfoundland.* English sea-captains in
particular sought new ways to reach the riches of the east without
crossing the sea-lanes of Spaniard and Portuguese. Thus Willoughby and Chancellor in 1553 sought a north-east passage
through the Arctic Sea. Poor Willoughby and his men, including
his Welsh carpenter, cook and purser, died in the frozen wastes.
But Chancellor reached the White Sea and Russia and clinched
a profitable trading arrangement which became the Muscovy
Company. Similarly the voyages of Frobisher, Davis and Hudson,
though they failed to find the north-west passage, led to the
establishment of the Hudson Bay Company in 1670. Gradually
profitable oceanic ventures like these served to move the centres
of commerce from the cities of the Mediterranean, like Venice
and Genoa, to the western seaboard and especially to England
and the Low Countries. To this the life of Richard Clough,
merchant of Denbigh and Bruges, bears witness.†

It was the import by Spain of vast quantities of bullion, gold
and especially silver from America that had the most immediate
effect on the economy of Europe. In the short-term it was a
major factor in the predominance of Spain in the sixteenth
century; in the long-term it caused her decay in the seventeenth.
It was a prime cause, secondly, of the disastrous rise in prices all
over Europe which impoverished monarch and peasant alike. It
led the rulers of Europe into accepting the misguided theories

* See below, p. 174.
† See below, p. 123.

which go under the name of Mercantilism: that bullion is the basis of national greatness; that wealth and trade are fixed quantities and one nation can get more of them only by robbing another; and, less misguidedly perhaps, that to import raw materials and export manufactured goods would increase a country's gold reserves. The monarchs and ministers of Western Europe, such as Elizabeth of England and her Welsh chancellor Cecil, accordingly set themselves to encourage trade and promote and regulate industry.

All this, of course, was merely to promote on a national scale the growth of individual enterprise for profit-making which had been a feature of agriculture and industry in England and Wales for more than a century.*

* See *The Defenders* p. 177.

ORIGINAL EXTRACTS

1   THE WORTH OF PRINTING:
    the admirable art of Printing . . . an inuention so excellent and so usefull, so much tending to the honour of God, the manifestation of the truth, propagation of the Gospell, restoration of learning, diffusion of knowledge.
              (Jourdan, 1610: from R. Brinley Jones: *The Old British Tongue*, p. 22)

2   THE WORTH OF THE VERNACULAR:
    Good cause have we therefore to gyue thankes unto certayne godlye and well learned men, whych by their greate studye enrychynge our tongue both wyth matter and wordes, haue endeuoured to make it so copyous and plentyfull that therein it maye compare wyth anye other whiche so euer is the best.
                                      (Sherry, 1550: *ibid* p. 27)

3   MACHIAVELLI GIVES ADVICE:
    there are two ways of contending—one in accordance with the laws, the other by force; the first of which is proper to men, the second to beasts. But since the first method is often ineffectual, it becomes necessary to resort to the second. A prince should therefore understand how to use well both the man and the beast.
                                      (*Il Principe*, chap. 21)

4a   REFORMATION STATEMENTS:

(a) ERASMUS ON MODERATION: The two parties are dragging at the opposite ends of a rope. When it breaks they will both fall on their backs. . . . let there be moderation in all things, and then we may hope for peace.

(J. A. Froude: *Life of Erasmus*, pp. 344–5)

4b   LUTHER ON INDULGENCES (in his 95 theses of 1517)
Thesis 21: Those preachers of indulgences are in error who say that by the indulgences of the pope a man is freed and saved from all punishment
Thesis 43: Christians should be taught that he who gives to a poor man, or lends to a needy man, does better than if he bought pardons

4c   CALVIN ON PREDESTINATION: (from his *Institutions*) We indeed attribute to God both predestination and foreknowledge. . . . By predestination we mean the eternal decree of God, by which He has decided in His own mind what He wishes to happen in the case of each individual . . . for some eternal life is preordained, and for others eternal damnation.

(H. Bettenson: *Documents of the Christian Church*, pp. 299–300)

4d   LOYOLA ON OBEDIENCE: That we may be altogether of the same mind and in conformity with the Church herself, if she shall have defined anything to be black which to our eyes appears to be white, we ought in like manner to pronounce it to be black.

(*ibid*, p. 363)

CHAPTER III

THE LAST MEDIEVALS

IT took many years for the great changes we described in the last chapter to reach Britain. During the reign of Henry VII, however, there appeared the first ripples of the tide that would come flooding in during the later years of his son Henry VIII. This chapter will tell the story of the first half-century of Tudor rule. In it 'adventures' are few; it is a period of preparation and promise on which the foundations of Tudor policy and of the New Learning are laid.

HENRY VII

Henry Tudor is the first of our adventurers. As we saw in *The Defenders*, he had lived dangerously for the first twenty-eight years of his life. Now in 1485 he had marched, greatly daring, through his native Wales into England and won its crown. Looking back over the previous thirty years of bitter warfare, the odds were against his holding it for long. He did not have our hindsight to know that the Wars of the Roses were over. Henry is thus like a traveller who walks slowly forward but keeps looking back over his shoulder, more concerned to hold what by good fortune he has got than to start new enterprises. In this sense he is the last of the medieval kings rather than the first of the modern.*

Henry's great aim was dynastic: to establish himself and his family on the throne. All his other concerns stem from this: restoring and keeping order at home: maintaining peace abroad by diplomacy and not by military show; building up the crown

---

* It is perhaps typical that Henry VII never used the new-fashioned cannon which he bought—he preferred the bow and arrow!

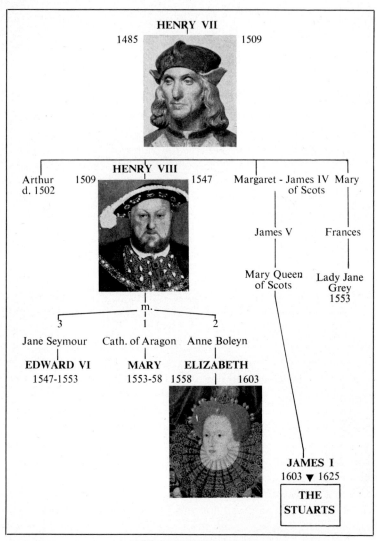

THE TUDOR FAMILY

Bust of Henry VII: 'Crown Copyright, Victoria & Albert Museum'. Portraits of
Henry VIII and Elizabeth by permission of the Radio Times Hulton Picture
Library.

finances by good accounting, by trade, and by barefaced extortion of money from those who had it to spare. All this he did, but not by methods that were new. The court of Star Chamber and the Statutes of Livery and Maintenance of 1504, which he used to put down 'strong-arm' gangs of overmighty nobles and their retainers, had both been employed before. So had the financial devices that made him a millionaire. Parliament was to him as to his predecessors merely an instrument to serve his sovereign will; he called it only six times in all, and only once in his last fourteen years. Justices of the Peace had been appointed in England long before Henry used them to maintain local government.

What made Henry's rule 'different' and 'new' was the fresh life he put into these older devices; what made him now an 'adventurer' was daring to rely on himself. He ruled in the strength of his victory in battle and of his own personality. This personal strength of the two Henries and Elizabeth is the secret of Tudor success. Henry had the Tudor shrewdness too for choosing helpers, a few from the nobility, more from the church and many from the middle-class; but in the end he relied on himself. Thus he recovered again the central power of the monarch which Edward I had possessed. On the forms and cere-monies that emphasize kingship this careful man *would* spend money. His one novel creation was the Yeomen of the Guard, 250 men, many of them Welshmen, sworn to defend the person of the king and thus 'the first permanent military force' in England.

Henry VII stands in history as a lonely, self-reliant figure; a man whom history respects but cannot love. Yet, two marks of a modern state England certainly had when he died in 1509: the predominance of the sovereign and the support of his people.

HENRY VII AND WALES

Henry's caution and conservatism is nowhere better shown than in his dealing with Wales. From there, two main factors had brought him victory at Bosworth: first, a wave of national enthusiasm; second, the support of a number of go-ahead and largely self-seeking gentry. The latter he quickly rewarded. His ever-faithful uncle, Jasper Tudor, became the duke of Bedford and was given great lands in South Wales including the earldom of Pembroke and the lordship of Glamorgan. Rhys ap Thomas, already knighted at Bosworth, also received wide estates and became the virtual ruler of the southern Principality of Cardigan and Carmarthen. The Stanleys similarly secured lordships in north-east Wales and control of the northern Principality. There were many lesser men too whose families rose to wealth and power thanks to Henry's favour: soldiers like Rhys ap Meredydd (founder of the Prys family of Plas Iolyn) and Llewelyn ap Heilyn (founder of the Meyricks of Bodorgan), lawyers like John Morgan, even abbots like Dafydd ab Owain of Valle Crucis. Scores of Welshmen too were freed from the Penal Laws by Henry's grant of letters of denizenship. This enabled them not only to accept good jobs in Wales but also to follow the king to England and there fill offices in the church, in the law courts, in business, and particularly at the royal court. A particular favourite was Charles Somerset whom Henry used at court and abroad. Rewarded with many offices and broad lands, he built up the great family of the earls of Worcester of Raglan which became the most powerful in all Wales, enormously wealthy and unique in keeping in effect the authority of a marcher-lord for two centuries in spite of the Act of Union and the Council of Wales. The several branches of their relatives, the Herberts, rose with the Somersets.

In this way Henry secured loyal friends who would have a vested interest in supporting him. He also gave direction to the 'brain-drain' to England which increasingly marks Wales of the Tudors.

But for the Wales which as a nation had shouldered him to Bosworth he did little. Probably he did not yet think of her as a nation in the way we would. It is true that he had his lineage traced back to ancient British kings, paraded the dragon of Cadwaladr on his coins and flags, and gave the name Arthur to his eldest son. All this, however, he did not so much to emphasize his Welshness as to indicate the antiquity of his family. Henry was a Tudor first and a Welshman only second.

His boyhood years as a fugitive moving between Pembroke and Merioneth and Chepstow must have shown him how much Wales needed a new deal. But his natural caution warned him that as yet it was too much of an Augean stable for him to clean. Politically Wales was backward and disordered. It still had the structure that Edward I had given it two centuries earlier :* the five shires of the Principality in the west, Flintshire in the north-east and the great jumble of marcher-lordships that claimed the remainder. The marcher-lordships with their own courts, taxes and officials had long been the breeding-ground of misrule, injustice and rebellion. Their bands of retainers acted like Chicago gangsters of our own times, intimidating juries, harbouring criminals, and exacting forced loans from their 'subjects', often to pay the fines imposed on the marchers for serious crimes like murder. Unfortunately for Henry, among them were many whom he had newly rewarded for their support. So that for the time being, gratitude tied his hands.

Social life had deteriorated in the political disorder. Wales had shared with England in the devastations of the Black Death and the Wars of the Roses; but even greater than either had been the awful ruin of the Glyndŵr Rebellion† which she alone had borne. By 1500, it is true, general prosperity had returned, as the revival in architecture‡ proves, but in the legal confusion which remained criminals, brigands and vagabonds prospered, life was insecure for the ordinary man, and the weak went to the wall. The Penal Laws§ too denied Welshmen equality before the law with Englishmen, and laid annoying restraints upon their movement and advancement. They were probably not rigidly enforced;

* See *The Defenders*, Chapter X.
† Ibid., pp. 180 and 187.
‡ See below, p. 28.
§ *The Defenders*, pp. 214–215.

but the stigma remained. Nor had Welshmen a voice in Parliament; only twice ever had representatives been summoned from Wales and then in the reign of the feeble Edward II.

In the second half of his reign Henry made some attempt to improve law and order by giving wider powers to the Council of the Prince of Wales which Edward IV had established in 1471. In 1501 he re-constituted the Council, and although Prince Arthur died within a few months, Henry's growing interest in Wales continued. The political position was easier too, for more and more marcher lordships came into his hands. In 1495 alone he took possession of Pembroke and Glamorgan at the death of Jasper Tudor, of lands in mid-Wales by purchase, and of a crop of lordships in north-east Wales by the treason of Sir William Stanley whom he summarily executed. Between 1505 and 1508 he granted charters to the people of the Northern Principality and all the lordships that later made up Denbighshire and much of Montgomeryshire. His aim was probably to please some of the gentry who were building up large estates or interests in trade; he certainly made them pay for them! But he did so in the face of loud protest from English burgesses in Wales. The privileges the charters bestowed included freedom from the Penal Laws, the abolition of serfdom, and the use of the English system of primogeniture (inheritance of the first-born only) instead of the outdated Welsh system of *cyfran* or gavelkind (inheritance by all male heirs). At least, in shedding these medieval remnants Henry showed that he was at last looking straight ahead!

HENRY VIII: FIRST PERIOD 1509–30

Henry VIII appeared a quite different 'adventurer' from his father whom he succeeded in 1509. He was young, athletic, exciting, popular, secure on his throne, and as carefree in spending money as the first Tudor had been careful in saving it. Yet, at heart, he was very much 'a chip off the old block', even more ruthless in meeting any challenge to his kingship, just as sensitive to popular support, equally shrewd in picking his helpers. In particular, as he grew older his concern to maintain his dynasty grew to be an obsession.

In his early years Henry acted the part of a medieval prince. He strongly defended the Pope against Luther. He sought military glory rather in the lavish style of the Middle Ages. Not for him the dreary details of state management which his hard-working father had handled himself. These he left to Thomas Wolsey, the remarkable man who for nearly twenty years was the 'general manager' in England.

Abroad, Henry's early victories in 1515 against the French at the Battle of the Spurs and against the Scots at Flodden cost him his fortune. Wolsey at first showed great diplomatic skill in trying to maintain the 'balance of power' between the new rival monarchs of France and Spain, while at the same time promoting his own advancement in the church. But in the end the cardinal showed himself over-clever, and by 1529 England had lost face abroad, and Spain was clearly victor, with Rome sacked (1527) and the Pope a prisoner in the hands of the Emperor Charles V.

At home, Wolsey did better. He pursued forward-looking policies with success. Through the Court of Star Chamber he brought the nobility to heel, and through the Court of Requests he gave cheap and speedy justice to humbler folk. He saw the need to reform the church, and closed fifty monasteries, using much of their wealth to endow colleges. He foresaw the evils of large-scale enclosures, and won praise from best minds like Sir Thomas More for his attempts to control them.

Wolsey at last fell a victim to his own and his master's insatiable pride and greed. Only a divorce from his first wife, Catherine of Aragon, would meet Henry's passion for Anne Boleyn and his anxious desire for a male heir. But Wolsey could get a divorce only from the Pope, and he was still held prisoner by Charles V, who had no wish to see his aunt Catherine belittled by a bankrupt king whom he had outwitted. So the cardinal failed, was discarded by his king in 1529, and died under arrest a year later.

Cardinal Wolsey was the last of the great medieval churchmen. Yet his one sure achievement was to direct the king in the way of a future Renaissance prince. As 'viceroy for Henry and deputy

for the Pope', he had shown that one man could rule both State
and Church. Henry could do the same. The changes the king
brought about after 1530 as a result will be described in the next
two chapters. They were revolutionary. —

HENRY VIII AND WALES

For Wales, Henry in the first twenty-five years of his reign did
even less than his father. He continued to give favour to Welshmen who were useful to him. Charles Somerset, for example,
was further rewarded with the earldom of Worcester for his
bravery at the Battle of the Spurs. But a generation had passed
since Bosworth, and the king could not go on for ever thanking
families who had then served his father well but had done nothing since. Nor could he ignore any challenge by them to his
sovereignty or any repeated breaches of the peace. Thus in 1521
he executed the Duke of Buckingham for oppressing his tenants,
and for boasting too often about his claim to the throne if Henry
died without an heir.

In 1525 the old warrior Sir Rhys ap Thomas died and his great
estate of Dinefwr, but not his offices, passed to his grandson
Rhys ap Gruffydd. In the same year Henry made his one con-
structive move of sending Princess Mary to Ludlow to revive the
Council of the Prince of Wales. Soon, however, he was involved
in the divorce question. He was aware too that a disordered west
Wales might be a channel for a Catholic rebellion on behalf of
Catherine, or for an invasion from Spain or from an even more
disordered Ireland. In 1529 Rhys ap Gruffydd, a staunch Catholic,
caused a riot in Carmarthen. He was tried and pardoned but
continued a trouble-maker. He was finally executed on 1531 on
a charge of plotting to overthrow Henry. The truth was probably
that he had made an enemy of Anne Boleyn, soon to be the king's
second wife.

The two executions showed Henry as the typical, ruthless
Renaissance prince. The point for Welshmen was that the Crown
was at last showing concern for the state of Wales and less for

By permission of Pitkin Pictorials

6. LLANDAFF CATHEDRAL: THE JASPER TOWER

Erected, it is said, by Jasper Tudor, and restored after bomb damage during World War II, the tower is a distinguished example of late-fifteenth century architecture. In that period "there was hardly a church in Wales, in however remote or bare a parish, which could not boast some degree of reconstruction or furnishing". (Glanmor Williams) the self-interest of great houses. Certainly with the disappearance of these two great marchers, the land of Wales was almost entirely the king's, to do with it as he wished.

THE SCHOLARS: LATE MEDIEVAL OR EARLY RENAISSANCE?

Many individuals of Welsh birth or connection displayed enthusiasm for the Italian Renaissance in the fifteenth century. John Blodwel, a native of Llanyblodwel near Oswestry, left his deanery in St. Asaph about 1420 to study law at the university of Bologna, where Renaissance thought was already moving powerfully. He served at the papal court in Rome for many years, greatly respected for his learning. His contemporary Andrew Holles, archdeacon of Anglesey, bought a magnificent Renaissance library in Italy. Thomas Langton, bishop of St. David's just before Bosworth, was such another enthusiast. But there is no evidence that the enthusiasm of these churchmen rubbed off on any Welshmen of their day.

There are signs in Welsh poetry of the latter half of the century of a growing concern with man as man which is the essence of humanism. Nor was the interest confined to literature and law but affected the visual arts of architecture and painting too. There was now an 'urge to build and beautify' churches in particular, with fine towers, windows, screens, lofts and stalls, and with colourful frescoes and costly chalices. Little of this enthusiasm, however, showed as yet a distinctive Renaissance style, and must be regarded as the final flowering of medieval religious culture.

These pre-Renaissance revivals in Wales began long before Bosworth and were mainly the result of the growing prosperity of the later fifteenth century. But Henry Tudor's accession gave them added impetus. It set the fashion for young Welshmen to flock to the English universities and schools of law. Here they came in contact with the new learning moving in from the continent. Richard Whitford, for example, left his native Flintshire to pursue a brilliant career at the universities of Cambridge and Paris. It was he with his pupil Lord Mountjoy (later tutor to Henry VIII) who first brought Erasmus to England in 1499.

7. ROOD SCREEN AT LLANWNNOG (MONTS.)

Whitford, Erasmus and Sir Thomas More, the great English humanist, became firm friends.[2]

Little, however, of this early scholarship, picked up in England, was now fed back to Welshmen at home in Wales. Not until the sixteenth century was half over can we say that there appeared a Welsh form of the Revival of Learning. Nor is this surprising. The Renaissance, as we have seen, was essentially the product of easy communication, of wealth, and of a flourishing town life. Wales had none of these ingredients. Moreover, conquest by England had robbed her of a central institution or idea—like, say, the National Eisteddfod in our own day—which could provide support and a focus for scholarship. Wales had lost its court and had not won a university. The Tudors were to give it a sort of court at Ludlow and strengthen it in an Act of 1543. But the earlier Act of 1536 was to discourage the use of the Welsh language.

Before the New Learning could be popular it was necessary to use the vernacular, the native tongue, to write in prose and to employ the printing press. Now the one advantage Wales had over England was a well-developed native literature reaching back unbroken for a 1,000 years, and treasured by prince and commoner alike. So far it had been expressed very largely in poetry; but it could easily turn to prose when the incentive appeared. The remarkable fact is that the printing press had been in use for a century before the first book in the Welsh language was printed in 1547, and then in London; and not till 1718 was a printing press set up in Wales—apart from the shortlived secret press at Rhiwledyn.* The reasons are clear. Printing is an expensive business which needs capital to start it, interested authors to feed it with material, and a wide reading public to support it. The young Welshmen now up at the English universities, however, preferred to write in English or Latin. Richard Whitford, for example, retired in 1506 to Sion House, a famous monastery near London, and lived there in strict seclusion for thirty years, writing a score of devotional books in fine English which were printed and published repeatedly. He resisted Henry VIII's changes, yet, unlike his friend Thomas More, managed to preserve his life. He died not long after Sion was dissolved by force in 1539. His fellow-Welshman Edward Powell, an Oxford scholar, was not as lucky. An out-and-out Catholic, he denounced in preaching and in print first Luther's actions and later Henry's divorce, and was imprisoned and eventually beheaded in 1540.

Whitford and Powell are men of the Renaissance only in that they moved among early humanists like Erasmus and published their views in print; in truth they are fine examples of the best in the Middle Ages. They bridge the interval between the two cultures. But they had little connection with Wales. Her Renaissance would come with a later generation of university men who would feel the urgent need to reach the ordinary people of Wales

* See pp. 107 and 262 below.

and not merely her scholars. The Reformation would provide
this need. In Wales, more perhaps than in any other country of
Europe, the religious awakening was its Renaissance.

THE WELSH CHURCH IN DECLINE

The church in Wales, as in the rest of Europe, had lost much
of its faith, its authority and its character in the fifteenth century.
Like a once-healthy tree, attacked by disease from within and by
creepers from without, the church was being drained of its
vitality by its own worldliness and the tightening grasp of lay
forces. Indeed there were factors operating in Wales that made
the situation worse than average.

One was the general poverty which we have already noted.
Poverty at least meant that Wales did not suffer from too many
churchmen; one person in a 180 was a cleric compared with
one in only a 100 or fewer in England. The bishops of Bangor,
Llandaff and St. Asaph drew the lowest incomes in all England
and Wales; a large English monastery like Westminster had
greater possessions than all the Welsh abbeys put together; and
nearly three-quarters of the Welsh clergy received less than £10
per year. Even so, the earnings of these Welsh bishops, abbots
and priests compared favourably with those of laymen in Wales
of the same social standing. The simple fact is that the country
as a whole was poor.

Poverty tended to make the clergy unsettled and so lacking in
interest. Bishoprics in Wales were too often given to ambitious
men, generally from England, who moved on as soon as possible
to some higher-paid see. Poor incomes encouraged pluralism and
the absenteeism which inevitably went with it. This did not
always mean neglect, for curates or deputies generally took
charge of the unattended churches, and many, we know, did
their work well. But earning, as so many of them did, less than
£5 a year, and having to find some additional employment to
make ends meet, they could spend little time on ministry and
study. Moreover, in Wales so many of the clergy were 'married'
and had families to think of.

Again, bishops and abbots increasingly yielded to the temptation of farming out their estates to laymen, among them of course
the new class of gentry now rising to prominence. The Carne
family, for example, leased the manor of Nash from the bishop of
Llandaff from 1432 until 1951! The result was that these bishops
and abbots tended to lose control of their estates and become
indifferent to the fate of their tenants. But it is they who would
be blamed, and the church discredited, if the lay 'farmer' were
neglectful or oppressive. So indifference by the church bred
indifference to the church.

Factors of race and language also accelerated the decline of the
church in Wales. The national revolt of Glyndŵr at the dawn of
the century had added enormously to the general poverty and
disbelief. Church buildings had been destroyed, estates ruined,
loyalties as between Wales or Canterbury divided, and, following Glyndŵr, Welshmen for political reasons had recognized the
'new' pope at Avignon rather than the 'old' one in Rome.* As a
result of the revolt not a single Welsh-speaking Welshman was
made a bishop in Wales during the fifteenth century, though
lesser offices, it is true, were filled increasingly by Welsh gentry.
The Welsh therefore lacked top-level leaders who could understand and guide them.

Language was a further difficulty. It tended to separate the
native parish priests from the higher officers of the church. It
also emphasized the universal lack of preaching. The Welsh
churchgoer always celebrated Mass, sung in Latin, but a sermon,
particularly in his native language, he rarely heard. The friars did
preach, but their number in Wales was small and dwindling
(about sixty in 1538); moreover, they now seldom wandered
from place to place. A few books in manuscript are known to
have been current to guide the parish priest in his duty, but they
were rarely available to him since no advantage was taken of
printing in Welsh until 1547. Thousands of English sermons in
manuscript have survived, but not one in Welsh!

* See *The Defenders*, p. 202–4.

A further result of the Glyndŵr revolt was a marked increase in the sale of indulgences in Wales in order to raise money for the restoration of desecrated churches.[1]

Wales too was comparatively remote. Even more so in the sense that communication by land was gradually becoming more favoured than the ancient sea-ways along which saints and pilgrims had moved. New influences from the continent accordingly came now more and more through England, and were slow to reach remote fringe-areas like Cumberland, Cornwall and Wales. On the one hand this isolation made church-going popular among the Welsh, for it had social as well as religious value. On the other it nourished superstition. We shall find both Catholics and Protestants complaining that superstitious practices were rife. Images or idols such as Mary Magdalene's at Usk and Derfel Gadarn's at Llandderfel, love-philtres, vows to the devil, charms to protect friends and curses to ruin enemies were widely current, often among the clergy themselves. (See extract 3 page 70).

Finally, a distinctive and, as we shall see, an important feature in Wales was marriage of the clergy. The law of the church was clear: a priest in holy orders should remain celibate. Yet, following the custom of the ancient Celtic church, so often denounced by Gerald the Welshman, marriage by the Welsh clergy both high and low was generally and openly practised. Their illegitimate children were acknowledged by public opinion and even by English law—but not by the church. Until he secured a papal dispensation no son of a priest could hope for promotion. Thus William Glyn, Mary's Catholic bishop of Bangor, and Rowland Meyrick, the Protestant who followed him, as well as Richard Davies the bishop of St. Asaph and later St. David's, were all sons of priests. Such men may well have had a personal interest in doing away with the authority of the pope.

THE MONASTERIES

The state of the 'regular' clergy in monasteries and friaries differed little from that of the 'secular' clergy described above. Wales had fewer religious houses in terms of its population than

England; they were also generally smaller and poorer. Yet compared with neighbouring laymen and even bishops their inmates
were certainly well-off. Most of the monasteries were situated
in the coastal lowlands of the south; of the 47 houses left in
Wales at the beginning of the Tudor period, 28 were in the
counties of Monmouth (11), Glamorgan (5), Carmarthen (5)
and Pembroke (7). The most important fact is that by 1500 they
were hopelessly undermanned. (See Exercise 3 to Chapter V
p. 307).

The Cistercians were easily the most numerous and wealthy.
Their wealth derived from both 'temporalities' and 'spiritualities'.
The former included their vast estates in farms and fisheries, their
mills and mines, their property in towns, and their income from
tolls, fees and fines and, not least, from the display and sale of
relics and indulgences. By Tudor times the monks had handed
over the care of most of these 'temporalities' to stewards and
bailiffs, nearly all drawn from rising families like the Carnes and
the Devereux, and merely claimed the rents themselves. The
monks thus lost touch with the countryside and gained no better
reputation as landlords than laymen. Moreover, when the dissolution came there were gentry at hand ready at once to take
over their property.

'Spiritualities' were mainly the income the monks could
claim in tithes from livings which had come into their possession.
Here again the monks had delegated their duties to 'vicars',
giving them the 'lesser' tithes on animals in return for looking
after the church, its parishioners and its land, but keeping the
'greater' tithes of corn and hay for themselves. By the sixteenth
century, however, they had fallen into the doubtful habit of
leasing out the whole living to laymen. This meant that the
appointment and payment of the priest, and so the essential life
of the parish, were in the hands of laymen. Little wonder that
other 'spiritualities' such as gifts from pilgrims and other pious
people had fallen markedly, though offerings at popular shrines
such as Holywell in the north and Penrhys (Rhondda Valley) in
the south continued to pour in. The few friars in Wales still

profited largely from gifts given them in wills, generally in return for continuing to pray for the soul of the giver. Henry VII, for example, made a grant of £8 per annum to Carmarthen Friary so that his father and he himself, when dead, should be daily remembered in prayer.

It is not easy to assess the character and behaviour of these men—and women in nunneries like Llanllŷr—sworn to vows of poverty, obedience and chastity. There is no doubt that the monks lived well; the poets tell us that they vied with each other in their lavish hospitality. Possibly too in impoverished Wales they spent more than the English average of 3 per cent of their income on charity. There is good evidence in the poetry of the time of their care for the aged, but little of their relieving the sick and needy or of educating the young. Nor did their conduct lift them far above the general level. They were occasionally guilty of serious crimes; a monk of Neath in 1496 stabbed a priest to death in the cloister of Whitland; another of Strata Florida was accused of counterfeiting money. In the half-century before the monasteries were closed, abbots or priors in Penmon, Conway and Basingwerk, in Carmarthen and Margam, among others, were charged with immorality.

But there were good abbots too like Dafydd ap Ieuan of Valle Crucis, later bishop of St. Asaph, who was as hospitable as any and yet remained a fine scholar and a sincerely devout man. Thanks to their abbots also, many monasteries such as Strata Florida, Conway, Strata Marcella and Valle Crucis shared now in the general revival of architecture we noticed above. It would be wrong therefore to assume that monks in general were immoral or criminal; lazy and pleasure-loving yes, but wicked no. Monks were no worse than laymen in general. The real point was that they were no better.

The early Tudors continued the medieval practice of using churchmen as the servants of the crown. They also used the church to reward their friends. Richard Kyffin and Robert ap Rhys are typical. Kyffin, the illegitimate son of a noble family, got himself a degree in law and supported Henry VII before and after Bosworth. In return he became vicar-general to the bishop of Bangor, dean of the chapter and rector of Llanddwynwen in Anglesey, and thereby enormously wealthy. Robert ap Rhys the son of Henry's standard-bearer at Bosworth, and also a lawyer, became Wolsey's chaplain and agent. His reward was to become vicar-general of St. Asaph and holder, it is said, of eighteen livings! He again became very wealthy and lavish in his hospitality at Plas Iolyn, high on the Denbighshire upland. Though a cleric, he had sixteen children, among them the notorious Dr. Elis Prys, Cromwell's henchman and father of Tomos Prys, Elizabethan poet and buccaneer.

Such king's-men brought no credit to the church. Nor were they in a position to defend it when threatened by Henry VIII, for whom they formed a 'potential fifth-column'. They had destroyed the church's defences from within before Henry attacked them from without.

Not that bishop or even pope mattered much to the average Welshman. He was happy to attend church and there meet his neighbours, and hear much of the Mass in an archaic tongue and a little preaching, generally in a foreign one. He accepted the blessing of the church at birth and marriage, and its consolation in trouble and in death from hireling parish priests, scarcely better off or more learned or more celibate than himself. For the rest, holy-days had become holidays, and pilgrimages and the monastic-life were all mixed up with superstition and sensation and the secular joys.

Yet there was more than a glimmer of hope. All around he saw churches being rebuilt, redesigned in the best Perpendicular style and beautified. There was a revival in poetry too, and a new attempt at religious plays. While down in Glamorgan a group of writers were turning out religious prose and starting to translate the Scriptures. There was a new sense of devotion in the air waiting for leadership. It would come not so much from politically minded Tudor rulers, however well-liked, certainly not from the monasteries, but from a school of Welsh humanists up at the English universities.

ORIGINAL EXTRACTS

1   THE STRATA MARCELLA INDULGENCE (see Illustration page 11)
Universis sancte matris ecclesie filiis ad quos presentes littere peruenerint
.... &c.
(*Reduced and translated it reads:*)
To all the sons of Holy Mother Church to whom this present letter may
come. We John by the sufferance of God Abbot of the monastery of the
Blessed Mary of Ystrad Marchell . . . send greeting and sincere love in the
Lord.

Whereas our most reverend Father, Lord Thomas (Wolsey), Cardinal of
York . . . and Chancellor . . . of England, also of our most holy Father in
Christ and Lord Clement, seventh pope of that name, has released ten
years and as many months and 140 days of indulgences from the penances
enjoined on all Christ's faithful people of either sex devoutly visiting the
said monastery which is to a large extent in a state of ruin . . . or (have)
extended helping hands to the same monastery . . . with power to absolve
them from all offences, excepting only those reserved to the said See (of
Rome), as often as occasion shall require . . . And also granted them leave
to eat eggs, butter, cheese and other milky products, and, on the advice of
a physician even flesh in Lent . . . we make known to all of you . . . that
we, the Abbot and Convent aforesaid have received and accepted our well-
beloved
(*name(s) of* 'buyer(s)')
(who, by their good offices have earned a right to participate in the things
aforesaid) to participation accordingly in the indulgence . . . aforesaid.
(*Y Cymmrodor* xxix (1919) pp. 1–18)

2   ERASMUS WRITES TO RICHARD WHITFORD IN 1506 (*asking him to
judge between Erasmus and their mutual friend More in a literary contest*): Utrunque
certo ex aequo amas, utrique vicissim ex aequo charus. (Both of us certainly
you equally love, to both you are equally dear).
(quoted in Glanmor Williams: *Welsh Reformation Essays*, p. 68)

CHAPTER IV

MAKERS OF MODERN WALES I:
THE POLITICIANS

Wolsey having failed him in the matter of divorce, Henry VIII
in 1529 turned to Parliament. In the next seven years the King
and his Reformation Parliament, in a tremendous burst of law-
making, brought about a veritable revolution in both religious
and political life and, as it were, bundled England and Wales
hurriedly into the modern era of history. Here we shall describe
the political changes they made, leaving the religious changes to
the next chapter.

The King's agents were three Thomases—More, Cranmer and
Cromwell. For the first three years Henry fought a kind of 'cold
war' with the Pope, in the hope of getting a divorce. He had
little difficulty now, with More's help, in passing acts which
fined the church in England and threatened to withhold the rich
fees paid to the papacy. But the Pope refused to yield to the
King's blustering.

Meantime two men had risen to power behind the throne.
Thomas Cromwell had been a loyal servant of Wolsey's but, unlike him, was a layman with a genius for working with Parliament.
He now rose in the King's service by his gift for administration,
his capacity for hard work, his speed, and his cold ruthlessness.[1]
His one aim was to make his master the unquestioned sovereign
over all his dominions. To Cromwell England owes the 130 or
so acts which were now passed and which gave Parliament its
apprenticeship in government. Thomas Cranmer was a scholar-
priest, gentle and unworldly, and a genuine reformer. For the
next twenty years he was to guide the country through the
Reformation.

Then came the critical year, 1533. In January Henry married Anne Boleyn in secret and named Cranmer his archbishop. Cromwell was already his right-hand man, for More, he knew, would not acknowledge Anne Boleyn as queen. Events now moved quickly. Within a year or so a series of acts of Parliament stripped the Pope of all his powers in England and gave them to the King. In 1533 the Act against Appeals settled the divorce question, and Cranmer duly married Henry and Anne officially. Early in 1534 other measures robbed the Pope of his payments from the clergy and his authority over them, and made Anne's children heirs to the throne (Elizabeth was born in September 1533). At the end of the year the Act of Supremacy declared that the King 'is and ought to be the supreme head of the Church of England', and the Treasons Act made anyone who denied it a traitor. Sir Thomas More and Bishop Fisher did deny it and were executed in 1535.

Then came the turn of the monks. They were now in an impossible position because of their vow of obedience to the Pope; more important, they had enormous wealth. Cromwell, who had previous experience of closing monasteries under Wolsey, sent two commissions hurrying round the remaining houses, one to value their wealth and a second to find evidence to justify taking it from them. Yet this human dynamo did not wait for justification; in 1536 he closed 400 smaller monasteries of less value than £200 per annum, and by 1539 he had closed the lot. The dissolution of the monasteries was not as great a calamity as was once thought. Only in the north of England, where there were other grievances, was there active protest—the Pilgrimage of Grace of 1536; but the King put this down with a firm hand.

Henry had seized the government of the Church and its wealth, but its beliefs he left alone. The majority of his subjects were pleased with this. Cromwell, a mild reformer, and Cranmer, a dedicated one, made some changes in the ritual of the church. They ordered relics and shrines and other tokens of superstition to be destroyed and preaching enforced. Their greater contribution was to authorize the English Bible, Coverdale's translation in 1535 and the Great (chained) Bible in 1539.

But Cromwell went too far and suffered the consequences. Jane Seymour, Henry's third wife, died in giving him, at last, a son. In order to establish friendship with the Protestant princes of Germany Cromwell persuaded the King to marry Anne of Cleves. But Henry loathed his fourth wife on sight, and vented his wrath on the man who, whatever his faults, had served him loyally. Beset by enemies and abandoned by his king, Cromwell was executed in 1540 with the same speed as had marked all his own whirlwind reforms and his master's marriages.

PREPARATION FOR UNION: ROWLAND LEE

Almost all the important institutions of modern Wales were given her by Henry VIII and his Reformation Parliament in two great statutes passed in the last third of his reign. Her division into thirteen shires (regrouped in April 1974), J.P.'s to administer local justice and M.P.'s to represent her in Parliament, her legal system and current law of inheritance—all these came now to Wales *because* of the Acts of Union of 1536 and 1543. They remain after almost four and a half centuries. The most distinctive of her present-day institutions, however—the Welsh language—she kept *in spite of* the Acts.

Praise and blame are still heaped on the Acts of Union. It must be remembered, however, that they did not initiate Tudor policy, good or bad; rather they are the final crystallization of a policy which, as we saw in Chapter Three, had been slowly evolving bit by bit over the previous fifty years. They gave form to many changes which were inevitable and had already taken hold of her people. In a curious way the Union gave Wales a distinctive character not enjoyed since the days of Llywelyn the Great. It completed the work of Llywelyn the Last in 1267 and of Edward I in 1284 and 1301 in trying to make one country of Wales under an acknowledged prince. There were two Acts, the first hurriedly set out general principles, the second, much larger, Act filled out the details and provided the machinery.

After about 1530 Henry VIII and his counsellors showed an acute interest in the affairs of Wales. Hitherto the reign had produced only one Act of Parliament particularly concerned with Wales, in 1529, but in the last third, 1534–47, there were twenty-two, most of them dealing with government. As we saw above, the immediate need was good order. The lawlessness of Wales at this time may have been exaggerated by earlier writers, as indeed by the Act itself. It still remains true that changes in the law were long overdue so as to bring order, security and fair play to all, and in particular to protect the vital cattle traffic from brigands and the king's revenue from those, natives as well as foreigners, who dodged paying the customs. But no doubt it was the divorce question and the consequent changes in religion that now compelled the king's interest.

When Henry met his counsellors in December 1533 to consider how best to defend his realm following the break with the Pope, one of the vital issues was the government of Wales. For opposition, rebellion and even invasion in support of Catherine and the papacy might well come from there. Henry's many spies reported, for example, that James ap Gruffydd, uncle to Rhys ap Gruffydd, beheaded in 1531, was actively trying to organize an invasion from Scotland or the continent. In the following June, Henry met the remaining marcher-lords at Shrewsbury and there agreed with them on methods to reduce crime in their lands. The Council, originally known as the Council of the Prince of Wales, and now in the absence of a prince called the Council of Wales and the Marches, must be strengthened and given prerogative powers and a new President. The man chosen was an Englishman, Rowland Lee, who, with Cromwell, had served under Wolsey. Lee was an able, firm and vigorous administrator. Nominally Bishop of Lichfield (though by his own confession he had never been in a pulpit) he was ruthless and often savage. Now from his headquarters at Ludlow he scoured the Marches for criminals, hunting them down indefatigably, convicting them in his courts, and often hanging them out of hand. Neither English 'blue blood' nor Welsh family pride carried weight with Lee.

By permission of the Radio Times Hulton Picture Library

8. LUDLOW CASTLE

The great Border fortress on a commanding site which housed a court and
'capital' for Tudor and Stuart Wales.

He is reputed to have compelled Welshmen to adopt the modern
practice of naming themselves after the English fashion of sur-
names, instead of by the long-winded Welsh style of 'ap's'.[2]

Lee probably initiated the sudden spate of legislation which
now followed, all designed to tighten up law and order—acts to
regulate the ferries crossing the Severn, to punish thugs who
attacked travellers along the border, and to compel lords to give
up criminals who had fled from neighbouring lordships. Law thus
began to bridge the border. Soon there was evidence that Lee's
work was paying off and crime slackening. But the 'stowte
bishop' was no statesman. He was content with the system as it
was; he had no intention of abolishing the marcher lordships for
ever.

In the summer of 1535 the King was back on the border again,
'hunting and traversing the country to gain the people'. In the
winter that followed there appeared a sudden change of policy.

It showed first in an act ordering the appointment of J.P.'s in the Principality and in the counties of Pembroke and Glamorgan. It seems that the government had switched to a more positive policy which meant trusting Welshmen to look after their own affairs. This was none of Lee's doing: he openly declared his opposition to Welshmen as J.P.'s to his dying day. Then in February 1536 an Act of Union was rushed through Parliament, apparently without Lee's knowledge.

Why this sudden change of policy resulting in the Act of Union? And who was responsible? The Act was clearly premature and hurried; it was incomplete, contained gross inaccuries, and had to be revised repeatedly until details were finally settled in the much larger Act of 1543.

No doubt the time was opportune. Tudor monarchs had a hunch for good timing. As we saw earlier* the majority of the marcher lordships were already, as the Act says, 'in the handes and possession of our soveraigne lorde the King', for him to deal with as he wished. For two centuries or more the social life of Wales had grown less dependent on the ancient tribal customs and more akin to English society.† Henry well knew that there were plenty of go-ahead men eager to risk their money in profit-able ventures in land, in industry or trade, provided they had secure conditions. A new class of gentry, small landowners and tradesmen, too was eager to lend a hand in local government in order to guarantee such security.

But all these factors had long existed and cannot explain the timing of this most important Act. Perhaps Henry's attachment to Jane Seymour gave him new hope of a son who would be Prince of Wales; it would be fitting that he should be given a consolidated dominion. More likely is the connection between the Act and the imminent dissolution of the monasteries. Cromwell had the dissolution in mind as early as 1534; in January 1535 he had appointed his two commissions of enquiry

* P. 28.
† See *The Defenders*, chapter 13.

into the monasteries. He was doubtless anxious about the probable reaction of the people of Wales to the drastic step he was
about to take. There was widespread criticism of the King, and
some local protests, all inflamed by an unusually bad harvest,
and he wished to forestall trouble by putting Wales under good
government. All the laws passed since 1529 to reorganize the
Church in England had already been applied to Wales. But to
Cromwell's tidy mind they might be better enforced if the two
countries were as one. So in the same month as he passed the act
dissolving the smaller monasteries, he also rushed through the
Act of Union.

It is probably true to say that the Act 'imposed' union on
Welshmen, rather than consult them as the Scots were to be
consulted in 1707 and the Irish in 1800. But we must remember
that consultation in government was not really possible until
Wales had parliamentary representation. Moreover, we know
that there was a strong desire within Wales itself for union and
uniformity. Cromwell, who had family connections and indeed
lands there, was well aware of it, and had consulted gentry who
could give voice to it. One was Sir Richard Herbert of Montgomery, a great friend of Bishop Lee and his companion in
hunting criminals in the marches. He was probably the author of
a petition received by the king early in 1536 asking him to grant
Welshmen 'the same laws and privileges' as his other subjects
enjoyed. Even better equipped was John Price of Brecon.
Through Cromwell, who was his wife's uncle, he had entered the
king's service and had soon become Henry's chief notary or
recorder, especially on all matters to do with the church. He
officiated in the king's wedding to Anne Boleyn; he too drafted
the papers for his divorce from her. He recorded the 'con-
fessions' of Sir Thomas More and Bishop Fisher and many others.
A man with great interest in all things Welsh, as we shall see, it
is more than likely that Price had a hand, with others at court,
in forming the new legislation.

However, the king may have tested his Welsh people's
approval, and John Price may have written in the details, but the

architect of union was Thomas Cromwell, who now hurriedly set it among the many statutes of his revolutionary Reformation Parliament.

THE ACT OF UNION 1536

We must now analyse the Act point by point.

A. THE DECLARATION OF 'UNION' OF WALES WITH ENGLAND. The first clause of the Act does not strictly create the union but reaffirms that Wales 'ever hath been annexed, united and subject to . . . this realm' (England). The Welsh princes had acknowledged a loose feudal overlordship of the English king since the days of Alfred, the Statute of Rhuddlan of 1284 had stated that 'the land of Wales had been united to the crown of England', and doubtless English kings and lawyers had since assumed it for two and a half centuries. In the strict legal sense, however, the statement was incorrect in that only the five western counties of the Principality were directly owned by the king as, or for, the Prince of Wales. It was a special kind of march-er lordship with a quite separate system of law and administration from that of England.[3]

However, union meant:

(1) that Welshmen were to enjoy all the 'freedoms, liberties, rights and privileges of Englishmen'. At a stroke the degrading Penal Laws were abolished.

(2) that English law should be used in Wales as from 1 November, 1536.

(3) that, in particular, land should be inherited by the English system of primogeniture as distinct from the Welsh system, already in decay, of *cyfran* or gravelkind. Thus Henry VIII achieved what outstanding Welsh princes from at least Llywelyn the Great had vainly striven for—to avoid the partition of their land between many sons rather than its consolidation under the eldest.

B. DIVISION INTO SHIRES. The Act rearranged the map of Wales to give it the form of thirteen shires which it kept, with

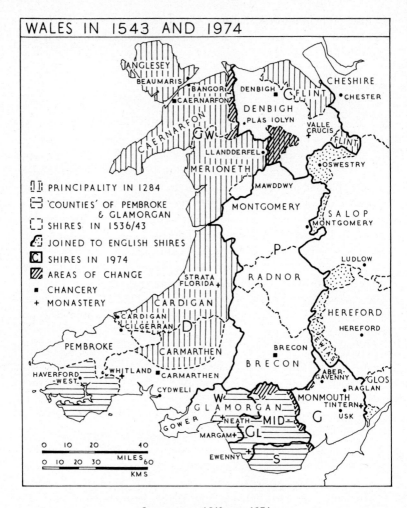

9. WALES IN 1543 AND 1974

Only the monasteries named in the text are marked here. See page 307 below, and *The Defenders*, pp. 20, 37 and 83 for full lists/maps. (After William Rees: *The Union of England and Wales*.)

small modifications until April 1974. This it did by abolishing the marcher lordships in three ways: (See the map on p. 46.)

(1) Joining some on the border to the nearby English counties; e.g. Oswestry to Shropshire, Ewias to Hereford-shire.

(2) Merging others in the south and west into existing Welsh counties. The Act assumes for this purpose that Glamorgan and Pembroke are already shires, which again was only partly true. To join, as it does, Gower with Glam-organ, Cydweli with Carmarthen, and Cilgerran with Pem-broke would seem good geography; but to join Mawddwy to Merioneth, from which it is separated by a mountain range, does not. Mawddwy, however, had a bad reputation for brigands, and probably it was thought that it would more quickly come under law from the old Principality than from newly created Montgomeryshire.

(3) Dividing the remaining middle belt, extending the whole length of central Wales, into five new shires—Denbigh, Montgomery, Radnor, Brecon and Monmouth, each with its shire town and centre(s) for shire courts.

In these arrangements we see Cromwell as the tidy administrator anxious to produce good order, but not as a great statesman. The line he drew between England and Wales was one of convenience, paying little respect to either the old ecclesiastical divisions or to language, both of which might have given Wales a greater sense of unity. But then Cromwell was not concerned with the unity of Wales nor with any boundary separating it from England. He was concerned with uniformity within Wales as a part of the general uniformity within Henry's whole realm.

C. JUSTICE AND TAXATION. The arrangements for justice to be done and tax to be collected were:

(1) Monmouthshire was treated distinctively. It was brought into the system current in the English counties and based on London and the courts at Westminster.

(2) Two new chanceries and exchequers were to be set up, one at Denbigh in the north and another at Brecon in the south, like the existing centres at Caernarfon and Carmarthen. This arrangement, said the Act, was necessary because of the distance of the Welsh shires from London, and because their inhabitants lacked 'substance, power and ability' to travel.

(3) English law was to be observed, but applied everywhere other than in Monmouthshire according to the manner current in the three shires of the former Northern Principality. Cromwell, it seems, was concerned to make the twelve shires not so much identical with England as identical with each other. Uniformity rather than union was the first requisite of good government.

D. LANGUAGE. The language to be used henceforth in all courts of justice was to be English, and no Welsh-speaking person could hold office in Wales or England 'or other of the King's dominions' unless he also spoke English. Probably English along with Latin and Norman-French, was already much used in the courts. Probably too this new ruling was not strictly enforced, and Welsh continued to be used for some considerable time. William Herbert, the first Earl of Pembroke and President of the Council of Wales and the Marches (and therefore the king's chief officer in Wales) could hardly speak anything but Welsh. Nevertheless, the native tongue, if used, was on sufferance. Not until 1942 was Welsh reinstated as a language to be used in courts of law.

E. PARLIAMENTARY REPRESENTATION was now granted to Wales thus:

County	No. of Members	
	Shire	Shire Town
Monmouth	2	1
Merioneth	1	none
The other eleven	1	1

Representation was therefore not as generous as in England, where normally each shire and shire town had two members. But few Welshmen of the day would take offence at this. A seat in Parliament was regarded as much a burden as a privilege, both by the M.P. himself and by the shire or town which had to finance him. Again because of its poverty, Cromwell decided that Wales should carry a lighter burden.

Finally, the Act of 1536 protected the rights of marcher-lords with regard to their customary rents, dues and petty civil courts. Two lords, significantly, are singled out in separate clauses, the Earl of Worcester, justice of Glamorgan, and Lord Ferrers, justice of South Wales. Two commissions were to be set up, one to divide Wales into hundreds and one to inquire into Welsh laws.

THE ACT OF 1543

Welshmen seem to have accepted the hurried first Act of Union of 1536 in spite of its errors, and there is little evidence of protest. There were again scares of invasion, and coastal defences were manned and troops mustered to meet them. But bluff Rowland Lee told Cromwell that Wales was now as quiet as England. Some amendments to the Act were made piecemeal in the following years, such as adjusting the boundary between Denbighshire and Flintshire. Then in 1543 came a long and comprehensive statute which finally laid down the details of government.

Who the author of the second act was we do not know. By 1543, Lee, Cromwell and Herbert were all dead. John Price is probably the likeliest person. The clauses of the Act are certainly the work of a lawyer with an eye for detail. They readjusted the boundary between the shires of Carmarthen and Pembroke; laid down the limits of the hundreds as decided by the recent commission set up in 1536; fixed upon 1541 as the operative year for the use of primogeniture in land inheritance; and curiously (perhaps as a mark of favour to a former mistress of the king's) gave the town of Haverfordwest an M.P. of its own, a privilege it retained until 1885.

The great achievement of the Act of 1543, however, was to establish two systems of law and administration that gave Wales uniformity of justice, and in a broad sense recognized it as a country distinct from England.

The Courts of Great Sessions formed one of these systems. These new courts were grouped into four circuits of three counties apiece, centred on Caernarfon, Carmarthen, Denbigh and Brecon. Each circuit would have its own Justice (two after 1576) who would hold sessions in each of the county towns for six days in every half-year. These courts worked quite independently of those at Westminster to try mostly civil actions under the common-law between person and person, and, to a small extent, crimes against the state. For nearly three hundred years these 'Assizes', as they are usually called, were to dispense justice quickly and cheaply. So they were popular with Welshmen, although few of their countrymen sat on their benches, and although the Welsh language was never officially accepted. In 1830, however, they were abolished and their work taken over by the jealous courts at Westminster. Then, and then only was Wales fully and legally swallowed up in England.

The distinctive character of Wales was recognized, secondly, by the re-establishment of the Council of Wales and the Marches. Hitherto, it had been an arbitrary court under the king's prerogative, like the Court of Star Chamber. It was now put on a proper statutory footing, directly responsible to the Privy Council for the good government of Wales. It had two functions. Primarily, it was an administrative and executive body for proclaiming and carrying out the orders of king and parliament, for appointing officials, for ensuring the defence of Wales, and for arresting vagabonds, pirates and recusants. It was, secondly, a court of justice dealing with those crimes against the state only partly dealt with by the Courts of Great Sessions—riots, assaults and any kind of disturbance likely to break the king's peace. Here too could the poor man come to seek justice against corrupt officials and grasping landlords, and obtain it without great expense. Some Welshmen, however, preferred to go directly to the Court of Star Chamber at Westminster, as increasingly did the people of the four English border counties of Salop, Hereford, Worcester and Gloucester, who resented more and more the authority of the Council of Wales under which they, with Monmouthshire, now came. The headquarters of the Council at Ludlow acted as a second royal court. Suspended at the outbreak of the Civil War in 1642, it was revived in part in 1660, only to be finally disbanded in 1688.

The sheriff remained the chief official of the shire. With his bailiff and his coroner he arrested criminals, mustered soldiers and collected taxes. He still held his monthly county court, his hundred court for small charges, and his 'turn' or court of inquiry twice a year. But now in Wales, as already in England, he acted, in all matters except debts, under the instructions of the J.P.'s. These had been appointed to the eight 'old' shires by the special act of 1536. All shires of Wales were now to have them, up to a majority of eight each. Appointed by the Council of Wales, they would carry out its work through their quarter sessions and petty sessions. They dealt not only with breaches of the peace, but with licensing, fixing wages and prices, mending roads and enforcing the poor law. In practice, this change of power from sheriff to unpaid justice meant very little, since the same landowners usually filled both offices.

The commission appointed by the act of 1536 had now done its work of dividing each county into hundreds. Every hundred had its high-constable. But increasingly the actual work of local government by the Tudors was done in the smallest unit, the parish. Once a year the parishioners met in their vestry meeting and there elected the local constables, the road surveyor and the poor-law overseer. This use of laymen or 'amateurs' in local government is one of the great successes of the Tudors.

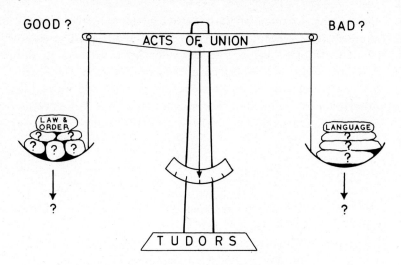

10. THE ACT OF UNION IN THE BALANCE
Complete loading the scales.

THE RESULTS OF UNION

Much has been said for and against Tudor policy in general and the Acts of Union in particular. In the short-term and to the people of the day its results would seem on the whole to be good. Undeniably, it brought a greater measure of peace and good order, which was the first priority. Tudor kings were thankful for the unusual absence of rebellion and the ordinary Welshman for security in his daily life. 'Welshman' no longer meant 'foreigner' nor even 'stranger'. The belittling Penal Laws had no force and Offa's Dyke no function. Welshmen poured over it in their hundreds to take their place in university and church, in law court and royal court, in soldiering and in trade, and in the current of adventurous life that was to be the mark of Elizabeth's day. The landowning gentry were given a new political status, trusted as J.P.'s to look after the affairs of home, and as M.P.'s in London, to share in the ever-growing part that Parliament was to play in the life of the two nations.

Security under the law brought favourable economic effects. The cattle trade quickly revived and flourished as never before. Men with capital to spare, many from England and some from the continent, now ventured to invest in trade and in new industrial enterprises in Wales, especially in mining and metal working. Stimulated by the current economic revival, town life too at last began to flourish. The old boroughs now lost their objectionable characters as English military bastions. A few like Cricieth dwindled as a result, but most took on a new life as natural centres of trade; their walls and castles decayed, but their markets flourished and their suburbs grew, often into new towns. Old or new, the towns tended to become more Welsh in language and character. Denbigh in the north and Abergavenny in the south are examples.

In a curious way, the legal steps whereby Wales was now merged with England gave recognition to her separate identity, with law courts and Council all her own.

However, these immediate, mostly material, benefits have to be balanced against serious social and cultural disadvantages in the long term. At home in Wales the landowning gentry had free rein to amass wealth and status, often by ruthless land-grabbing. Union with England, was not wholly responsible for this, nor even Tudor policy in general; the process had begun at least a century before and would be accentuated by chance events like the dissolution of the monasteries. But as old Bishop Lee had warned, the gentry took advantage of the offices given them by the union to line their pockets. As the century wore on the poor became poorer and the rich became richer, and the growth of a middle class was too slow to bridge the widening rift between them.

The lure of fame and fortune outside Wales robbed her of some of her best minds. Thus many of those who should be her natural leaders ultimately became too absorbed in their own advancement 'abroad' in England to concern themselves with the national life at home in Wales. After a century had passed, they would no longer patronize the arts nor speak the language except, if they could, to their servants. In joining Monmouth-shire and Welsh-speaking border areas to English counties, and especially in making English the official legal language, the Acts ignored national and cultural considerations. Nothing in them condemns the language as such, and there is no evidence of a conscious attempt to eradicate it—the preamble of 1536 merely states the undeniable fact that Welsh speech 'is nothing like nor consonant to the natural mother tongue used within this realm' (England). Nevertheless the Acts had sacrificed the status of the language in all matters of law on the altar of uniformity. The natural poverty of Wales had already delayed her use of the printing press; the Acts only accentuated the delay.

Finally, for good or ill, the stream of cultural thought from the continent would now flow to Wales not directly but through England. And that, at the time of the Renaissance and the Reformation, was an all-important consideration.

ORIGINAL EXTRACTS

1 SIR RICHARD BULKELEY ADMITS TO FEAR OF CROMWELL:
I know right well it lieth in your hands to undo me for ever with a word of your mouth . . . I would not have spoken one word against the simplest groom in your stable . . . for though I be not very wise I am not so stark mad to contend in anything that is appertaining to your lordship.
(from Glanmor Williams: *Welsh Reformation Essays*, pp. 40, 43)

2 ROWLAND LEE—*by a member of the Council of Wales and the Marches:*
. . . stowte of nature, readie witted, roughe in speeche, not affable to anye of the walshrie, an extreme severe ponisher of offenders.
(from Penry Williams: *The Council in the Marches of Wales*, p. 16)

3 THE ACT OF UNION 1536: 27 Henry VIII, c. 26
(Title) An Act for laws and iustice to be ministered in Wales in like fourme as it is in this realm.

(Preamble) . . . by cause that in the . . . Principalitie . . . dyvers rightes usages laws and customes be farre discrepant frome the lawes and customes of the Realme (England) And also by cause that the people of the same dominion have and do daily use a speche nothing like ne consonaunt to the naturall mother tonge used within this Realme some rude and ignorant

people have made distinccion and diversitie betwene the Kinges Subiectes
of this Realme and hys subiectes of the said dominion and Principalitie of
Wales . . . his highnes therefore of a singular love and favour that he
beareth towardes his subiectes of his said dominion of Wales . . . and to
bring his said subiectes of this his Realme and of his said dominion of
Wales to an amiable concorde and unitie hath . . . (on the advice and
authority of Parliament) . . . enacted that his said countrey or dominion
of Wales shalbe stonde and contynue for ever fromehensforthe incorporated
united and annexed to and with his Realme of England . . .

(from William Rees: *The Union of England and Wales*, pp. 55–56)

CHAPTER V

MAKERS OF MODERN WALES II: THE EARLY REFORMERS

DURING Henry VIII's reign more and more Welshmen thronged to the English universities and schools of law. There they absorbed the new Humanist influences and later the new Protestant beliefs. Then they left to pursue the distinguished careers as churchmen and politicians in which we shall meet them. Most of them eventually returned to their native land, or kept contact, and in their persons the Renaissance and Reformation first came to Wales.

Richard Gwent—whose name suggests he came from Monmouthshire—studied law at Oxford before the German Reformation begun. He served as Cromwell's agent and the king's chaplain, but his real religious views are not known to us. Of the others up at the university in the twenties there is no doubt. Luther in the meantime had made his dramatic protest against abuses in the church, and his ideas were all the rage among students. Men of high qualification in the arts, divinity and the law, they all agreed on the need to correct abuses in the church, and on the all-important part that printed books would play in the work of reform. But beyond that they divided into two camps, Catholic and Protestant.

Two of the Catholic group were (Sir) Edward Carne of Glamorgan and Bishop William Glyn of Anglesey. Both had fine careers at Oxford and Cambridge respectively, and became heads of colleges there. Both went along with Henry's seizure of church government; but no more. They held fast to the old faith. The Protestant enthusiasts, however, rejected it, not merely because it was abused and discredited, but because at best it could not satisfy their religious thirst. So they urged essential changes in belief and in ritual. Two such were Hugh Price and John Price, both Brecknock men (but apparently of different families) who were reading law at the same time at Oxford in the early twenties. Hugh returned there in 1571, at the end of his long life, to found Jesus College, which has been the Mecca of Welsh students ever since. Sir John we have already met, playing his part in shaping the Act of Union. His was a busy life. He was secretary to the King in church matters during the all-important years 1530–55, and then a commissioner of inquiry into the monasteries. Later he served as secretary to the Privy Council on Welsh affairs and to the Council of Wales, as sheriff in the counties of Brecknock and Hereford, and as M.P. for Hereford and Ludlow.

Yet in all this he found time for Wales and its culture. Born of a family of Welsh bards, he combined their teaching with the new learning. He was one of the first to collect old Welsh manuscripts, many of which are fortunately preserved in the National Library of Wales, the British Musuem, and other collections. So he made some redress for the loss of monastic

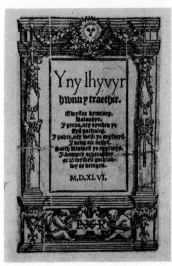

11. YN Y LLYFR HWN

The title-page of the first book to be printed in Welsh. Explain the discrepancy between the date on it and that given on page 58 here. Decipher the monogram below. (Henry VIII died on 27 January, 1547.)

By permission of the National Library of Wales

records. But he is best remembered as a pioneer in print. He despaired of his countrymen ever learning the new beliefs through Latin or even English. So in 1547, just as he was knighted by Edward VI, he produced for them the first printed book in Welsh, known from its opening words as *Yn y Llyfr Hwn*. It is a translation of the Creed, the Lord's Prayer and the Commandments. These, he declared, were the very minimum of belief which the clergy 'either cannot or will not reveal to their parishioners'.

Up at Oxford together during 1527–31 were four Welshmen who were to become firm Protestants. One of them stands on his own as the very pattern of a Renaissance man. William Thomas was a native probably of Radnorshire, and possibly the son of Walter Thomas, Cromwell's faithful servant. After graduating in 1529 he spent much of his life in Italy, but remained a Protestant. He became an outstanding Italian scholar, and wrote many books including a history of Italy, an Italian grammar, a dictionary of Boccaccio, Petrarch and Dante, and a defence of Henry VIII in Italian. Yet he pleaded the worth of English as a language in its own right and not simply as a means of learning Latin and Greek. He too was the first to advocate the teaching of English in the schools. Nor was he a mere bookworm, but an active politician who appreciated the teaching of Machiavelli and used it, as we shall see, in high office under Edward VI.

Thomas was firstly a man of affairs and only secondly a man of religion; moreover, his connection with Wales was very thin. His three fellow-students, however, Richard Davies, Rowland Meyrick and Thomas Young became devoted to Protestantism, suffered for it, and, as bishops under Elizabeth, played a major part in establishing it in Wales.

While this last group of early humanists were graduating at Oxford, a boy was growing up in his native Llanrwst tutored in the ancient craft of the bards of Mynydd Hiraethog. A generation later William Salesbury (1520–84) would be the brightest star of the Renaissance in Wales.

HENRY VIII: A KING IN HASTE

All the major acts of the Reformation Parliament were applied
to Wales as to England. In this sense the Reformation, like the
Act of Union, was imposed on Wales. Yet Welshmen gave no
sign that they objected to the 'imposition'. In fact, they seemed
to accept the changes in church leadership more quietly than
any other of the king's subjects.

The clergy of Wales, almost without exception, obediently
took the oath under the Acts of Supremacy and Succession.
Edward Powell, like More and Fisher was one who refused. He
was put in the Tower and finally executed in 1540. But others,
even good Catholics like William Glyn (Bishop of Bangor under
Mary), accepted Henry's changes. Sir Edward Carne, Richard
Gwent, and Sir John Price actively promoted them, the first as
a diplomat in Rome and the other two as lawyers for Cromwell
and Cranmer. All three were later handsomely rewarded for
their support with offices, lands and livings.

None of the Welsh Bishops was likely to oppose the king's
will except the Spaniard, Bishop Athequa of Llandaff, who had
been Queen Catherine's confessor. In any case during the critical
years 1534–37 all four would be succeeded by new men chosen
for their support of their new master. Two of them owed their
jobs to Anne Boleyn: Salcot made bishop of Bangor in 1534 and
Barlow of St. Asaph in 1535 and St. David's in 1536. Both made
sincere attempts to reform their sees but were prevented, partly
by their inability to speak Welsh, and partly by local jealousies
and conflicts. In Bangor the long-standing quarrel between
Sir Richard Bulkeley and the archdeacon, another William Glyn,
both minions of Cromwell, led to violence even in the cathedral,
itself. As a result the parish clergy, said the poet Dafydd Trefor,
were like 'poor terrified oxen' who would be mad 'to venture
among such great bulls as Glyn and Bulkeley'. Barlow at
St. David's was a real, go-ahead Protestant who tried to rid his
flock of their superstition and idolatory, to reorganize his
diocese, to encourage Bible reading, and to found grammar
schools to provide preachers. But he was further hindered by his

own greed and arrogance, and by the bitter quarrel between him and the canons at St. David's, who were over-concerned for the reputation of the cathedral and for its very profitable pilgrim traffic.

It is difficult to say how Welshmen in general felt about Henry's changes. Their taking the oath was no proof that they were actively keen on his reformation; it merely showed perhaps that they feared his anger. There is little evidence either way. One priest of Caernarfon is recorded as saying in 1533 that he would like to get hold of the king on the top of Snowdon and there 'souse him about the ears!' But he is an exception. The quarrel of distant pope and king, or even of local 'bulls' meant little to the Welsh peasant. He cared more probably for the sudden predicament of the poor parish priest who ministered to his daily needs. The much-married king now clamped down firmly upon the marriage of his priests; they had to give up either their 'wives' or their livings. On this the clergy of Caernarfonshire dared send a protest to Cromwell in 1536. But in general Welshmen did not feel strongly one way or another about Henry's 'takeover'. The Reformation could have little real meaning for them while it appeared to be an excuse for their betters to score over their rivals, and while the Bible was read to them in English, however fine, and not in their homely Welsh.

Nor, apparently, did they care a fig about the fate of the monks. Closing monasteries in their day is rather like the closure of the railways in our own: both had served their purpose well, both had lost 'business' alarmingly and were no longer 'profitable', both were cluttered up with outworn 'rules' and regulations, both have marked the countryside with ruins, and both have left a great body of nostalgic sentiment! One difference, however, is that while Wales has kept her main-line railways, she then lost all her monasteries, and most of them at a stroke in 1536. The first of Cromwell's commissions produced the Valor Ecclesiasticus, a remarkably accurate estimate of the annual worth of each abbey. (It has been aptly called 'the Domesday Book of the English Church'). This valued the income of all the Welsh houses at less than £200 each per year, though Tintern at £192 and Valle Crucis at £188 came pretty near.

The second commission of three men followed hard on the heels of the first, nosing out the way of life of the monks themselves. Of two of the commissioners, John Vaughan and Adam Becansaw, we know very little; the third was the notorious Elis Prys of the rising family of Plas Iolyn who had won a doctorate of law at Cambridge the previous year (hence his nickname of 'Y Doctor Coch' from the colour of his college gown), and who lived well into Elizabeth's reign to win a doubtful reputation in his native Denbighshire and at court.[3] The trio started their work in North Wales in September 1535; they were still in South Wales in April 1536 by which time the act to dissolve the monasteries anyway had long been pased! Naturally they uncovered some grave scandals: the abbot of Basingwerk had been employing his monks as a 'strong-arm' gang to keep his family's hold on the abbey; the abbot of Valle Crucis was the

Copyright British Rail

12. A RUINED MONASTERY: FROM MONKS TO MINERS
As the canal in the foreground of this recent print suggests, the dissolved abbey of Neath became the centre of a busy mining and smelting scene.

ringleader of a band of highwaymen in Oxfordshire, and was imprisoned while the commissioners were at his abbey. But these are glaring cases. The inspectors found that most of the monks were harmless enough, lazy and pleasure-seeking but not criminal.

The returns given by the Valor show that Wales in 1535 had forty-seven religious houses and some 246 monks, nuns and friars. The low average of a little more than five inmates per house shows dramatically that these institutions were under-manned and the monastic life no longer popular. (Further Statistics are given in the Exercise on p. 307). Of course monk and gentry had wind of Cromwell's intentions long before even he could carry them out. Some monks had doubtless left before the Valor was taken, and abbots had disposed of much of the wealth, and given favoured tenants long leases of monastic land. Gentry too, like Sir Richard Bulkeley in Anglesey and Sir Rice Mansel in Glamorgan, had already tried to stake a claim to monastic land, often with bribes to Cromwell.

Usually, within weeks of the passing of the act for the dis-solution Cromwell, this 'hammer of the monks', had sent his men to wind up the affairs of the monasteries and eject the monks. Most of the monasteries and all the nunneries went in 1536 and all the friaries in 1538. Some of the Benedictine houses like Ewenny which were cells of greater monasteries in England went one by one after 1537, while three favoured Cistercian abbeys, Whitland, Neath and Strata Florida were reprieved on payment of a heavy fine. By 1539 they had all gone and nobody seemed to care.

What now happened to the buildings and property, the lands and the monks? The case of Margam provides a good example. It was valued by October 1535 and visited by Becansaw and Vaughan in the winter. On 20 June, 1536 an auditor, a receiver, a clerk and three local gentry arrived and over a period of two months made a careful inventory of the monastery possessions. Here are the main items:

	£	s.	d.
Cash receipts from 'temporalities'	235	4	9½
Lead from roofs melted down	372	5	6
Six bells melted down	52	18	9
Goods and chattels sold by auction	51	8	0
Debts to be debited	32	7	11½

Plus corn, 131½oz. of plate, and manuscripts.

The proceeds, the plate and the manuscripts were sent to the king. On 24 August, the agents broke the seal of the monastery and handed over the buildings to Sir Rice Mansel in the name of the king. Margam abbey was no more.

Usually, enough of the buildings would be pulled down to make them unusable, leaving the local people to complete the demolition by looting the stone. Margam was lucky. It had already been 'booked' by Mansel, and, as he moved in almost immediately, its buildings were better preserved. So its grand chapter-house remained intact until the eighteenth century, and its church in part has served the local parish until today.

The king of course took over the vast lands of the monasteries, in much the way that Middle-East rulers have taken over the oil interests of outsiders in our own day. This has been called 'the biggest piece of land nationalization in English history'. At first it seemed as if Henry would keep it 'for the nation', since the great bulk of it was only put out on lease. Later, however, new debts compelled the king to sell outright; Mansel doggedly bought the whole of the Margam estate piece by piece between 1540 and 1557. Henry did not sell the land cheaply, nor give much of it in gifts (Tintern Abbey to the Earl of Worcester is an exception), yet it did not fetch anything like the price it later could.[1] Who knows, had the king been able to wait until the huge rise of prices that would come in a few years—like property inflations in our own day—he and his descendants might well have been able to live without Parliament's help, and democratic rule might have been delayed in Britain by a century at least!

It was the local gentry almost inevitably who profited from Henry's difficulties, families such as the Mansels, the Carnes of Ewenny, and, on a smaller scale, the Cromwells (ancestors of Oliver) at Neath, and the Bulkeleys and Salusburys in North Wales.[2] Two points must be made here, however. Firstly, this wholesale transfer of land only rarely created *new* gentry; usually it merely enhanced the wealth of already established families. Thus it widened the gulf between them and the local peasantry. Secondly, selling them land did not necessarily win these families over to the king's Reformation. The Mansels, Carnes, Stradlings, and above all the favoured earls of Worcester all remained good Catholics. Nevertheless, the sale ensured that any return to Roman Catholicism could only be a limited one. Not even Mary would hope to make these 'adventurers' disgorge their gains and with them open new monasteries.

And what of the monks? Few of them suffered real hardship. All were given reasonable pensions that put them at least on an equal footing with parish priests. Leyshon Thomas, the good abbot of Neath, was given a handsome 'handshake' of £40 a year. Many monks became priests, others returned to their families and lay occupations. Many of the nuns married.

Finally, the results of the dissolution were not all that dramatic, any more than were those of its contemporary, the Act of Union; for both mainly recognized, ordered and accelerated processes begun long before. Religious life did not suffer unduly, for the great majority of the monks had long lost sight of the monastic ideal and were failing in their spiritual work. Nor was their part in social and economic life important any longer. Laymen had taken over their work as farmers, and, after the dissolution, showed themselves at least the equal of, if not better than the monks as considerate landlords. Possibly travellers and the aged found life more difficult when the monks had gone; but the poor and the young in need of schooling saw little difference.*

The transfer of monastic land, however, had one grave result; it tightened markedly that hold of laymen on the tithes and livings of the church which, as we have seen, had been choking it for a century. The established church in Wales was thus condemned for centuries to be at the beck and call of the gentry, and parson along with peasant must touch his forelock to the squire.

Culturally, the dissolution was a disaster that ranks with the furious destruction of the monasteries by the Vikings six centuries earlier. The loss to architecture, art and scholarship was tremendous. The monastic buildings had architecturally been the biggest and finest; they had housed the best of medieval art in sculptures and work in wood, silver and fabric. The greatest sacrilege of all was the wilful destruction of monastic libraries with their rare and priceless books and manuscripts. Margam was fortunate in this again; much of its collection was preserved, its *Annals* is now safe in Trinity College, Cambridge, and its copy of Domesday Book in the British Museum. But hundreds, perhaps thousands of valuable records are lost to scholars for ever, thanks to the indifference of a king. To Wales with its long literary heritage the loss may have been greater than to England, and a factor in delaying the Revival of Learning. We are not to know. But at the time not a voice in Wales was raised in protest. Even good Catholics and men of learning like Sir Edward Carne were content to see the monasteries die and to take the pickings of the carcase.

EDWARD VI SPEEDS UP

— During the reign (1547–53) of the boy Edward VI, his kingdom was ruled by two regents, the Dukes of Somerset and Northumberland, in turn. Now the stream of the Reformation

---

* Occasionally education benefited from the dissolution. In Mary's reign Geoffrey Glyn, the brother of her loyal bishop William of Bangor, used the Dominican Friary there to endow Friars School.

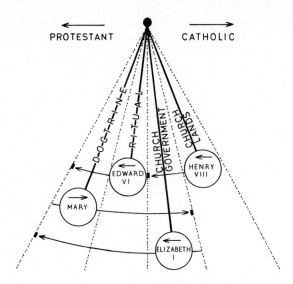

13. THE PENDULUM OF THE REFORMATION
Devise a 'see-saw' chart to show the same features.

became a flood which swept away not only the headship of the
pope but most forms of doctrine and worship as well. Protestant
refugees from the continent in their hundreds flocked to England,
bringing with them not only the beliefs of Luther but the more
extreme and militant creed of Calvin also. A new Prayer Book
in 1549 and an even more advanced one in 1552 set out the
reformed articles of belief, and Acts of Uniformity accompanied
each in order to compel people to conform. The Mass was
abolished, the marriage of clergy again allowed, shrines and
images savagely destroyed, and pilgrimages forbidden. Both
regents, and especially Northumberland, used the tide of events
to gather power and wealth by land-grabbing and debasing the
coinage.

At the same time economic changes accelerated and brought
acute distress. The suppression of the guilds in the towns and the
rash of enclosures in the country brought unemployment. Prices
rose everywhere. Inevitably the peasantry suffered most. The

Reformation had always been a movement of London and south-east England. At last in 1549 English country folk, who now saw both their old faith and their daily living lost to them, could stand it no more. Rebellion broke out in Norfolk and in Devon and Cornwall. The Duke of Somerset failed to deal firmly with the rebels, largely because he had much sympathy with them, and was displaced by Northumberland who had no scruples. Under him the country suffered the worst wave of political, religious and economic confusion since the Wars of the Roses.

But there was no revolt in Wales. William Thomas, the Italian scholar, became clerk to the privy council and the boy-king's political adviser, for which he was given lucrative offices in his native Radnorshire. Good catholics like Sir Edward Carne, however, withdrew from court, and William Glyn resigned his chair at Cambridge. The Prayer Book, rendered in French for the benefit of the inhabitants of Calais and the Channel Islands, was not officially translated into Welsh. Sir John Price printed his version of the Creed, Paternoster and Commandments in the first months of the reign, and William Salesbury in 1551 made further amends with his *Kynniver Llith a Ban*, a translation of the Gospels and Epistles used in the Prayer Book. But it is doubtful if these pioneer works were widely used. To the Welsh peasantry the new English was about as unintelligible as the old Latin. So Edward's Protestantism, like his father's Catholicism, passed over their heads. When the regents attacked their beloved shrines and other 'superstitious practices', however, they grumbled, and the government feared revolt. But none came. Instead, thousands of Welshmen marched with William Herbert, Earl of Pembroke to put down the rebellion of priests and peasants in south-west England in 1549.

MARY GOES INTO REVERSE

When Edward died in 1553 the reformers in Wales as else-where tried unsuccessfully to continue the new faith by making Lady Jane Grey queen. She was proclaimed queen in Beaumaris on one day, but Mary was proclaimed there on the very next.

Now came a complete 'about-turn'. William Thomas lost all his offices, supported Wyatt's ill-fated rebellion in 1554 on behalf of poor Lady Jane, and was imprisoned and beheaded. Carne and Glyn, however, emerged to the full limelight, the first as Mary's diplomat-in-chief and the second as bishop of Bangor. The stream of refugees reversed too. A few Welshmen of real Protestant conviction like Richard Davies and Thomas Young were among the 500 or so clergy who fled to the continent, and the queen let them go.

Mary now tried to enforce a return to the Catholicism of her father, and, after her marriage to Philip II of Spain, to the supremacy of the Pope. The Mass was restored, the Prayer Book banned, married clergy expelled from their livings, and bishops deposed. But the devout queen could not swing the pendulum back all the way. She could not restore the abbey lands nor recall the monks. Nor could she easily get the clergy to leave the wives they had hastened to marry in her brother's reign.

It was this question of clerical marriage that caused such com-motion as arose in Wales, indeed the most general one of the whole century in Wales. And not without reason. A poor woman who had been 'married' in say, 1534, unmarried by Henry VIII in 1535, restored by Edward VI in 1547 was to be disowned once more! One priest in every eight in the diocese of Bangor was 'sacked' for refusing to abandon his wife, and even one in six in St. David's. These were far higher proportions than for England generally. Scores of others, however, chose to abandon their wives and be moved to other livings in a sort of clerical musical-chairs. Of course there was much 'dodging' of the law. Even devout Bishop Glyn, son and grandson of priests, and him-self a father, dared to wink his eye at much that went on.

In other respects Glyn was a model bishop; he resided in his diocese and regularly moved among his clergy instructing them in their duties. Doubtless there were many others who were Catholics by real conviction, such as the young scholar Morys Clynnog, chaplain to Mary's great reforming Cardinal Pole, and his friend Gruffyd Robert. Both were robbed of high office by Mary's death in 1558, and chose lifelong exile rather than serve under Elizabeth.

When Mary, in 1555, turned to the wholesale burning of heretics like Cranmer, there were apparently only three in South Wales and none in the North who were prepared to die for their Protestantism. One was Robert Ferrar who had succeeded Barlow as bishop of St. David's, and like him had quarrelled bitterly with his canons. He died in the flames in Carmarthen square with great courage, which lifted him above the petty prejudice and bickering that had frustrated his genuine attempts at reform. Rawlins White, a poor fisherman, was burnt at Cardiff. William Nicholl of Haverfordwest, of whom we know little, was the third. We cannot safely argue from the fewness of martyrs that Protestantism had necessarily taken less root in Wales than elsewhere. Two-thirds of the 300 who died in England and Wales were from London and the towns of its near counties; only one died in the north of England and only one in the west country. The Reformation was a product of the south-east and of towns. In the remote rural west and north the older practices lingered undetected, no matter what king or bishop came or went.

Very little drama and no rebellion had attended the religious changes of the three reigns in Wales. Why? The remoteness of the country, its poverty and lack of communication provide one answer. The lack of leadership from a self-seeking, 'adventuring' gentry is another. The absence of a real identity in a prince, a court or a university of its own is a third. Loyalty to the house of Tudor, which had given the Welsh not only a sentiment but also the solid gain of law and order, must also go far to explain the absence of rebellion. The key fact about the Reformation in Wales is not what Welshmen believed about religion but what they believed about their king. Above all, Wales would remain indifferent to Protestantism and Catholicism alike until the Bible in her own language would give her people real conviction.

ORIGINAL EXTRACTS

1   JOHN LELAND VISITS TWO MONASTERIES RECENTLY DISSOLVED:
At Goldclif a iii. myles from Newport on the Severn shore was a priory of
monkes of the French ordre, suppressed, and the landes given to Eton
College.

Lanternham Abbay of White Monkes a ii. myles from Cairlion lately
suppressed.
                        (L. T. Smith: *Leland's Itinerary in Wales*, p. 45)

2   THE GRAB FOR MONASTIC LAND: Sir Richard Bulkeley writes to
Cromwell:
    (*a*) (*If Cromwell will support Bulkeley's candidate for the abbey of Aberconway,
he promises to pay him £100 —*) . . . to be paid unto your hands at such a
day as it shall please you to appoint.

    (*b*) (*He begs for monastic land at Penmon, Anglesey*) I beseech you that I may
have it to farm according to the king's books, for it lieth hard at my nose,
and I and my elders have ever been stewards of the said place.

    (Glanmor Williams: *The Welsh Church from Conquest to Reformation*, p. 407)

3   DERFEL GADARN'S IMAGE DESTROYED: Elis ('Red-hot') Prys
writes to Cromwell re his commission to destroy images:
    . . . there ys an image of Darvelgadarn (at Llandderfel) . . . in whome the
people have so greate confidence, hope, and truste, that they cumme dayly
a pilgramage unto hym, somme with kyne, other with oxen or horsis, and
the reste withe money: in so muche that there was fyve or syxe hundrethe
pilgrames, to a man's estimacion, that offered to the saide Image the fifte
daie of this presente monethe of Aprill. The innocente people hathe ben
sore alured and entisid to worshipe the saide Image, in so muche that there
is a commyn sayinge as yet amongst them, that who so ever will offer anie
thinge to the saide Image of Darvellgadarn, he hathe power to fatche hym
or them that so offers oute of Hell when they be dampned.

    (*Later Prys reports that he has taken down the image, having—surprisingly for
him!—refused a bribe of £40 by local people not to do so. The Welsh, said the
chronicler Hall, had a prophecy that the image would set a whole forest on fire. It
was burnt on 30 May, 1538 at the same time as a friar named Forest!*)
                        (*Archaeologia Cambrensis*, 1874, pp. 152–4)

CHAPTER VI

THE PROGRESS OF THE REFORMATION:
WARS OF RELIGION

THE last years of the 1550s provide a convenient milestone in the history of Europe. The treaty of Cateau-Cambrésis of 1559 brought a truce in the wars between France and Spain that had left them both bankrupt. New monarchs appeared: Philip II of Spain in 1556, Elizabeth of England in 1558 and Francis II of France in 1559. The Peace of Augsburg in 1555 gave Germany a period of uneasy religious calm. The Catholic church, regenerated by the Counter-Reformation, was ready to move to the attack against heretic Protestants in the west and heathen Turks in the east. Its sworn leader, Philip II, dominated Europe and indeed the New World, for Spain was now entering her golden age. And in southern France, in Scotland, in the northern Netherlands, and in many a Rhineland state, equally militant Calvinism was ready to take up the challenge. Europe was poised for religious warfare on a grand scale.

For a century there would be almost unbroken strife. France, the Netherlands and Germany, in turn, would be torn apart. Nor would their neighbours go unscathed, but would be drawn in for religious reasons, or choose to interfere for political or commercial advantage. France especially had a bad record in this respect. Emphatically Catholic herself, she was prepared to support both Protestant and even Turk elsewhere in her own selfish national interest.

THE RELIGIOUS WARS IN FRANCE

France herself was the first to suffer. Civil war raged here for thirty-six years (1562–98) between rival houses of jealous nobles, themselves divided Catholic or Huguenot. The queen-mother Catherine de Medici at first strove to maintain a middle ('politique') position, and give enough toleration to the Huguenots to ensure that her three puppet sons in turn would rule in peace. She was nevertheless a Catholic at heart, and when it seemed that her second son Charles IX was falling under the influence of the Huguenot leader Coligny, she acted swiftly. On St. Bartholomew's Day (24 August) 1572, with her approval, the Catholics fell without warning on the Huguenots in Paris and massacred 4,000, including Coligny; as many more died elsewhere in France.

Protestants all over Europe were horrified; Elizabeth of England, with typical showmanship, went into mourning. Catholics everywhere, led by the Pope and Philip II, rejoiced. But the Massacre of St. Bartholomew was in fact a blunder which stiffened the Huguenots to resist, and perpetuated the wars for another generation, attended by further faction and killings. In 1589 old Catherine died and the last of her sons Henri III was assassinated. The rightful claimant to the throne was now the Huguenot leader Henri of Navarre, of the house of Bourbon. Now, too, Philip II of Spain joined in, not only as a good Catholic but as the father of Isabella the next claimant. Henri proved a victorious general in battle; moreover, the tide of national feeling against Spanish interference flowed his way. Only one snag remained, and he removed it by becoming a Catholic in 1593. Five years later the Spaniards made peace and left, and the Edict of Nantes gave the Huguenots generous freedom of worship and civil rights, especially in the important towns of the south-west. Henri, it is often said, declared 'Paris is worth a Mass'. What he meant was that to the rulers of France national interest was more important than religious principle. This was to be the code for the long line of Bourbon kings who followed him for two centuries.

THE REVOLT OF THE NETHERLANDS

Meanwhile, strife raged in the Netherlands. Here at the gateway to the Rhine was the wealthiest area in Europe, thanks to the industry of its large population in manufacture, mining and especially commerce; here in its many cosmopolitan towns and international ports flourished a high culture which had readily absorbed the Renaissance influence from Italy. Here, we shall find, came merchant bankers and their agents like English Thomas Gresham and Welsh Richard Clough, spies like Hugh Owen of Llŷn, and scholars and map-makers like Humphrey Llwyd of Denbigh.

The seventeen provinces by 1559 fell roughly into two groups distinguished by both language and religion: those of the north and west, speaking Flemish or Dutch, had with their spirit of free inquiry quickly adopted the sturdy creed of Calvin; those of the east and south speaking Walloon (a form of French), remained Catholic. However, the nobles and merchant princes of all the provinces, though often jealous of each other, were as one in their fierce guardianship of their local liberties.

The Netherlands formed part of Charles V's inheritance from his grandfather, and were now part of the Spanish empire. Charles regarded them as his homeland and, though he taxed their wealth heavily, he treated their liberties and their religious differences with respect and tolerance. Not so Philip II, who left the Netherlands in 1559 and never returned, leaving their government to a succession of regents. He now imposed heavier taxes and showed his determination to stamp out heresy, if necessary with the use of the Spanish Inquisition. The nobles in reply banded together under William of Orange (or 'the Silent') who, though born in Nassau on the middle Rhine, had in fact been brought up a Catholic in Brussels. The struggle here, therefore, when it came was not strictly a civil war over religion as in France, but a revolt against a tyrannical foreign king in defence of national and local liberties and of commercial privileges.

In 1567 Philip sent the able but ruthless Duke of Alva with a Spanish army, the crack troops of Europe, to enforce his will. William, for the moment, was forced to flee, and Alva, by his own confession, put some 18,000 people to death. But in fact opposition was mounting, organized from outside by guerilla

bands who had taken to the sea. In 1572 Elizabeth closed the
ports of England to these 'sea-beggars'. They crossed the North
Sea and seized the port of Brille. The revolt had begun.

In the next year Alva was recalled. Even so William's invading
army failed to hold the south, but Holland and Zealand in the
north were secure behind their water-defences of river, flood-
dyke and sea. Gradually too differences of religion and speech

14. MEDAL TO COMMEMORATE THE DEATH OF WILLIAM THE SILENT
On the obverse Balthazar Gerard, instigated by Philip II, is firing at William,
and on the reverse the Spanish wolf leaps at the Dutch shepherd. The inscription
promises vengeance and declares distrust of Spain.

began to show. In 1578 Philip sent the Duke of Parma, the ablest
general of the day, as regent. In the next year the southern
provinces gave up but the United Provinces of the north held out.

For six years the conflict was bitter. William, struggling ill-
armed in the Flanders mud against the well-equipped regiments
of Spain, lost battle after battle but still came back fighting.
Neighbouring Protestant countries gave little help, though volunteers came as mercenaries in their thousands, including Welshmen led by Roger Williams and Thomas Morgan. Then in 1584
the blow fell. William was assassinated at Delft by a fanatical
Catholic hireling*. As he lay dying he whispered 'Dear God,
have pity on my soul, have pity on my poor people'.*

* See p. 82 below.

William was no great general but he was an outstanding patriot who, like Elizabeth of England and Henri IV of France put national liberty above all religious bigotry.

The United Provinces were now desperate. Elizabeth at last interfered officially and sent a force under Leicester and Williams to help. But still Parma advanced steadily, besieging and winning town after town. By 1587 he had crossed the great rivers and was at the back door of Holland, the rebels' last stronghold.

At this eleventh hour the Dutch were saved by three factors. Firstly, in the immediate emergency, England indirectly came to the rescue. Philip was set on sending his Armada against her and withdrew Parma from the north to organize it. Secondly, a year later, Henri of Navarre became king of France and the civil war there turned into a popular campaign against Spain. The third was a more positive factor than these two distractions of Philip. The United Provinces found a fine war minister in Oldenbarneveldt and a general of genius in Maurice, the eighteen-year old son of William the Silent. While the first reorganized the resources of the Dutch, the second drove the invader back relentlessly in a series of victories won by strategies and tactics that changed the art of war. The struggle lasted another twenty years, but there was never doubt about the issue. By the Truce of 1609, while the south remained as the Spanish Netherlands, the independence of the United Provinces (Holland) was tacitly recognized and their trading rights protected. These they had won partly because of geography, partly from religious fervour, partly because of Maurice's generalship, but mainly because of the patriotism that burned nowhere brighter than in one undistinguished, quiet-eyed adventurer, William the Silent.

THE RISE OF FRANCE

In the first half of the seventeenth century Spain declined, her every enterprise stifled by royal stupidity and religious bigotry. Holland, with the momentum of her tremendous effort against the tyrant, rose to leadership in commerce, colonization and culture. But she was too small to maintain it for long. In the second half of the seventeenth century England challenged her dominance in three Dutch Wars. But not yet was it the turn of England. This was the heyday of France.

The foundations of French greatness were laid before 1660 by three great statesmen—Henri IV and Cardinals Richelieu and Mazarin, all pursuing the one policy: to make the king master in France and France master in Europe. All were fortunate in their times in that all France's neighbours were weak or distracted: Spain was in decline, Italy divided, Holland recovering after her religious war, the states of the Empire torn by the terrible Thirty Years' War, and England crippled by the growing struggle between the stupid Stuart kings and a truculent Parliament.

Henri IV realized that his task was one of reconciliation and reconstruction after the civil war. Three bodies might hinder the work of reconciliation and challenge the will of the king: the Huguenots, the nobles, and the States General (a sort of undeveloped Houses of Parliament). To the first he gave toleration and rights in the Edict of Nantes of 1598; the second he disarmed by inviting them to court where they spent their energies in frivolous activities; the third he simply ignored. For his council he chose able middle-class men, and to carry out its wishes he employed paid civil servants. His right-hand man was the Duke of Sully. Together they pursued a policy of economic reconstruction. By rigid economy and supervision, the system of taxation was made efficient and the exchequer filled; positive encouragement was given to agriculture, to industry, to roads, to trade and to exploration, especially in Canada. Foreign complications they avoided. In many ways Henri's tolerant, cautious, intelligent reign resembles closely the first ten years of Elizabeth in England. Unlike hers his reign was cut short in 1610 by an assassin's knife.

He was succeeded by Louis XIII, a boy of nine years. For fourteen years his mother, a Catholic, ruled as regent, for Sully, a Huguenot, had retired. One event only stands out in this confused period. In 1614 the queen-mother called the States General. Like the Addled Parliament of the same year in England it settled nothing and was soon dismissed. The story of the two bodies was to be very different however; in England Parliament steadily rose to supreme power, in France the States General was not to meet again until 1789, and then only to herald the Revolution.

Richelieu came to power in 1624. During the next eighteen years he fashioned what remained the policy of France for a century and a half. At home he robbed the Huguenots of their political rights and kept the nobles down by means of a spy-network and summary execution. Every department of state was centralized and administered by *intendants* or travelling agents. For finance or social reform he cared little. His great obsession was to make France dominant in Europe. For this he built up a powerful army and navy. He saw the Hapsburgs of the Empire and Spain as the enemy, and was ruthless in his determination to make trouble for them wherever he could. Machiavelli never had a better disciple. Though a Catholic cardinal, he sided with the Protestants in the Thirty Years' War by subsidizing their leader Gustavus Adolphus while trying secretly to bribe Wallenstein, the Catholic general, to leave the service of the Emperor. When Gustavus was killed, he deliberately prolonged the savage conflict for a dozen years by active military interference. When Richelieu died in 1642 France was supreme in Europe and Germany a ruin.

Mazarin continued the policies of his master Richelieu, also for a period of eighteen years. The two men differed in style; where Richelieu would compel, Mazarin, an Italian, would persuade. The latter's difficulties too were greater. Within six months of his taking office, Louis XIII died, and Mazarin was left to rule France with a boy-king, Louis XIV, and yet another queen-mother. He was also left the legacy of hate which Richelieu had won by his ruthlessness. The outstanding event of his period is the Fronde, a series of revolts against the government in which the middle-class now joined with the nobility to rouse the Paris mob. Twice Mazarin and the court had to flee the city. He waited until his opponents, alarmed by mob rule, fell out among themselves, then acted. Meanwhile the armies of France had proved victorious over the Spaniards, both in the south and in the Netherlands.

Mazarin died in 1661 and the personal rule of Louis XIV began. The two cardinals had succeeded well in their avowed aims: one man ruled France and France towered over Europe. But in the fields and in the streets there was welling up such a tide of resentment at injustice and crippling taxation as would one day overwhelm monarchy and nobility in the torrent of revolution.

THE THIRTY YEARS' WAR

The Thirty Years' War of 1618–48 was fought out in Germany which was laid waste as a result. This, however, was no local struggle, but the first of the great international conflicts on a grand scale. At some point or another almost every country in Europe was involved. Certainly not until the Great Wars of the twentieth century was such a useless holocaust of carnage and destruction committed.

15. TWO RIVAL GENERALS
(a) Gustavus Adolphus   (b) Wallenstein.

Nominally it was all over religion, a revival of the quarrel between Catholic and Protestant, particularly Calvinist. In fact it was also a tangle of the Emperor's quarrels with France, with his Princes, and with the Pope. As it progressed, the war itself unfortunately created new issues: the vested interests of mercenary generals like Wallenstein, commercial ambitions, and the question of the control of the Baltic.

Both the military treaty of Cateau-Cambrésis and the religious Peace of Augsburg had been compromises and temporary. Minor squabbles there had been but none had led to war. Nor need an incident of 1618 in Bohemia have done. Here the Czechs, independent and increasingly Calvinist, had broken with long tradition and rejected the Hapsburg Ferdinand as their king, thrown his agents bodily through the palace window in Prague, and elected instead Frederick of the Palatinate, the son-in-law of James I of England. It was a challenge that Ferdinand, a keen Jesuit, and newly-made Emperor, could not refuse. By 1620 his mercenaries had completely defeated Frederick's, and Bohemia was made a subject state and Catholic by force. So it remained until 1918 when it at last regained its liberty as part of Czechoslovakia.

The matter could have ended there. But the mercenaries had to be paid and disbanded, Ferdinand's allies had to be rewarded, and above all the princes were alarmed at the Emperor's success. The Lutheran Protestant princes stayed neutral but the Calvinists now sought help from foreign powers and especially France. Richelieu readily organized an alliance of France, England, the United Provinces and Denmark. A local rebellion had become an international struggle.

Ferdinand now employed Wallenstein, a brilliant mercenary general who was determined to make war a paying 'business-racket'. He defeated the forces of the Protestant alliance, pressed northwards, and by 1629 had won much of the coastal states of Germany and the title of Admiral of the Baltic. Here at the Peace of Lubeck the war could again have ended.

16. EUROPE IN 1648.
Compare this with an earlier map on page 4.

But the Emperor's success had alarmed even the Lutheran princes. Moreover, Gustavus Adolphus, Sweden's rising king and brilliant soldier, could not allow the Baltic to become a German lake. So he contracted with Richelieu to keep an army in the field subsidized by France. Thus the struggle went on and worsened. The suffering of the civil population became enormous. At the sack of Magdeburg in 1631 alone, 24,000 people, mainly Lutherans, were killed. Gustavus now pushed south-west into Germany. In November 1632 his forces faced Wallenstein at Lutzen and defeated him. But Gustavus was killed. A little more than a year later Wallenstein himself was assassinated. The two great protagonists dead, it should have been clear that no side could any more win complete victory. In 1634 the Emperor, helped by Spain, defeated a combined Protestant army at Nordlingen, and in the next year peace was again signed at Prague, a compromise on the lines of 1555. Again the conflict could have ended. But Richelieu had spent too much on subsidies to let it. He must interfere actively. He made new alliances with Sweden and the United Provinces, and the war went on for another thirteen years. Thanks to the French generals, Turenne and Condé, the military dominance of Spain was shattered and that of France established. It was at last wrested from her by England's Marlborough in 1704.

After international war came the international peace of Westphalia in 1648. The right of the Princes of the Empire to decide the religion of their states was now extended to include Calvinists. France gained rich possessions in the Rhineland, Sweden a controlling influence along the southern shores of the Baltic, and the state of Brandenburg scattered lands in North Germany. These three would be the rising continental states of the future. But for the moment poor Germany was a desert, her culture and economy set back at least a century and without the ready means of recovery which the Netherlands and France enjoyed. For her the war had truly been a Second Black Death.

England played little part in the Thirty Years' War. The initial revolt centred on James I's son-in-law, Frederick of the Palatinate.

But both he and his son Charles I sent little effective help. After 1629, Charles trying to rule as an absolute monarch, had neither time nor money to spare for Europe. Hundreds of his subjects saw service as volunteers and mercenaries, however, and many like Prince Rupert of England and Sir Thomas Morgan* of Wales returned as veterans to fight for King or Parliament in the Civil War. This, in a way, was England's own religious war. It too ended in 1648. The political struggle between France and Spain went on till 1659, but Europe's 'Reformation wars' were all at last at an end.

* Lived 1604–79. Not to be confused with the earlier Sir Thomas Morgan (1542–95), the friend of Sir Roger Williams. See pp. 117–9 below.

ORIGINAL EXTRACTS

1   THE DEATH OF WILLIAM THE SILENT:

. . . the sudden loss of the Prince of Orange, who on Tuesday in the afternoon as he was risen from dinner and went from the eating place to his chamber, even entering out of a door to go up the stairs, the Bourgonian (Balthasar Gerard) . . . making show as if he had some letter to impart and to talk with his Excellency with a pistol shot him under the breast, whereof he fell down dead.

After having done the deed, he (Gerard) fled towards the rampart behind his Excellency's lodging, thinking to escape by climbing the walls. And being taken by Captain Willems (Roger Williams), with a boy and several others following, the wicked traitor cried 'What is the matter, have you never seen a man killed before now? It is I who have done the deed, and would do it (again) if it were still to do'.

. . . The same evening he was beaten with ropes . . . notwithstanding there was no sign of distress or repentance . . .

. . . On Saturday 14 July he was publicly put to death . . . At the time when he was in the greatest suffering, having his flesh torn off with red-hot pincers in many places, the minister asked him if he did not yet repent. The traitor answered: 'Leave me to finish my prayers', and remained obstinate till death.

(*Calendar of State Papers, Foreign* 1584, Nos. 715 (2 July) and 721 (4 July))

CHAPTER VII

THE PROTESTANTS

ELIZABETH'S accession to the throne in November 1558, was almost as much an adventure as that of her grandfather, Henry VII. Now, however, the kingdom was divided not by the jealousies of two great feudal houses but by religion. Religion indeed was the basis of all the problems that faced her: of the struggle of Anglican, Catholic and Puritan at home, of the succession to the throne, and of the hostility abroad first of France and Scotland and then of Spain. Even the discontent caused by the acute poverty of the day often expressed itself as unrest over religion. Like all her family, Elizabeth was an opportunitst—one who solved her problems and took her chances as they arose, and worried little about principles, except the one principle of remaining queen over a united nation. This last and greatest Tudor could be as vain, ruthless and self-willed as her father, as frugal, shrewd and peace-loving as her grandfather, and as courageous as both. It was these qualities in the queen, imitated nationwide by her subjects, that made her long reign a period of unequalled excitement, colour and adventure.

Elizabeth also had the Tudor gift for choosing the right helpers.[1,2] Three of her nearest advisers in 1558 were of Welsh origin, all members of a family with widespread connections in Brecknock and in Ewias, the Welsh-speaking district that had been joined to Herefordshire by the Act of Union. Blanche Parry was the Queen's chief gentlewoman for a half-century until her death in 1590; she kept the Queen's books and jewels, and had considerable influence over her. Her kinsman, Sir Thomas Parry had also attended Elizabeth since the days of Edward VI; on her accession he was made a member of the Privy Council of eight and became

By permission of Pitkin Pictorials   *By permission of the National Portrait Gallery, London*

17. THE QUEEN'S WELSH CONFIDANTS
(a) Blanche Parry   (b) William Cecil, Lord Burghley.

the most influential of her counsellors until his death in 1560. He was followed by none other than William Cecil, the great Lord Burghley (1529–98). Cecil came of a Norman-Welsh family which had a seat in Ewias at Allt-yr-Ynys, an estate which bridged the river Monnow and the new boundary between England and Wales. Able, wise, utterly loyal to queen and country, Cecil was the power behind the throne for forty years. Proud of his Welsh descent, he kept an active interest in the affairs of Wales throughout his lifetime, as we shall see.

For the first eleven years of the reign the queen and Cecil played for time. In religion, firstly, they compromised. 'Elizabeth', said the great historian Macaulay, 'founded a national church halfway between Rome and Geneva', halfway, that is, between Catholicism and Puritanism. An undoubted Protestant, she was nevertheless tolerant to both Catholics and Calvinists; as long as her subjects took the oath of supremacy and accepted the new Prayer Book of 1559 and the Act of Uniformity that went with it, she asked no question, imposed the lightest of fines, and certainly burnt nobody. In foreign policy, secondly, she played her enemies one against the other; refusing to commit herself in marriage, she used the question of her successor to pit France against Spain, and the Presbyterian Scottish lords against their fickle, half-French Catholic queen Mary. Thirdly, she brought order to economic and social life by restoring the coinage and by a new Statute of Artificers in 1563 which controlled the wasteful move-, ment of labour, regulated wages and did much to combat the steep rise in prices.

In 1570 the Pope finally excommunicated Elizabeth. He was too late. The wise, firm measures of the previous years had brought order and contentment to the great majority of her subjects, who now stood solidly behind her. The Catholics then brought to Britain priests specially trained on the continent, and, later, fanatical Jesuits in an attempt to stem the tide of Protestant belief, but without any great success. Now too in desperation they plotted to kill the queen; but Ridolfi's plot in 1571, Throgmorton's in 1583 and Babington's in 1586 all failed, largely because of the watchfulness of the secret service organized by Francis Walsingham, the queen's principal secretary. Elizabeth, now sure of her ground, imposed increasingly heavy penalties against recusancy, that is, religious disobedience. These measures, together with the help which the queen, at first secretly and then openly, gave the rebels in Philip II's Spanish Netherlands, her refusal to marry him, and the attack of English seamen upon his treasure-ships infuriated the 'most Catholic king' of Spain. Finally, in 1587 Elizabeth agreed to the execution of Mary Queen of Scots, who had been at the heart of all the plots. It was the last straw. In the summer of 1588 Philip sent a huge fleet of galleons loaded with soldiers to invade England. But the skill of the English seamen, Catholics as well as Protestants, the quality of their cannon (many cast and bored in Welsh foundries), and a 'most Protestant' gale wrecked the Spanish Armada, and with it any hope of reconverting England again to the old faith. For the rest of the reign Elizabeth remained unchallenged; abroad it was she who now took the attack to Catholic Spain and Catholic Ireland, though not always with success.

The work of the Protestants in Elizabethan Wales will occupy the rest of this chapter. The next will follow the stirring story of their Catholic contemporaries. A third will describe the part played by Welsh 'adventurers' in the varied and exciting 'high-life' of Elizabeth's day, a fourth, the pattern of society and politics, and a fifth the less colourful but even more important features of everyday life and labour.

THE ANGLICAN CHURCH IN WALES

Elizabeth's first task was to discover the state of the clergy. She divided England and Wales into regions each with its group of visitors or inspectors. Wales, Herefordshire and Worcester-shire formed one region with five visitors. Three of these did the work in Wales: Richard Davies, Thomas Young and Rowland Meyrick—the first two newly returned from exile. Bishop Kitchin, who had held Llandaff under Henry VIII, Edward and Mary, agreeably trimmed his conscience for the fourth time and took the oath! The other three Catholic bishops resigned, and two of them, Morys Clynnog of Bangor and Goldwell of St. Asaph, together with Gruffydd Robert chose exile abroad. But, rather to the visitors' surprise, the rest of the clergy, almost to a man, conformed without a murmur and the lay people, largely un-comprehending and uncaring, duly followed suit.

The three visitors themselves took over the vacant sees. Davies went to St. Asaph, Meyrick to Bangor and Young to St. David's. Within a year Young was translated Archbishop of York, and Davies took his place in St. David's. They were all sincere, hard-bitten reformers, anxious to stir the lukewarm conformity of their flocks into a burning zeal for Protestantism. In their reports, as a result, they probably give us an over-black picture of the religious state of Wales—the age-old superstition and idolatry, much of which had returned under Mary, the pluralism (of which indeed they themselves were not guiltless), absenteeism and lack of preaching.

There major difficulties barred the way to reform: the reluctance of the gentry to give a lead, the poor quality of the clergy, and the lack of printed books in the Welsh language. Slowly but surely over the forty-five years of Elizabeth's reign, the Welsh church improved in every one of these three aspects.

The gentry swung steadily to overwhelming support for Protestanism. As the long conflict with Spain developed, and Catholics became identified with treason and plotting, the loyalty of the upper classes to the Queen grew and with it their liking for her church, for it stood for order and stability. Moreover, the gentry became better educated in grammar schools and universities where they came in touch with new ideas and new books which were mostly religious in character. Both the landed gentry and the 'new gentry' of trade and commerce played an active part in the publication of books. Without the support of landowners like Sir Edward Stradling and of merchants like Humphrey Toy, and in the next century Thomas Myddelton and Rowland Heylin, much of the religious literature of the period might never have been written.

There was, secondly, a marked improvement in the character of the clergy by the end of the reign. The bishops, now playing a smaller part in the affairs of state, devoted more time to the care of their dioceses. They were usually resident and in constant touch with their clergy. They were mostly Welshmen and aware of the needs of their flocks. Sixteen bishops were appointed to Wales by Elizabeth, and of these twelve were Welshmen and all resident. There was a marked rise also in the number of ordained clergymen, the majority of whom were better educated. They lived better lives too; for one thing marriage of the clergy was no longer a 'shady' business. Of course there were still indifferent priests. John Penry, as we shall see, complained bitterly about their shortcomings and especially of their neglect of preaching. But, burning zealot as he was, he at the end of Elizabeth's reign, like the bishops at its beginning exaggerated the failings of the clergy and set standards of good preaching that were too high.

18. WALES 1558-1760.

The chief place-names referred to. Maps on pages 184, 278 and 279 show additional details.

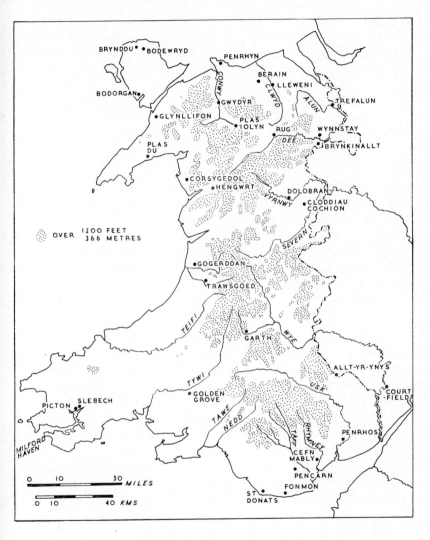

19. SOME SEATS OF THE GENTRY

The most dramatic improvement, thirdly, came in the provision of religious literature. Both Protestants and Catholics had long realized the value of the printed word as a means of winning first the clergy and then the laity to their beliefs. Now in the queen's reign the printing press came into its own in Wales.

THE TRANSLATION OF THE SCRIPTURES:
THE NEW TESTAMENT 1567

The translation and printing of the Scriptures and other religious works in the second half of the sixteenth century is Wales's particular contribution to the Renaissance. Many had earlier tried their hand at turning parts of the Bible into Welsh. Around 1500, for example, there flourished in Glamorgan a group of prose writers whose translations have been preserved for us in manuscript copies. But none were printed. It remains a curious fact of Welsh history that it was almost entirely North Walians who translated the Scriptures in print in the sixteenth century, and equally South Walians who publicized them in the seventeenth and eighteenth.

The translators were of course Protestants to whom the open Bible is the very basis of belief. The introductions they wrote to their works tell us a great deal about their minds and motives. They bitterly attack the clergy for their inadequacy; they bemoan the decline in moral standards and the scarcity of printed books; they point with pride to the ancient glories of the Welsh, especially as pioneers in the Christian faith in these islands; they rejoice in the antiquity of their literature, and beg their countrymen to find and preserve old manuscripts in which it lies; they all press for the use of the native Welsh language in religious services and books. These were the pleas of humanists everywhere in western Europe, and they show that at last Wales had been drawn into the fast-moving current of Renaissance learning.

We have already met the two pioneers in the business—Sir John Price and William Salesbury. 'God', said Price, 'has given the printing press in our midst to multiply knowledge of His blessed words'. He, however, was writing at the end of an ever-busier life as a politician. So the onus fell upon the young William Salesbury. He has been justly called 'the greatest Welsh scholar of the century'. Certainly, it was he who energized the movement for translation.

Of Salesbury's many books we know a great deal; of his life sadly very little. He was born of a good family about 1520 at Cae Du, Llansannan, high on the Hiraethog hills of Denbighshire, but spent most of his life at Plas Isaf, Llanrwst. About 1540, probably, he went to Oxford. There he drank in the new Protestant beliefs, and developed a burning zeal to make them known to his countrymen in printed Welsh. During the reign of Edward VI he was in London, now the Mecca of Protestant refugees. Indeed he may now have met Price while he studied there. In his first year in the capital he produced two printed works, of apparently contradictory aim. The first was a dictionary, which from its Welsh-English layout was intended, it seems, for Welshmen learning English. In the second book, *Oll Synnwyr Pen Kembero* (Collected sense from a Welshman's Head) Salesbury puts into print a collection of Welsh proverbs compiled by his friend and co-humanist, Gruffudd Hiraethog. In the preface to this he emphasizes that their own language is itself a perfectly good medium for Welshmen to learn the Protestant ideas. But time is running out:

'Go on pilgrimage barefoot to the King's Grace and to his Council to desire that you may have authority to have the Holy Scriptures in your own language'.

This sense of urgency for action marks all Salesbury's writings in these years. In 1550 he produced three books: one a guide to the pronunciation of Welsh, and two others attacking Catholic practices. In the next year, as we have already seen, he published his *Kynniver Llith a Ban*, a translation of the gospels and epistles in the Prayer Book. His preface to this begs the bishops of Wales to compel their clergy to use it. How far they complied we do not know. Unfortunately, Salesbury already shows in this book the curious ideas about word-forms that were to mar his later work. Nevertheless, its use was enforced in his home diocese of St. Asaph in 1561.

In 1552 another petition, probably by Salesbury, was presented to the bishops, pleading for a Welsh translation of the New Testament. Before the bishops could act, however, Edward VI died, Catholicism returned, and the scholar retreated home to Denbighshire. For some six years there is silence, though we may guess that Salesbury used his seclusion to get on with the work of translation on his own. Then in 1558 Mary died and Richard Davies, another native of the Conway valley returned from exile in Frankfurt, and possibly Geneva, to become bishop of St. Asaph. He and Salesbury were now near neighbours, and probably discovered, or perhaps renewed, their mutual interest in producing a Welsh version of the Bible. It was important that they had the queen's backing; only she could give permission to print, and only she could compel the translation to be read. Now Davies was an active member of the House of Lords and of the Council of Wales and the Marches, and a trusted agent of the Privy Council. He also had influence with Cecil and with Arch-bishop Parker. Elis Prys, Salesbury's brother-in-law, could doubt-less 'lobby' the House of Commons and ensure the help of his patron and the queen's favourite, the Earl of Leicester. There were many other influential Welshmen at hand to help, such as Humphrey Llwyd of nearby Denbigh, the celebrated antiquarian and map-maker, and Gabriel Goodman of Ruthin, now Dean of Westminster.

As a result an act of Parliament was passed in 1563 ordering the five bishops of Wales and Hereford to ensure that the Bible and Prayer Book were translated into Welsh by St. David's day 1567, and put alongside the English version in every church in Wales. Meantime during services the clergy were to read the Epistles, the Gospels, the Lord's Prayer, the Articles of belief, the Litany and the Ten Commandments in Welsh, presumably from the works of Price and Salesbury. But no grant of money was made to help the work, and the time allowed was all too short. Nevertheless, this Act, in denial of that of 1536, had given official recognition to the Welsh language.

Davies alone of the Welsh bishops took action. At his palace at Abergwili, near Carmarthen, he kept 'a typical Renaissance household' where poets and scholars, priests and politicians all found open house and a congenial atmosphere in which to exchange views. Here he invited Salesbury and Thomas Huet, precentor or dean of St. David's, to come. The three settled to the task of translating the New Testament from the Greek, having first shared out the work between them. Davies was to tackle five epistles (Hebrews, I Timothy, James and I and II Peter), Huet the Revelation and Salesbury the rest, which was by far the lion's share. Salesbury too (and not Davies, as was once thought) was mainly responsible for the Prayer Book. In May 1567 he was back in London, the guest of Humphrey Toy, a bookseller and a nephew of a rich Carmarthen merchant of the same name who was a friend of Bishop Davies. There presumably he supervised the Queen's printers at their task of setting type for the unfamiliar words of Welsh. Both the Testament and the Prayer Book, paid for probably by the younger Toy, were published before the year was out.

Now the essential books of the Protestant faith were available in Welsh for priests to make public and anyone to read who could. The Testament, unfortunately, is marred by Salesbury's pedantic ideas about the language. The Renaissance scholar in him took precedence over the Reformation zealot. Not content with giving the meaning in simple Welsh words, he must show their derivation too. Thus he gives many words the Latin form from which they come, probably in order to show the proud classical origins of the Welsh language; for example he writes 'Deo' for 'Duw' (God) 'descendent' for 'disgynnit' (they descended), 'eccles' for 'eglwys' (Church). Again he often does not mutate the second element of a compound noun (writing 'anduwiolion' for the usual, smoother 'annuwiolion') and ignores the nasal mutation of the initial consonant (giving 'yn dyddiau' for the spoken 'yn nyddiau'). Pedantically, he restores many

20. TWO PROTESTANT TITLE-PAGES

(a) The New Testament, 1567. (b) The Bible, 1588. Note the dragon on the right of the coat of arms at the head of the page and the Queen's 'imprimatur' (or licence to print) at the bottom.

words to their older, clumsier form (writing the full 'cyfododd' for the customary 'cododd'). As a result Salesbury's Welsh, read as written, is stilted and harsh on the ear and his print distracting, although we know from his other works that he could write perfectly smooth prose when he chose. He would probably answer his critics by saying that he did not intend to have his words read publicly as written, but relied on the priest to read them in their usual spoken forms.

Unlike Salesbury, the fussy young scholar of independent means, busy bishop Davies had only one aim in mind: to provide his all-too-limited priests and their congregations with the Scripture in a form they could at once understand and enjoy. So his Welsh flows naturally, like the language of the best medieval poets. It was he who wrote 'A Letter to the Welsh People' which prefaces the Testament. The Welsh, he complains, have forgotten their heritage and their duty: learning and nobility are in decay. 'The lust of this world', he declares, 'has overwhelmed Wales today . . . the hall of the gentleman has become the sanctuary for thieves'. Wales which led the field in the first coming of Christianity is now the last in its second coming. 'Awake thou therefore, good Welshman, my beloved brother in Christ; remember the former times when once you were honourable and high in esteem'.

It must be remembered, however, that Salesbury was the moving spirit, and his the largest share of the work. It was he, said the poet Edmwnd Prys, who had 'broken the ice'. He had shown that Welsh, no less than the other vernaculars of Europe, was a fit vehicle for the new learning and the essential language of public worship in Wales. He was thus not only a theologian and a scholar; he was a patriot. In the person of this urgent, industrious lawyer and litterateur, humanist and Protestant, the Renaissance came of age in Wales.

THE BIBLE 1588

Davies and Salesbury no doubt intended to fulfil the commitment of the Act of 1563 and further translate the Old Testament. But they never did, and we can only guess why. Sir John Wynn said they quarrelled over a word; this may be his dramatic way of saying that Davies could no longer accept Salesbury's fads about spelling, etc. Enthusiasts are often touchy, moreover, and Salesbury may have been utterly discouraged by the criticism levelled at his work in his own day. Certainly he published nothing more in print before his death sometime between 1584 and 1594. Bishop Davies, moreover, was probably too busy to think of doing the work unaided. The care of his large scattered diocese alone was enough for one in his late sixties, but he was also active as a J.P., as a member of the House of Lords and the Council of Wales, and, on top of all this, the Queen and her Privy Council gave him tasks ranging from helping to write the English Bishops' Bible of 1568 to catching pirates in Milford Haven!

It was left to yet a third native of the Conway valley to translate the whole Bible twenty-one years later. William Morgan
(1545?–1604) was the son of a tenant farmer in Wybrnant, Penmachno, high in the hills about the source of the Conway, where
the three counties of Caernarfon, Denbigh and Merioneth met. In
1565, helped by his father's landlord, Maurice Wynn of Gwydir,
he entered St. John's College, Cambridge as a 'sub-sizar', that is
a student paying for his studies by 'fagging' for others. Edmwnd
Prys (1544–1623) joined the same college in the same year and
became Morgan's lifelong friend. Both took their bachelor's and
master's degrees at the same time; both became clergymen.
Prys was eventually made archdeacon of his native Merioneth
and settled to a long literary life. Morgan, a brilliant Hebrew
scholar, probably began to translate the Old Testament before
leaving Cambridge. Then he held many livings, but made his
home after 1578 as vicar of Llanrhaeadr-ym-Mochnant. The prolonged and violent enmity of some influential but malicious

By permission of the National Library of Wales

21. TWO PROTESTANT TRANSLATORS
(a) Bishop William Morgan   (b) Edmwnd Prys.

parishioners, ending in a law-suit, doubtless discouraged his work of translating. It served, however, to bring him to the notice of Archbishop Whitgift, who not only declared him guiltless in the matter but thereafter took a keen interest in his work.

Translating the whole Bible was a tremendous task for one man. Fortunately Morgan could marshal much support. He had Salesbury's New Testament, the Geneva Bible of 1560 and the Bishops' Bible at his elbow. In Wales he had his old friend Edmwnd, and in London another graduate of St. John's, Richard Vaughan, then canon of St. Paul's and later bishop of Bangor and of London. There too, ready to help, was David Powel, the historian. By the end of 1587 the great task was finished, and Morgan moved to the capital where he lived with Dr. Gabriel Goodman, a native of Ruthin and yet another brilliant Cambridge scholar, now dean of Westminster and most influential with the great Cecil. Picture then in July 1588, Morgan, this quiet, resolute cleric from the Berwyn hills, elbowing his way to the Queen's printers through the crowds of Londoners on the Strand, all agog with the news that the Spanish Armada had been scattered in the gale of the previous night! A month or so later his Welsh Bible was published.

The 'adventure' of Morgan's Bible has a place of greater importance in the history of Wales than has even the Armada in that of England. Firstly, it achieved the immediate aim of buttressing the Protestant Reformation in Wales.[3] There it sounded the knell of the old faith more effectively than the defeat of the Spaniards. Secondly, it rescued the Welsh language, which Tudor keen-ness for uniformity had implicitly condemned. Thanks to his liberal education in a university which made him familiar with many languages, ancient and modern, Morgan resisted the temptation both of writing in the Welsh of his native Gwynedd, and of mixing the many dialects of Wales. Helped by Edmwnd Prys he chose the classical Welsh of the princely poets of the Middle Ages. Had he not done so, the Celtic language in Wales might well have crumbled into degenerate dialect forms as it did in Brittany, or disappeared altogether as it has in Cornwall.

Thirdly, the Bible put new life into Welsh literature. It gave to prose a standard and a prestige that hitherto had belonged to poetry alone. The prose of the Bible preserved the language and idioms of medieval poetry which might have been lost in the definite decline of verse in the later sixteenth and seventeenth centuries.

In all, the work of these sons of the Conway valley, Davies, Salesbury and Morgan together stands as the greatest single factor in the history of modern Wales, for it knit and preserved the nation. In the address to the queen with which Morgan prefaced his Bible he refers to those who believed with sincerity that it were better that all Welshmen should learn English. 'Let them beware', says he, 'lest they obstruct the truth in their eagerness for uniformity'. Likeness in language, however desirable, would take so long to achieve that religion (Protestantism) may die. 'There is no doubt' says Morgan, 'that likeness in religion is a far stronger bond of union than uniformity of language'.

Wales has survived and made her contribution to the British fellowship of nations largely because her language has made her different, has given her an identity, a bond within her own borders. So the Bible achieved what Glyndŵr and the Tudors had failed to do: it gave Wales, in effect, a focal point for the life of the nation. Perhaps Morgan's Welsh was rather too correct. It was certainly not the tongue spoken on the town square of Caernarfon or Carmarthen. But then it was not intended for selling sheep and cattle, but for the written page and the pulpit. As such, it eventually provided Wales with an exalted point of reference. The Bible in Welsh made more than a little recompense for the Act of Union.

ORIGINAL EXTRACTS

1   THE DEATH OF BLANCHE PARRY:

On Thursdaye last Mrs. Blanshe a Parrye departed; blynd she was here on earth, but I hope the joyes in heven she shall se. Her Majestie, God be praysed, is in helthe, My Lord Triserar, (Cecil) by mayne of some present grief, kipethe his chambar; the gowte, and wynd in his stomake, is the cawse—From Westmynstar, the xvii of Februarye, 1590. Thomas Markham.

(C. A. Bradford: *Blanche Parry*)

2   THE QUEEN'S WELSH APOTHECARY IS SCARED: Hugh Morgan writes to Cecil in 1596:

I myself, walking . . . here in the great hawle of the court Mr. Oliver St. John came unto me with a sterne countenance saying unto me, 'What is the matter that you have set your hand ageynst me unto my Lord Treasurer?'. I beholdyng his countenance sayd 'I wyll answer you before his Lordship'. 'And not else?', said he. 'No', said I, and with that he clapt his hand upon my shoulder, saying in my Eare 'Thou are an old Raskavilia', and fearyng his fury, as God knoweth I do, I went from him as fast as I could.

(C. A. Bradford: *Hugh Morgan, Queen Elizabeth's Apothecary*)

3   GEORGE OWEN REJOICES IN THE WELSH BIBLE:

We have the light of the Gospel, yea the whole Bible in our native tongue . . . whereas the service and sacraments in the English tongue was a strange to many or most of the simplest sort as the mass in the time of blindness was to the rest of England.

(Geo. Owen: *The Dialogue of the Government of Wales* (1594), printed in *The Description of Penbrokshire* pp. 56–7)

CHAPTER VIII

CATHOLICS AND PURITANS

MANY Welshmen refused to conform with Elizabeth's religious settlement, take the oath and attend the Anglican services. The story of these non-conformists is one of the most colourful and exciting of the age; a story of daring deeds and escapes, of spies and martyrs, of sacrifice and devotion, of betrayal and tragedy.

At the start of her reign all the queen demanded of her subjects was an outward show of conformity with the Anglican church. And this the great majority gave. Later, however, as Elizabeth became surer of herself and her people, and the Catholic plots more dangerous, she imposed increasingly severe fines on the recusants, that is on people who refused to attend church. An Act of Parliament of 1587 imposed on a recusant the huge sum of £20 per month or the loss of two-thirds of the profit from his estate. The law was particularly severe on priests and teachers who might actively persuade others to disobey. In the eighties Jesuit priests became the arch-enemy, and in 1581 and again in 1585 fresh laws made helping them treason, punishable by death. Of the 189 Catholics who suffered death under Elizabeth, 123 of them, including 96 priests, were condemned under the act of 1585.

Of course these penalties were not always enforced; they were strictly applied only at times of especial tension, such as the discovery of a plot at home or news of a momentous event abroad like the Massacre of St. Bartholomew in 1572 or the assassination of William of Orange in 1584. It would be difficult to assess the number of the recusants; there was so much 'dodging' and 'winking of the eye' by those in authority from Sir Henry Sidney, the august president of the Council of Wales, down to the humblest J.P. Such officers were happy to tolerate Catholicism but not to suffer for it. Many recusants openly defied the law and paid their fines or lost their lands. Edward Morgan of Llantarnam (Mon.) paid £7,760 in fines between 1580 and 1633. John Williams of Tremeirchion (Flints.) and his family owed a total of £19,200 for over eighteen years' absence from church.

There were clearly defined pockets of recusancy, generally concentrated around certain well-to-do families: the Owens of Plas Du in Llŷn, the Pughs of Penrhyn Creuddyn near Llandudno, the Edwardses of Chirk, the Griffithses of Cwm on the borders of Herefordshire and Monmouthshire, and of course the Somer-sets of Raglan. The old faith continued strong in these areas well into the seventeenth century.

SEMINARY PRIESTS AND JESUITS

Many Catholics, however, preferred exile abroad to the shadowy life of a recusant at home. Most of them were univer-sity men of good family, scholars who had given serious thought to their religion and were prepared to dedicate their lives to it. In them the counter-reformation gathered its forces to regain England and Wales for Rome. The obstacles they faced were great indeed: difficulties of transport and communication; privation; disagreements amongst themselves; spies; fear of capture; lack of printing presses. Their greatest fear was that the great body of Welshmen would become Protestant through the habit of years of regular church-going while there was no longer a Catholic bishop in Wales to consecrate clergy.

Priests must therefore be trained on the continent and ex-ported to England and Wales. But ten years of Elizabeth's reign went by before the first of such 'seminaries' or colleges was set up in 1568 at Douai in the Spanish Netherlands. Its founder was William Allen, a Lancashire man, together with two of his dis-tinguished fellows at Oxford—both Welshmen, Owen Lewis (1533–95) a native of Anglesey and Morgan Phillips (d. 1570) from Monmouthshire. The three-year course they set for their students was hard, and designed to equip them for the dangerous and rigorous life they would face, moving about, each on his own, in Britain.

Not surprisingly, more than one in every five of the students at Douai in the early years were Welshmen. Altogether a hundred Welshmen entered the college in Elizabeth's reign, and some sixty-four of these returned to Britain as 'seminary priests'.

Meanwhile another Catholic trio had given up the high offices in Wales they had held under Mary, and journeyed to Italy, where they were to spend the rest of their lives. They were Thomas Goldwell, bishop of St. Asaph, Morys Clynnog, bishop-elect of Bangor, and Gruffydd Robert, archdeacon of Anglesey. They arrived in Rome in 1561 and were given posts in the English Hospital there. Goldwell took an active part in the work of the Council of Trent in 1562; Gruffydd Robert entered the service of the saintly Cardinal Borromeo at Milan.

In 1574 Owen Lewis visited Rome and proved himself so useful to the Pope that he was pressed to stay there. Four years later, he persuaded the Vatican to set up a second seminary, the English College in Rome, with his fellow countryman Morys Clynnog in charge. But, within a year, Clynnog was forced to resign because of the opposition of the Jesuits, supported by the English students, who claimed that he had been favouring the Welshmen among them. In the same year, and again probably because of the enmity of the Spanish Jesuits, Lewis failed to get financial support from the Pope towards getting Welsh translations of Catholic books printed in Rome.* Gruffydd Robert had already had the first part of his pioneer 'Welsh Grammar' printed in Milan in 1567 and had also helped Morys Clynnog produce his little catechism *Athravaeth Gristnogawl* there the following year.

Two more seminaries were set up, both significantly in Spain, Valladolid in 1589 and Seville in 1592, by the Jesuit, Robert Persons who had come to England in 1580. None of these later

---

* Owen Lewis, after joining his friend Gruffydd Robert in the service of Cardinal Borromeo for a period, returned to Rome where he remained for the rest of his life in high favour with the Pope in spite of Jesuit intrigues. He died in 1595, when about to be made a Cardinal in succession to William Allen. Morys Clynnog left Rome in 1580 for Rouen; in the next year he was drowned while on a voyage to Spain.

colleges, however, proved nearly as popular with Welshmen as the pioneer at Douai (moved to Rheims 1578). Of forty-six students from North Wales attending the four seminaries during Elizabeth's reign, twenty-six went to Douai. This was partly because of the distance, but mainly because of dislike of the Jesuits.

The Spanish Jesuits hated Elizabeth on both religious and national grounds. The Welsh exiles and priests, however, while they differed from the Queen in religion and hoped to reconvert her and their homeland to the old faith, were generally loyal to her person. Thus Morys Clynnog in 1567 warned Cecil in a letter written in Welsh that the Pope was about to excommunicate Elizabeth.[1] In 1570 he was proved right. Now the Queen became fair game for plotters. Hugh Owen of Plas Du was involved in the Ridolfi Plot of 1571 to remove Elizabeth and put Mary, Queen of Scots on the throne. When the plot failed, he fled to the continent where he remained the arch counter-spy of the Catholics for almost another fifty years.

In 1574 the first ordained priests from Douai arrived in Wales. They landed secretly, probably under cover of darkness in some quiet cove, often in disguise and with false names. They moved from one friendly Catholic household to another, celebrating Mass in secret by night with the squire who, by day, openly attended the Anglican church. They lived hazardously indeed, in peril of torture and death, relying on friends, often J.P.'s themselves, to 'tip them the wink' that the Queen's men were about, and to bundle them into a hiding place, often purpose-built in the thick panelled walls of manor houses. A certain Nicholas (John) Owen was expert at making such priest holes in houses all over England and Wales until he was finally caught and died under torture in the Tower of London in 1606.

The government had its spies too, like William Parry, a rascal from Northop in Flintshire, who was saved from the hangman's noose for burglary on condition that he entered Elizabeth's secret service. He made frequent journeys to the continent, spying on Papists and feeding back information to Walsingham. In 1584,

22. A PRIEST HOLE
From a country-house on the Welsh
border.

however, he was said to have turned Catholic, became a 'double agent' and joined a plot to kill the Queen; all of which may be true or merely trumped up by Walsingham, who had no further use for him. He was beheaded in March 1585. The government had many other, more respectable voluntary agents; merchants like Richard Clough, and many well-to-do young men who wandered apparently foot-loose on the continent like William Vaughan of Golden Grove in Carmarthenshire. In 1602 Vaughan warned the Privy Council that new priests, among them at least three Welshmen, were about to leave Valladolid for these shores. As a result, one at least of them was captured at sea.

Gradually the work of the priests bore fruit. Many families like the Pughs of Creuddyn, who had hitherto conformed, became resolute recusants. The Privy Council became more and more alarmed. Repeatedly in 1579 they charged Sir Henry Sidney, the Lord President of the Council of Wales, to search out and punish the priests. Walsingham, probably knowing full well that he was too lenient towards the Catholics, warned him: 'Your lordship has need to walk warily, for your doings are narrowly observed'.

Hugh Owen and two of his brothers who had joined him on the continent continued to pass secret information to Thomas, his one remaining brother at home in Plas Du. The papers were said to be hidden in the messenger's walking stick or in the hollowed heel of his shoe. The mansions of Llŷn became almost openly a main route of entry for the Papists. At last in 1578 the Privy Council pounced. They ordered the Bishop of Bangor and Dr. Elis Prys to search four houses in Llŷn, Plas Du among them. They found nothing suspicious. And no wonder; all the owners had been warned of the search before-hand, it was said, by a clerk of the Council of Wales! But the incident had badly shaken the gentry of Llŷn, who were afterwards at pains to show that they were conforming Protestants.

In 1580 the first Jesuits began to arrive in Britain, led by Campion and Persons. In the next year the government replied with an act which made it a treasonable offence, punishable by death, to seek to convert people to Catholicism. Campion was captured and executed; Persons escaped. In 1582 John Bennett, a native of Holywell and a Douai priest, was arrested and banished; he later became a Jesuit and returned first to Holywell and then to London. The religious situation grew more tense.

Meantime, Richard Gwyn (or White), a young Wrexham schoolmaster, had been in prison since 1580 for openly professing his Catholicism. It seems clear that Gwyn had been acting as an agent between a number of seminary priests and local families. It is equally clear that he was hunted by the extreme Protestants or Puritans in the area. They forced the hand of the authorities, who seemed reluctant to condemn him. Eight times he was made to stand trial; for four years he was moved from prison to prison, sometimes suffering torture but at others allowed to walk freely in the streets of Wrexham with his family. Then in June 1584 the great Dutch leader, William the Silent, was assassinated by a Catholic, and immediately there were renewed fears for the safety of the Queen. In October Gwyn was put to a cruel death in the market square of Wrexham, bravely declaring 'I die in the old Catholic Faith (but) . . .

innocent of all treason'.[2] His cry echoed the feelings of those who were divided in their loyalty to the old faith and to their much-loved Tudor Queen.

South Wales too had produced an arch-spy in the person of Thomas Morgan. As secretary to Mary, Queen of Scots, he knew all her secret companions and was involved in both the Ridolfi and Throgmorton plots. From exile in Paris he now organized Babington's plot to murder Elizabeth and replace her with Mary. Walsingham was probably 'tipped off' by spies set to operate in France after the discovery of William Parry's treachery in 1585. Babington was caught red-handed in August 1586. Among his young confederates were Thomas Salusbury, heir to the great family of Lleweni, near Denbigh, and Edward Jones of Plas Cadwgan near Wrexham. Both were executed on Tower Hill in September 1586. Catholic supporters in Denbighshire were cruelly shocked.

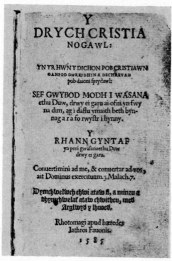

By permission of Gwynedd Archive Service   *By permission of the National Library of Wales*

23. A SECRET PRINTING PRESS AND ITS PRODUCT

(a) Rhiwledyn (Little Orme, Llandudno);
(b) Title page of *Y Drych Cristianogawl*.

THE RHIWLEDYN CAVE

So much for Llŷn, Denbigh, Holywell and Wrexham. Now came the turn of Penrhyn Creuddyn, probably the toughest centre of recusancy in North Wales. Already before Salusbury and Jones were executed the government acted.

The priests from Douai and the Jesuits realized, no less urgently than the Protestant reformers, the value of the printing press in their propaganda. But printing was by statute a monopoly of the Stationers' Company of London and required a licence from the Queen. The penalties for breaking the law became increasingly severe. As a result the Catholics resorted to secret presses.

The discovery of one of them in a cave at Rhiwledyn on the Little Orme, one of the promontories that enfold Llandudno (then only a poor fishing village), is the most exciting of stories. Scholars are still not sure of the details, but the events as pieced together by their clever detective work are broadly these:

The moving spirit was almost certainly Robert Gwyn who had been active in North Wales since his return from Douai in 1576. Four years later the Jesuits Campion and Persons arrived and Gwyn was at a meeting in Uxbridge where they decided to set up a secret press. Gwyn now persuaded Robert Pugh of Penrhyn Creuddyn near the Little Orme to house a press for publishing papist material for Wales. Then in August 1586 Babington's plot was discovered; the authorities were alarmed and the Earl of Pembroke, newly made President of the Council of Wales, was ordered to tighten up on recusancy. In the early autumn Penrhyn was searched and Pugh fled to Rhiwledyn cave, taking the press with him and accompanied by others, including William Davies.

The cave can no longer be found and has probably been quarried away. It is said to have had a narrow entrance some 90 feet down the cliff face from the summit. Inside, it opened into a wide chamber 18 feet deep with a convenient fissure at the back which served as a chimney and possibly an emergency exit. Here they lived for seven months producing copies of *Y Drych Cristianogawl* (Part 1) (The Christian Mirror), which urges

Catholics openly to refuse to conform. This is probably an adaptation by Robert Gwyn of Persons's *Christian Directory*. Yet this printed version ascribes it to 'Gruffydd Robert of Milan'; the title page, which is shown on p. 106, says the book was printed in Rouen (Rhotomagi); it is dated 1585 though we know the printers were at work in 1587; the preface too, signed 'from Rouen by your loving countryman is ascribed to R.S. i.e. Rhosier Smyth, another Welsh Catholic author who was known to be on the continent at this time. All these items were probably falsehoods, however, designed to deceive the authorities as to the whereabouts of the press, a device often resorted to by the Catholics.

However, on 14 April, 1587 smoke from the cave was seen by some local men, probably from the sea, and they reported it to the nearest J.P., Sir Thomas Mostyn. He, however, was slow to take action, and when next day his men entered the cave the printers had fled, leaving their heavy equipment behind, but having first thrown their lead type into the sea, where it was recovered at low tide.[3]

Other recusant papers may have been printed at the Rhiwledyn press but there is no evidence of any. There were certainly other secret presses. One is said to have been set up shortly afterwards at Brecon in the home of Dr. Sion Dafydd Rhys, a fine Renaissance scholar and Catholic sympathiser. Possibly Gwyn fled there to try to complete his *Drych*. Another press was probably set up in a cave in English Maelor (Flints.). However, the *Drych Cristianogawl* remains the first extant book to be printed in Wales. One hundred and thirty years were to pass before a press would operate there legally.

In March, 1592 Pugh, Davies and four students, on their way to Valladolid via Ireland, were seized at Holyhead. Pugh escaped to lead a fugitive life for some years. But William Davies was moved from prison to prison for over a year, openly declaring his faith, and refusing every opportunity given him by his tolerant captors to recant and even to escape. He was finally hanged, drawn and quartered at Beaumaris on 27 July, 1593, watched by a sorrowing crowd. He was in fact the only seminary priest executed in Wales in Elizabeth's reign. He was beatified by the Catholic Church in 1929.

One by one the smouldering fires of recusancy in North Wales were being stamped out. The government was doubtless fully aware of the sympathy shown by very many of the local inhabitants. Nevertheless, faced by open defiance of the law, it was determined to show its teeth. And sympathy never became open rebellion.

THE CATHOLICS IN SOUTH WALES

The seminary priests were even more active in South Wales and on the border. (In fact of the thirty-three priests whose homes were in North Wales, a majority were sent on mission to South Wales). One of the earliest was known by the name of Morgan in Monmouthshire but as Vaughan in Herefordshire. With him in the vital year 1587 was Morgan Clynnog, the nephew of Morys, and also a priest named Griffith Ellis and all were said to be doing 'well and some much good'. The Vale of Glamorgan was a favourite haunt of recusants, amongst them William Griffith the devout squire of Llancarfan, who squared up to the law and forfeited two-thirds of his lands. When he moved to Cwm Llanrothal in the remote hill country west of Hereford, it became, in the next reign, a Jesuit headquarters under Robert Jones, Founder of the English Jesuit mission, and under his successor John Salusbury it became a college. Raglan Castle, the home of the devout Edward Somerset, Earl of Worcester, was the power-house of the movement in 'Monmouthshire and the skirts of the shires of Wales'. It was the lesser gentry and the yeomen who suffered most for their faith; in one year alone, 1593, the government seized the lands of nineteen people in Monmouthshire and threatened another thirty-eight unless they paid their fines. The greater families, the Stradlings, Carnes, Mathews and Somersets were never fined. They conformed most dutifully outwardly, no matter if they harboured priests and celebrated mass in the privacy of their own mansions.

Contrary to what one would expect, in central and west Wales
there is little evidence of recusants; Pembrokeshire was strongly
Protestant. Life in these remote parts was more private, and
beyond the reach of both the greater gentry on the one hand and
of government informers on the other.

In 1603, the year in which Elizabeth died, a report gave the
number of recusants in Wales as 808, or in fact fewer than one
in every 260 of the population. Doubtless there were far more
Welshmen who were Catholic at heart; the declared recusants
were only the hard core of the faithful. Even so, the effective
Catholics formed but a small minority. The work of the seminary
priests doubtless had its effect. They had kept the faith alive in
Wales, and the many records made of their suffering at this time
stiffened the resolve of the more lukewarm Catholics. Many like
Morys Clynnog and Gruffydd Robert had under great difficulty
made a considerable contribution to Renaissance writing in
Welsh.

Yet as a movement to re-establish the dominance of the old
religion and replace the authority of the Queen by that of the
Pope, the Counter-Reformation in Wales was 'a resounding
failure'. The reasons are clear; the patient yet firm policy of the
government compared favourably with the badly organized
campaign of the Catholics; there was the extreme difficulty of
getting printed books and of teaching Welshmen to read them;
but, above all 'the Catholic faith failed in Wales for want of
Welsh priests'. Time, geography and lack of funds were all
factors working against the priests. Not least among their difficulties, finally, was the envy of the militant Jesuits, the failure
of Welshmen, Englishmen and Spaniards to work together in
harmony, and the disagreements between Catholic priests from
abroad and Catholic gentry at home. William Allen's aim for the
Douai students had always been 'to train Catholics to be plainly
and openly Catholics'. Clearly he had failed in Wales. The young
Welshmen who were trained later around the turn of the century
inevitably went to Spain and became Jesuits like Robert Jones

and John Salusbury, or Benedictine monks like John Roberts
from Trawsfynydd and John Leander Jones from Pembrokeshire,
men committed to a shadowy and often sinister existence.

THE PURITANS: JOHN PENRY

Not all the recusants were Catholics. As the reign progressed,
the extreme Protestants or Puritans came more and more into
prominence. The little evidence we have of them in Wales,
however, comes from the border lands where strangely enough,
as we have seen, Catholic recusancy too was strongest. It was the
Puritan element in the Wrexham area that had tracked down
the Catholic martyr, Gwyn. The pioneer Welsh Puritan, however, was John Penry (1563–93) from Llangammarch in central
Wales. While yet a student at Oxford and Cambridge, he
developed strong views about religion. The church, he said,
should be run not by bishops with their authority handed down
from the pope or queen as in the Catholic and Anglican
churches, but by a democratic assembly of presbyters or elders
as in Scotland, guided by the Gospels. He condemned the superstition still rife in Wales, and despised mere attendances at
church services as a means of grace. Real religious conviction
could come only through an understanding of the Scriptures
explained in preaching. Only in one church out of every twenty,
he claimed, was this done.

In 1587 Penry published a *Treatise* to draw the attention of the
Queen and Parliament to the critical state of Wales. Archbishop
Whitgift's answer was to imprison Penry for a month. Like the
Catholics, he turned to a secret press which was at the same time
printing the *Martin Marprelate* tracts, attacking the bishops. At
the outset of 1588 he published *An Exhortation unto the Government
and people . . . of Wales*, pleading for a translation of the Scriptures.
William Morgan in fact was at this very time in London setting
the type for his Bible. In August 1588 Penry published his third
book *A Defence*. The secret press was soon afterwards discovered,
and Penry fled to Scotland where he wrote *A Briefe Discovery*
defending the Church of Scotland. By now, however, he was

convinced that not even Presbyterianism would serve; every congregation of believers should be an authority in itself. In 1592 he dared return in secret to London. There he joined a community of Separatists, or extreme Puritans. He was betrayed, tried, and finally beheaded on 29 May, 1593.[4]

Penry, like the earlier patriot Owain Glyndŵr, had 'risen too early'. Puritanism was nourished best in the towns and in industrial areas. So another half century would pass before it took a firm hold on rural Wales.

John Penry, the Puritan and William Davies, the Catholic, both young men, suffered the death of martyrs within two months of each other. Extremists at opposite poles as they were, they bear strange resemblances; both pressed for more ministers; both pinned their faith on the dissemination of religion through literature and turned to a secret press; both were strangely obdurate. Before his trial, Penry appealed to old Cecil, his countryman. But his appeal was ignored. Elizabeth's government could not brook such bare-faced stubborness, however sincere.

ORIGINAL EXTRACTS

1   MORYS CLYNNOG WARNS CECIL: *(in a letter of May 1567 from Rome, written in Welsh and 'in parables' ('ar ddameg') for secrecy, warning him of the 'dangerous condition' of England:)*

For God's sake, as you love Her Grace the Queen and the kingdom, and yourself also, consider seriously what can and is likely to follow if the Queen is excommunicated and adjudged a wrongful possessor of the kingdom.

(*Cymmrodorion Transactions*, 1901–2, p. 114)

2   A CATHOLIC MARTYR: The death of St. Richard Gwyn, 15 October, 1584:

Well, well sayd the sherriefe, no more of that, dispatch hangman . . . who prepareing himself to execute their bloody willes asked the prisoner forgiveness the second time whereupon the martyr takeing him by the hand kissed it saying, I do forgive thee with all my heart . . . Ffynally as ye executioner offered to put the rope about his neck he smiled adviseing him to leave the occupation, for it was but simple . . . So the executioner

came down and the Sherriefe commaunded ye Jaylour to bid him turn the
ladder . . . In the end as he (Gwyn) was saying the prayer of the publican—
Deus propitius esto mihi peccatori, O God be mercifull to me a sinner,
the executioner turned the ladder, and so he hanged.

(D. Aneurin Thomas: *The Welsh Elizabethan Catholic Martyrs*, pp. 119–20)

3   THE SECRET PRESS AT RHIWLEDYN: *William Griffith, J.P. writes to
Archbishop Whitgift on 19 April, 1587:*

    . . . . ther is a place called Gogarth that buttethe upon Denbigh Sheire . . .
& ther is a cave bye the Sea side about 3 faddomes deepe . . . & the xiiiith
of this Apriell ther weare in the aforesaid Cave twelue or more Jesuites
Seminaries & recusantes the which weare discovered by a neighbour
therbye who sawe at the Caue mouth one or twoe of them with pistoles
whom he spake with & fownd them strangers & such as cared not for
officers wherfore he wente to the next Justice . . . Master Thomas Mostyn
(who) Raised people xl or ther aboutes (and) came to the Caue mouth.
(He) durst not or tooke on hime not to dare to enter the Cave the mouth
therof was soe narrowe but lefte a Watch ther ouer nighte to the number
of xxtie wherof some weare his owne men. I wott not howe by the next
morninge all weare suffered to escape & none of the wach is committyd;
the Justice dwelleth within a myle. Ther was fownde the next daye in the
Cave Weapons within a myle. Ther was fownde the nekt daye in the Cave
Weapons Victualls & the Cave borded & theire Alter. . . .

(Geraint Gruffydd: *Gwasg ddirgel Rhiwledyn, Jnl. Welsh Bibl. Soc.* ix, 1958)

4   A PURITAN MARTYR: *John Penry, the pioneer Puritan, a week before his
execution on 29 May, 1593, writes to Cecil, his countryman:*
I am a poore young man borne and bredd in the mountaynes of Wales.
I am the first since the last springing up of the Gospell in this latter age
that publicly laboured to have the blessed seed thereof sowen in these
barrayn mountaynes . . . I leave the successe of these my labours unto such
of my Contreymen, as the Lord is to rayse up after mee for the accom-
plishing of that worke, wch in the calling of my contrey unto the knowledge of Christs blessed Gospell I beganne.

(David Williams: *John Penry,: Three Treatises* p. xxvi)

CHAPTER IX

ELIZABETHAN AND JACOBEAN ADVENTURERS

THE life-span (1564–1616) of Shakespeare, England's greatest poet, is regarded as one of the most vigorous, exciting and colourful in the whole of our history. Now the Renaissance, in its broadest, sense really flowered—in literature, religious thought and scholarship, as we have seen; in enterprises also in trade and industry; in daring deeds of soldiering and seamanship; and in new fashions of architecture, dress and furniture.

It was a period of outstanding individuals. Welshmen shared fully in this varied activity, and many are represented in Shakespeare's plays. We have met some 'adventurers' like Salesbury or Morys Clynnog already. Here we shall deal with a variety of other Welsh characters who played their part on the broad stage of Elizabethan and Jacobean life. The one talent that links them all is their liking for literature in one form or another.

POETS AND PROSE-WRITERS IN WALES

The Renaissance apparently had little effect on the traditional literature of Wales. In fact poetry in the strict metres, which had reached a pinnacle of achievement in the fourteenth and fifteenth centuries, fell into decline in the sixteenth. There were poets, so-called, in plenty but few showed real talent and training in the craft. Many who now followed the ancient practice of moving from one mansion to the next were little more than vagabonds, hardly different from the many other 'sturdy beggars' who vexed Tudor governments. Thus in 1523 and again in 1568 a few chief bards and gentry were ordered to hold *eisteddfodau* at Caerwys in Flintshire, in order to decide which minstrels deserved a licence to wander and which did not. Another 'bread and butter' practice of the bards at this time was to write heraldic and pedigree poems and elegies as 'status symbols' for prosperous gentlefolk.

Such poets were Siôn Tudur, Simwnt Fychan and Wiliam Cynwal, all of whom were licensed at Caerwys in 1568. Their teacher Gruffudd Hiraethog (d. 1564), however, was a poet of real talent, who rose above these practices and may well claim to be a Renaissance humanist. He compiled a Welsh dictionary, and is ranked with Salesbury who put Gruffudd's fine collections of proverbs into print, and who called him his 'foremost companion' in the campaign to uphold the Welsh language. Another of Gruffudd's pupils, William Llŷn (d. 1580) showed real artistry and sincerity, especially in the elegies he wrote, notably one to his old master. The greatest name, however, is that of Edmwnd Prys, the friend of Bishop Morgan. He represents the new university school of poets who emphasized the need for standards of learning, language and sincerity in poetry, and scorned the old-fashioned and pedestrian writing of men like Wiliam Cynwal.

Elizabethan Wales produced a new kind of 'free' or popular poetry. This had still its set forms, metre and rhyme but was no longer fettered by *cynghanedd* (alliteration). Poems of this kind must have been composed and passed on orally in earlier centuries by lesser bards, but there is no record of them before the sixteenth century. Edmwnd Prys wrote in this way too and so did many of the gentry. The themes of this new poetry were broader. Thomas Jones, a Monmouthshire cleric, for example, in 1588 wrote two poems of thanks, one for the defeat of the Armada and the other for the Welsh Bible. A Lieutenant Peilyn wrote a dramatic ballad poem describing the adventures of a crew of Welshmen who went at Elizabeth's command to harry the Spaniards in the West Indies.[1]

Free communication with England and the printing press had their effect even on poetry. Many poems were doubtless translations from the English. Welsh words too were fitted to old traditional English airs. The professional bards wished to keep their poetry a close secret and disliked the publicity of print. But there was a popular air about this new poetry: it was meant to entertain and to involve a wider public in both its making and its enjoyment. A great deal of the 'free' poetry was of course religious. Its wide appeal was proved by the popularity of Edmwnd Prys's Psalms in this metre printed in 1621. The regular singing of these by Welsh congregations down to today has probably done as much as anything to set down strong roots for Protestantism in Wales.

The greatest advance in Welsh literature at this time, however, was in prose. It was devoted almost entirely to two topics: religion and studies of the Welsh language. Almost all the religious prose was translation. It included of course the Scriptures, the Prayer-Book and the Psalms; the Protestant viewpoint in Morris Kyffin's *Deffynniad Ffydd Eglwys Loegr* and Huw Lewys's *Perl mewn Adfyd* (both in 1595); and the simpler Catholic appeal of Morys Clynnog's *Athravaeth Gristnogawl* (1568) and Robert Gwyn's (?) *Drych Cristianogawl* (1585).

But Catholics and Protestants were of the same mind regarding the Welsh language; it must be preserved and refined at all costs. So they produced books of Welsh grammar, by Gruffydd Robert in 1567, by Siôn Dafydd Rhys in 1592, by Henry Salesbury in 1593 and, best of all, by the great scholar Dr. John Davies of Mallwyd in 1621; dictionaries by Salesbury, Thomas Wiliems of Trefriw and again by Dr. John Davies; and Midleton's manual on Welsh *cynghanedd* in 1594.

The Renaissance may have had little influence on traditional Welsh poetry, but in their prose these devout men, many of whom had wandered far from Wales and drunk deeply of other European cultures, were in the true line of Humanists.

SOLDIERS AND SAILORS

It is remarkable how often Elizabeth's soldiers and sailors were also poets and authors. Perhaps they found relief from the harsh realities of their profession in the fanciful flights of literature.

Sir Philip Sidney, courtier, soldier, poet, and translator of the Psalms, is a typical case. There were several multi-gifted Welshmen like him; notably Morris Kyffin, Will Midleton and Thomas Prys. Sir Roger Williams, the greatest soldier of them all, however, was no poet, though an author of several books on the art of war.

The careers of these four men illustrate for us the whole of Elizabeth's foreign policy. After 1567 it became increasingly evident that Spain presented the greatest threat both to England's safety and to the Protestant cause in Europe. Some, like Sidney, pressed the Queen to attack the Spanish mainland. Others thought it more urgent and practicable after 1572 to send help across the narrow seas to the rebels, mainly Protestant, now resisting Spain under the great patriot William the Silent of Orange, in the Netherlands. At first the Queen refused to commit herself, and England remained officially at peace with Spain; while unofficially her sea captains harassed Spanish shipping, and thousands of volunteers went to fight for the rebels in the mud of Flanders.

Roger Williams was born at Penrhos near Newport (Monmouthshire) of a good family about 1537. He was already an experienced soldier-of-fortune before he was twenty. By 1572, when the Sea Beggars began the Revolt of the Netherlands, he was a hardened veteran. Now he joined with his contemporary and lifelong comrade-in-arms, Thomas Morgan (c. 1542–95) of Pencarn in Glamorgan, to lead the first company of English volunteers to support William of Orange. The Welshman quickly won a name for his dash, gallantry and leadership, but the expedition was a failure. Soon after, on his way to join Morgan in Ireland, he was captured by Spaniards and persuaded to join them, since officially they were not at war with England. For four years 1574–78, he served under Spanish generals, the finest in Europe, and learned from them the art of war. This knowledge he later put into his two books *Brief Discourse of Warre* and *The Actions of the Low Countries*.

In 1578 he rejoined the rebel forces of William the Silent, and over the next years of desperate fighting against the military might of Spain, became his close friend. Williams was with the great leader at his home in Delft when, on 10 July, 1584, he was shot and killed by a hired Catholic fanatic, Balthazar Gerard. It was the Welshman who chased after the assassin and caught him just as he was about to scale the garden wall.* The shock of the tragedy may have converted Williams from a mercenary to a patriot and an ardent Protestant. It certainly persuaded Elizabeth to take direct official action at last and send a force to the Netherlands under Leicester. In spite of the earl's incompetence, the disagreements between the English and the Dutch, the want of money and equipment, and the difficulties of the terrain, Roger won the admiration of friend and foe for his courage and generalship.[2] He was at Zutphen in 1586 when another of his friends, Sir Philip Sidney, was mortally wounded. 'Roger Williams', wrote Leicester, 'is worth his weight in gold'. Both he and Thomas Morgan were now knighted. It was his heroic but fruitless defence of Sluys in 1587 against the Duke of Parma, Spain's finest general, that made Sir Roger a national hero at home, and made his opponent, Parma, beg of him to change sides. But the patriotic Welshman refused, although exasperated by the envy of English courtiers and the continued refusal of the English Queen to listen to him and send more help.

Then came 1588, the year of the Armada, and the English soldiers in the Netherlands flocked home to the defence of Queen and country. Sir Roger joined Drake and Howard on Elizabeth's council of war. But as cavalry commander in the defending army at Tilbury he, unlike them, did not engage the enemy, to his regret.

In the next year Williams with Drake led an ill-fated expedition to Portugal, and incurred the fury of his Queen because he allowed the quixotic earl of Essex, Elizabeth's new favourite, to join the venture against her wishes. Fortunately Drake ignored his Queen's order to imprison Sir Roger, but rather than face her anger the Welshman went to France to help her ally, Henri of Navarre, and his Huguenots against the Catholic League, which

* See extract page 82.

was supported by Philip II. Here for the next four years Sir Roger enhanced his reputation as a daring captain and military strategist. He gained the affection of Henri, and at long last the forgiveness and the gratitude of the Queen. In 1593, Henri turned Catholic in order to win his crown, and Sir Roger came home to a hero's welcome. He was now the 'Queen's Soldier' and the idol of her Londoners. One of them surely would be Shakespeare, walking the streets of the capital in search of 'character' for his plays. It is highly probable that he found in Sir Roger his prototype for Fluellen, the brave, honest Welsh captain of 'Henry IV' and 'Henry V'. But before these plays were performed Sir Roger had moved off the stage of life. He died on 13 December 1595 and was buried in St. Paul's. His lifelong companion Sir Thomas Morgan died the next day. Soldiering was the whole life of Sir Roger.

Our other three soldiers, though never of his European stature, had more varied interests, and kept closer contact with Wales. All three came of good families in the North-east. They were all tutored in Welsh bardism in their youth, all served in the Netherlands with Sir Roger, and all were probably in England at the time of the Armada. All were caught up in the fashionable literary pursuits of the day.

In Morris Kyffin (c. 1555–98) the distinction between Welsh-man and Englishman disappears. Born at Oswestry, a Welsh-speaking part of England since 1536, Kyffin was the friend of William Morgan, translator of the Welsh Bible, on the one hand, and of distinguished English writers like Spenser and Camden on the other. He was also as happy composing poetry in English as in Welsh. A year before the Welsh Bible appeared and the Armada sailed, he published a song in English, *The Blessedness of Brytaine*, praising Queen Elizabeth for, among other things, 'Granting Christ's Gospel in their Country speech'.

After busy years as recruiting officer to the English army in the Netherlands and Normandy, he returned to London, and there in 1594 completed the prose work that was his master-piece—*Deffynniad Ffydd Eglwys Loegr*, a translation of Bishop

Jewel's great *Apologia* for the faith of the Church of England. Its substance shows him to be a man of the Reformation and an ardent Protestant; in its vigorous, smooth, homely Welsh it ranks with the Testament and the Bible as the outstanding prose work of the period. Alas, Kyffin exhausted himself as an over-keen army officer in Ireland, which had now become the focus of Elizabeth's foreign policy, and died in 1598.

William Midleton (*c.* 1550–*c.* 1600) is perhaps our best example of the cultured gentleman of the Renaissance. A native of Llansannan in Denbighshire, he served in the household of the Earl of Pembroke. In 1583 we find him at sea with Thomas Prys, Pirs Griffith and a Captain Koet capturing a rich prize, probably Spanish, off the Canaries. Among the cargo they seized was a quantity of tobacco which they smoked—the first ever—in public, when they returned to their old tavern haunts, to the amazement of the Londoners who watched them. After the defeat of the Armada, Midleton seems to have taken to the sea

24. PIONEER SMOKERS

Thomas Prys and his friends are said to have smoked tobacco not in pipes but with the tobacco leaves twisted together 'like the Indian segars (cigars)'.

again either in the Queen's service or as a buccaneer with Thomas Prys. He perhaps was the Captain Midleton who went to warn the fleet under Lord Howard, in time to save all but Sir Richard Grenville's gallant little ship 'Revenge' from the huge Spanish fleet that lay in wait for them. What is certain is that he whiled away the long hours at sea writing poetry. When ashore, he hurried to publish his compositions. In this he was a pioneer, for the Welsh poets were usually reluctant to commit their work to the printed form which anyone could buy. Midleton, however, wished to popularize poetry, and in a book which he published in 1593–4 he writes about the craft in such a way as any layman of reasonable education could understand and practise it. On the other hand, when he translated the Psalms into Welsh, he used the strict metres which made them difficult for ordinary folk to sing. He died before they appeared in print in 1603.

The youngest and most colourful of the trio was Thomas Prys. Born, probably in the same year as Shakespeare, the son of the notorious Elis Prys of Plas Iolyn, he drank as deeply as any Welshman of the pleasures of Elizabethan life. As a youth he spent an abandoned life in London, roistering, drinking, gambling, brawling. He later expressed his regrets in two odes, one of which is entitled *An Ode to show that London is Hell*! He then turned soldier, and served in the Netherlands, France and Spain, and in Scotland and Ireland. In the 90s he found excitement again in piracy with his bosom friend, Pirs Griffith of Llandegai near Bangor. After some reverses of fortune off the Spanish coast they set up a lair on Bardsey. In the end, however, this wine too turned sour, and Prys expressed his chagrin in another ode, *To show the Misfortunes a Man Suffered at Sea*, which is a comic mixture of English and Welsh, expressed mostly if not always correctly in *cynghanedd* or alliteration. It has all the drama of the chase:

Be Miri!¹ I see a sayl   (1. *By Mary*)
Gif sias, er a gefais i!²   (2. *Give chase for all my worth*)
Owt topsail, yw lowt tipsy
Gif way, er y gauaf wynt³   (3. *before the winter wind*)

But in the end the buccaneer is worsted and vows:

> 'Before I will, pill or part
> Buy a ship, I'll be a sheaphart!'

In spite of his roaming, Prys seems never to have lost contact with his home in the Denbighshire hills. He often returned to roister with the home-keeping lads of Llanrwst, and to engage in friendly competition with local poets. On his father's death about 1595 he came home for good. He settled to the life of squire at Plas Iolyn, bringing up a large family and winning a high reputation for his poetry and especially his elegies. Perhaps his best is that to poor Pirs Griffith, who, to his friend's regret, never abandoned the sea, and lost his ancestral estates at Llandegai as a result. Thomas Prys, almost alone among Welshmen, wrote in his poetry about the exciting, world-wide enterprises which produced heroic giants in his own day. When he died in 1634, the Elizabethan age had passed away; but few men were more typical of it than Thomas Prys, man-about-town, pirate, soldier and poet.

Kyffin, Midleton and Prys were but three of a large band of Welshmen who found excitement and some renown in adventures on land or sea. Among those who ventured with Willoughby in search of the north-east passage in 1553 and died in the Arctic ice were Richard Gwyn, carpenter, Robert Gwyn purser and Richard Morgan, ship's cook. A well-known merchant trading off the African coast was a certain Thomas Evans. When Hawkins was trapped at San Juan de Ulloa in 1567, among the poor wretches he had to abandon to the tender mercies of the Spaniards and the Inquisition were 'Richard Williams, Humphrey Roberts and Thomas Ellis'. When Drake voyaged to the Spanish Main in 1585, he took with him Anthony Powell, his sergeant-major, and Captains Mathew Morgan and Robert Pugh.

MERCHANT 'ADVENTURERS' AND OTHERS

In the second half of the sixteenth century England moved into a period of growing commercial prosperity, thanks to Elizabeth's long peace at home and abroad, the wise financial policies of her advisors like Cecil and Sir Thomas Gresham, and the remarkable urge of her people to venture to all corners of the earth in search of new trade or merely for the joy of voyaging. Merchants accordingly became a new class of gentry, who, by the sheer power of their wealth, could challenge the old in the social, economic and even political life of the country. They formed powerful livery companies at home, such as the Goldsmiths Company in London. Abroad, they invested in chartered companies which traded either as a loose association of individual merchants, such as the Company of Merchant Adventurers, or as a joint-stock venture into which a number of traders pooled their resources and drew their profits in proportion to their 'shares'. Their royal charter gave them the monopoly of trade within specified areas, the Merchant Adventurers to Western Europe, the Eastland Company to Eastern Europe, the Muscovy Company to Russia, and the Levant Company to the Near East. As the monopoly which Spain and Portugal claimed was challenged and broken, companies ventured further afield to form the Africa Company, the East India Company—the most powerful of all—and, early in the next century, the London and Plymouth Companies to North America.

Carmarthen in South Wales was an important centre of commerce in Elizabethan times. Humphrey Toy was one of a group of merchants there who opposed Bishop Ferrar, one of the three Protestant martyrs. It was Toy, or his nephew, a London bookseller of the same name, who bore the cost of publishing the Welsh New Testament and Prayer Book in 1567.

A more eminent group centred round the fast-growing town of Denbigh. Outstanding among them was Sir Richard Clough who, after some travel (including a pilgrimage to the Holy Land where he was made a Knight of the Holy Sepulchre), settled about 1552 at Antwerp as factor or agent to Sir Thomas Gresham. Antwerp was now the centre of the trade and commerce of Western Europe, a city without equal for its wealth, culture and splendour. Here Gresham and Clough served Elizabeth by borrowing money to re-build England's badly depleted finances, by

By permission of the Welsh Folk Museum

By permission of the National Museum of Wales

25. DENBIGH AND THE NETHERLANDS
(a) Richard Clough's chest;   (b) Humphrey Llwyd.

smuggling out arms and munitions, and above all by keeping Cecil informed about events on the continent.³ Thanks to Clough's long-winded letters, no country had a better intelligence service than England in the critical years leading up to the Revolt of the Netherlands. The Welshman supplied Gresham with all sorts of goods, from strings for his lute to materials for his new Royal Exchange, which was now to challenge and eventually to capture the commercial supremacy of the Low Countries.

In 1567 Clough made a brief visit to London where the Exchange was nearing completion. Then he journeyed on to Denbigh where he married Katheryn of Berain* and then returned with her to Antwerp. An international figure of note and immensely wealthy, Clough evidently meant to settle in his native Wales. He bought lands there and built two new mansions in the Dutch style near Denbigh. He also proposed deepening the Clwyd estuary to enable ships of some size to come up to Rhuddlan. But he died suddenly in Hamburg in 1570 and Katheryn returned to bury his heart at Denbigh's parish church.

Clough had served Elizabeth well. His greatest service to Wales was probably the support he gave to his friend and townsfellow Humphrey Llwyd, as we shall see.

The Myddeltons too came from Denbigh. No family supplies better examples of younger sons having to turn to commerce for a living and winning political power by so doing. The chart on p. 126 shows that the whole history of the seventeenth century can be told in the adventures of this one family. Richard Myddelton was the governor of Denbigh in the days of Clough and Llwyd. Of his nine sons, two who became London merchants stand out. Thomas (1550–1631) rose to be a freeman of the Grocers Company, a financier and a shareholder in both the East India and Virginia Companies, and a lord-mayor of London. Hugh (1560–1631)† first established himself as a goldsmith in Elizabeth's reign, and then in James I's turned to ambitious industrial schemes and public works. His great success was the New River

* See p. 136–7.
† See p. 154.

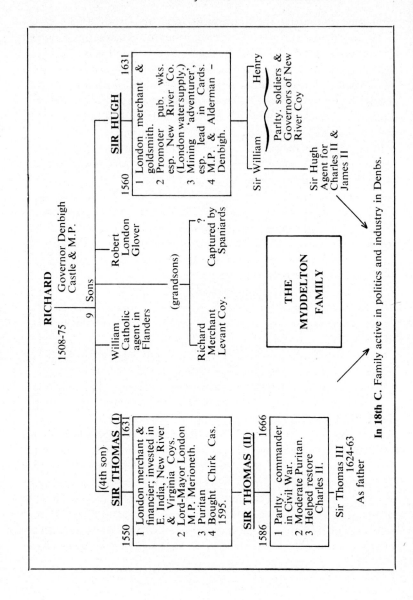

RICHARD
1508-75
Governor Denbigh
Castle & M.P.
9 Sons

William
Catholic
agent in
Flanders

Robert
London
Glover

(grandsons)

Richard
Merchant
Levant Coy.

Captured by
Spaniards
?

SIR HUGH   1631
1560
1 London merchant &
   goldsmith.
2 Promoter pub. wks.
   esp. New River Co.
   (London water supply.)
3 Mining 'adventurer',
   esp. lead in Cards.
4 M.P. & Alderman –
   Denbigh.

Sir William   Henry

Parlty. soldiers &
Governors of New
River Coy

Sir Hugh
Agent for
Charles II &
James II

THE
MYDDELTON
FAMILY

(4th son)
SIR THOMAS (I)   1631
1550
1 London merchant &
   financier; invested in
   E. India, New River
   & Virginia Coys.
2 Lord-Mayor London
   M.P. Merioneth.
3 Puritan
4 Bought Chirk Cas.
   1595.

SIR THOMAS (II)   1666
1586
1 Parlty. commander
   in Civil War.
2 Moderate Puritan.
3 Helped restore
   Charles II.

Sir Thomas III
1624-63
As father

In 18th C. Family active in politics and industry in Denbs.

project for bringing fresh water to London. Both these busy brothers, however, took an active part in the affairs of their native town and country. The large sums of money that Thomas loaned to his neighbours in North Wales won for him considerable power over the county families; Hugh was a leading figure in the town of Denbigh and its M.P. for a quarter of a century. Thomas was a sincere Puritan, and with Rowland Heylin financed the re-printing of the Bible and other religious books around 1630.

TOPOGRAPHERS AND MAP-MAKERS

'Some to beautify their Halls, Parkes, Chambers, Galeries, Studies or Libraries with; others some, for things past, . . . some other for their own journeys directing into far lands, or to understand other men's travels, . . . liketh, loveth, getteth and useth, Maps, Charts, and Geographical Globes.'*

The new interest in man which we call Humanism produced a similar interest in the study of his surroundings which we call Topography. Scholars everywhere now produced descriptions of their native lands, both of their present state and of their past history or 'antiquities'. Maps were of course the obvious accompaniment to such studies.

Giraldus, the pioneer Welsh topographer, is said to have made a map 'laying down rivers, mountains and sea coasts . . . with forty-three towns of Wales', but no copy of it has been found. The 'mappa mundi' (maps of the world) of the medieval monks (a fine one is to be seen in Hereford cathedral) and even the later Portolan charts drawn for seamen after *c.* 1350 were very crude attempts, largely based on hearsay and guesswork and not at all on accurate measurement. Then in 1533 Henry VIII made John Leland his Royal Antiquary and ordered him to spy out the whole land of England and Wales. Leland did so most diligently, journeying through Wales sometime between 1536 and 1539,

---

* John Dee: *The English Euclid*, 1570. Dee was a Welshman from Radnorshire and one of the greatest mathematicians of his day.

the critical years of the Act of Union and the Reformation. In his report to the king he claimed:

> '. . . there is almost neyther cape nor baye, hauen, creke, or pere, ryuer or confluence of ryuers, breches, washes, lakes, meres, fenny waters, mountaynes, valleys, mores, hethes, forestes, woodes, cyties, burges, castles, pryncypall manor places, monasteryes, and colleges, but I haue seane them, and noted in so doynge a whole world of thynges verye memorable.'

His detailed notes certainly give us the best description of the Wales of his day. He too clearly intended to produce a map, but again none can be found. However, his notes, and particularly the distances he records between various places, provided a most useful basis for a number of maps which were made in the early years of Elizabeth's reign. These for the first time resemble the accurately-surveyed maps of today. They are: a manuscript map of England and Wales by Laurence Nowell, Dean of Lichfield; a map of the British Isles by Mercator; and Humphrey Llwyd's two engraved maps, one of Wales and another of England and Wales.

The two leading Welsh topographers of the day were again Denbigh men. Humphrey Llwyd was probably a boyhood friend of Richard Clough's at Denbigh. After a fine career at Oxford, he returned to live at Denbigh castle and practise as a doctor. But his great interest was topography, and he quickly won a fine reputation for the many antiquarian studies of Wales he soon produced. The Netherlands were now the centre of the printing and engraving trade of Europe. Two friendly rivals in the business, both living at Antwerp, are best known by the Latin 'trade-names' they adopted—Mercator and Ortelius. Mercator drew a map of the British Isles in 1564 but it was never engraved.

Richard Clough told Ortelius, his fellow citizen at Antwerp, about his friend Llwyd's work. Llwyd then visited Ortelius in 1566–67 as he journeyed to Italy in the retinue of the Earl of Arundel with Hugh Owen (soon to become the leading Catholic conspirator*). They became great friends. Alas, in 1568 Llwyd

* See p. 103 et seq.

27. HUMPHREY LLWYD'S MAP OF WALES, 1568-73.

was taken ill. Knowing himself to be dying, he packed up his papers and maps and sent them by Hugh Owen to Ortelius with a most touching letter:

'Dearly beloved Ortelius.

. . . neither the dayly shakynge of the continuall Feuer . . . neither the lookyng for present death . . . could put the remembrance of my Ortelius out of my troubled brayne. Wherefore, I send vnto you my Wales, not beutifully set forth in all poynctes, yet truly depeinted, so be that certeyn notes be obserued, which I gathered euen when I was redy to die. You shall also recaue . . . an other England also drawne forth perfectly enough. . . . Which, also (if God has spared me life) you should haue receaued in better order, and in all respects perfect. Take therefore, this last remembrance of thy Humfrey, and for ever adieu, my deare friend Ortelius. From Denbigh in Gwynedh, or Northwales, the XXX. of August 1568.

Yours both liuying and diyng:
Humfrey Lhuyd.'

A few days later Llwyd died, a comparatively young man. But his papers arrived safely, and the maps were printed by Ortelius first as loose sheets (though no copies remain) and then in a re-issue in 1573 of his famous atlas, *Theatrum Orbis Terrarum* (Theatre of the Whole World). Thus Llwyd's maps became the first of England and Wales to be engraved and printed.

His map of Wales has obvious faults (see p. 129); the parrot's beak tilt of the Llŷn peninsula, for example, and the shapeless coast of Glamorgan. The detail of North Wales is good—as one would expect of a mapmaker whose home was at Denbigh; but as one moves away from that point the less accurate the map becomes. Poor Llwyd must not be blamed for the curious spelling of many place-names, for he was dead before he could correct the work of the Dutch engravers, unfamiliar with Welsh.

Llwyd probably made no personal survey of his own, but relied on the work of someone who had. It is likely that both he and Mercator used the copious notes (and possibly a map) by Leland. It was left to Christopher Saxton to make an official and accurate survey of England and Wales beginning in 1574. He first published maps of the counties and then of England and Wales in an atlas of 1579. John Speed in his well-known maps of counties

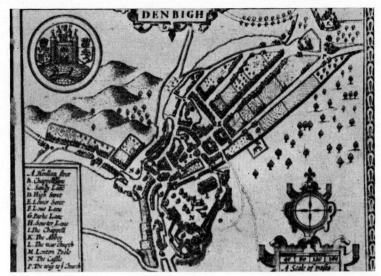

By permission of the National Library of Wales

28. SPEED'S MAP OF DENBIGH

The great castle and old town stand on a hill. The new town lies mainly on the slopes dropping away to the north-east. Speed drew many valuable maps of towns in Wales.

and towns (see above) of 1611 drew a great deal on Saxton's work. Between them they established a modern English school of map-makers. Yet Humphrey Llwyd's maps continued to be printed for another 170 years.

Another Denbighshire topographer and historian was David Powel (*c.* 1552–98). He is said to be the first graduate from Jesus College, Oxford. At the request of Henry Sidney, the President of the Council of Wales in 1583, he edited Llwyd's translation of *Brut y Tywysogion* (The Chronicle of the Princes). Powel added to it very considerably, however, with works of his own and a history of Norman Wales by Edward Stradling, which he got from Blanche Parry and her kinsman the great Cecil. This, when printed as the *Historie of Cambria* remained the standard history of Wales until Professor J. E. Lloyd published his fine

History in 1911. In it Powel is at pains to glorify both his native land and the Tudor family. He repeats, for example, the legend first told by Llwyd that America had been discovered in 1170 by a Welshman, Madog, son of Owain Gwynedd. Thus he makes out that Queen Elizabeth had a better claim to the New World than the Spaniards. He was equally patriotic (and prejudiced!) when in 1585 he issued the first printed version of Giraldus's *Itinerary* and *Description of Wales*, for he deliberately omitted the author's pointed criticisms of the Welsh! Powel too helped Bishop Morgan with his translation of the Welsh Bible.

The new enthusiasm of Elizabethan gentlemen for topography was not confined to Denbighshire. Glamorgan had its historian in Edward Stradling, as we have seen, and in his friend Rice Merrick, a landowner of St. Nicholas, who about 1578 wrote *A Booke of Glamorganshire Antiquities* which gives us a valuable picture of the county in his day. A similar group of landowner-scholars lived in Pembrokeshire, the most important being George Owen, the leading squire of the north of the county. His *Description of Penbrokshire* (*sic*) of 1603 is probably the best account of social life in Tudor Wales that we have. Last, but not least, was Owen's friend Thomas Jones (*c.* 1530–1609), better known as Twm Sion Catti, a legendary figure in Cardiganshire and Carmarthenshire.

ORIGINAL EXTRACTS

1   THE BALLAD OF LIEUTENANT PEILYN: (see page 115)
(The 'gang') Captain Billings, that fierce Hector, is our chieftain; Captain Roberts is the second to venture boldly like Jason or like great-headed Theseus; Hugh Middleton in every place spares no pains to do his utmost; and the two lieutenants in every fray, Salisbury and Peilyn; Robert Billings and Sergeant Hughes—they'll make no truce with the blackfaced foe; Will Thomas, William Jones, and Hugh—that's the lot of us Welshmen

(The natives of Dominica) . . . there came to meet us a crowd of naked men with painted skins, with bows in their hands, like devils: Hellish imps of fierce rude mien, their skins painted like Satan's own. With wires in their nostrils like boars, they chanted their war-songs with foam-flecked jaws. . . . the cruel cannibals.

(E. R. Williams: *Elizabethan Wales*, pp. 55, 57)

2   RECKLESS SIR ROGER WILLIAMS IS WOUNDED: *The Earl of Leicester*
writes after the battle of Duisburg, 1586:

Roger Williams hath gott a blow thorow the arme . . . I warned him of
(the danger), being in trench with me, and (he) would need run upp and
downe so oft out of the trench, with a great plume of feathers on his gylt
morion (helmet), as so many shott (were) coming at him, he could hardlie
escape with soe little hurt

(J. X. Evans: *The Works of Sir Roger Williams*, p. xxvi)

3   RICHARD CLOUGH, SECRET AGENT: (*In their letters back to England
about the armaments they were secretly smuggling out of the Netherlands, Gresham
and Clough often used a form of 'code'; 'velvet', for example, meant 'gunpowder'.
Sir Thomas Challoner, England's ambassador in the Spanish Netherlands, used
Clough as the 'courier' for confidential letters to the Queen. In 1559 for example,
he writes, enclosing a package, asking Clough to find a 'trusty berer'*—)

Mr. Cloughe, the packet sent herein is of great importans with lettres out
of france to the Queen's Majesty . . . yf the Frenche shulld offerr to bourd
the vessell (the messenger) goeth in, then seinge non other Remedye he
(must) tye the packet to a stone and throwe it over bourd.

(R. Gwyndaf Jones: *Sir Richard Clough, Denbs. Hist. Soc. Trans. 1971*, p. 69)

CHAPTER X

SOCIETY AND POLITICS

THE SOCIAL CLASSES

LAND was still the basis of Tudor and Jacobean society, for it gave a living to the vast majority of Welshmen. Wales could boast of very few 'nobles' apart from the Earls of Worcester and Pembroke. More numerous were the 'esquires' or upper gentry, some of them old-established like the Stradlings of Glamorgan[1] and some comparative newcomers like the Bulkeleys of Anglesey, but all owning considerable land, much of it formerly the property of the monasteries. Lower in the social scale were the 'gentlemen' or lower gentry owning less property, some of it let out to tenants but most of it still needing their own working. Unlike their counterparts in England, they could not always afford 'to live idly and without manual labour'. Next down in the social charts were the yeomen, generally descended from freemen and owning some land in freehold which they worked themselves. Last of all came the tenant farmers or 'tyddynwyr' and labourers, working on land they did not own.

But in the changing conditions of the sixteenth century the distinction between one class and the next became less definite. A man could now easily improve or even lose his status. But whatever their standing, Welshmen were still as touchy about their pedigree as they were in Gerald's day*, and were now as ready to defend it in the law courts as formerly with the sword. The records of the Courts of Star Chamber and of the Council of Wales and the Marches are full of petty actions taken by one Welshman against another. The underlying cause was their concern over land, which was now changing hands at such speed. The

* *The Defenders*, p. 41.

same concern showed in the anxiety of the Welsh gentry to preserve records of their ancestry in manuscripts and on gravestones, and to make 'good' marriages for their children, and probably to equal Englishmen in the proportion of their sons sent to universities and schools of law in England.

POLITICIANS AND LAWYERS

To hold office had by now become a fashionable and highly prized status symbol and a major cause of family rivalry. Each family had its own sphere of influence. Flintshire was dominated by the Mostyn family of Mostyn Hall (see map on p. 184). In Denbighshire five great families competed, often violently, for power—Salusbury, Thelwall, Trevor, Myddelton and Edwards. Even different branches of the same family sometimes quarrelled bitterly. In March 1593 John Salusbury of the senior house of Lleweni fought a duel at Chester with Owen Salusbury of the junior house of Rug. Farther west in Denbighshire the notorious Dr. Elis Prys of Plas Iolyn extended his estates over the high moorlands around Ysbyty Ifan and oppressed its people. The Wynn family of Gwydir did the same in the Conway valley and Caernarvonshire, until in the next century they were ousted by the Griffiths of Cefnamwlch in Llŷn. Anglesey was held by stalwart Sir Richard Bulkeley, head of the family for fifty years in the reigns of Elizabeth and James I.

Two junior branches of the Herberts held sway in mid-Wales, while the senior branch, now earls of Pembroke, were powerful in west Monmouthshire and east Glamorgan. Mid Glamorgan was the domain of the Mansels and Stradlings, while the Devereux family, earls of Essex, had wide estates in Brecknockshire and Carmarthenshire and shared influence in Pembrokeshire with the Perrots.

A few Welsh gentlemen increased their capital by investing in trade or industry. Most grew rich, however, by extending their lands, especially by intermarriage with other wealthy families of the same class. At all levels of society marriage was as yet less a romantic and private affair of the heart than a business deal made public. Notable in this respect was much-married Katheryn of Berain (*c.* 1534–91) often known as the 'Mother of Wales', both for her personal goodness and for her wide-ranging family connections. The sequence of her four marriages is well told in a charming if fictional story by Thomas Pennant, the famous eighteenth century traveller. Maurice Wynn of Gwydir, he says, proposed to Katheryn as he escorted her from the church after the funeral of her first husband, John Salusbury. But she refused him graciously, saying she had already accepted Sir Richard Clough of Denbigh as her second husband on her way *to* the church. She promised, however, that if she had to perform 'the same sad duty' for Clough (i.e. attend his funeral) Maurice might depend on being the third! And so he was! Edward Thelwall was her fourth husband and she his third wife. The network of family connections thus made was further meshed by marrying many of her children to children of her successive husbands by their earlier marriages.

Many families tightened their grip still further by taking sides with powerful English families. Thus Elis Prys was 'a creature of the Earl of Leicester' (Elizabeth's favourite) 'and devoted to all his bad designs' in seizing crown lands and oppressing his tenants. Both were sworn enemies of Richard Bulkeley, who nevertheless retained the favour of the queen. The Meyricks of Pembrokeshire similarly served the Earls of Essex. The soldier Sir Gelly Meyrick was the devoted follower of the second earl, Elizabeth's favourite after the death of Leicester, and was executed with him after his rebellion in 1601. The Trevors of Trevalun in Denbighshire were 'hangers-on' of the Lord Howard of Effingham, the admiral who led the English forces against the Armada. They secured thereby offices in the navy and 'pocket-boroughs' in the House of Commons. These were the families who for centuries were to serve as J.P.'s, M.P.'s and sheriffs for their counties and as members of the Council of Wales and the March. The Bulkeleys, to take only one example, supplied both county and borough members for Anglesey over an unbroken period of 300 years. All the marrying and even the feuding served to knit the Welsh

AN DNI 1568

By permission of the National Museum of Wales

29. KATHERYN OF BERAIN

There are a number of portraits of this 'royal, rich and beautiful gentlewoman'. This one was painted in Antwerp in 1568, probably for her second husband, Richard Clough, whom she had married the previous year. Has the skull any significance.?

gentry into a well-defined class with a code and loyalties all its own. So under James I they became a powerful political force and under his son an equally united military one.

THE COUNCIL OF WALES AND THE MARCH

The orders of the Queen and her Privy Council could be issued directly to the Welsh sheriffs and J.P.'s or they could be filtered through the President of the Council of Wales and the March. Ludlow, where the Council almost always met, was a second or vice-regal court for Wales although strictly outside its boundaries. It was in many real senses a capital for Wales. The courts and court functions held there were splendid social occasions and especially so at Christmas. Throughout the year the ordinary work of supervising J.P.'s and sheriffs and of finding and punishing pirates, smugglers, recusants etc., went quietly on. Ludlow, too was a court of law and, like the Star Chamber, a prerogative court, and, unlike the ordinary courts, unencumbered by juries and thus speedier and cheaper. The power of the President was all the greater because he had his part in the appointment of the justices of Great Sessions, some of whom always sat on the Council. Through them he had a further channel of spreading orders and of testing the feeling of the localities along their circuits.

The reign of Elizabeth was the 'golden age' of the Council of Wales and the March. For a long term of twenty-seven years (1559–86) its president was the able Sir Henry Sidney, father of Sir Philip Sidney, the soldier poet. He 'ruled' his 'province' much as Elizabeth herself ruled England, firmly yet wisely; winning the respect of the gentry; healing their quarrels and avoiding extreme action especially in religious matters, as we saw above. His policy must have been responsible in large measure for the remarkable freedom from disturbance that marks her reign in Wales. This Englishman from distant Kent made Ludlow his family home, and won the affection of Welshmen for his sympathy with the national life of Wales, its antiquities, its

literature and its growing industries.[2] Absences in the Queen's
service on the Continent and in Ireland disturbed his 'rule', but
they lent belief to his declaration about Wales that 'a better
country to govern Europe holdeth not'. Sidney's body lies buried
at Penshurst, Kent, but his heart, by his own request, at
Ludlow.

His policies were continued by his successor, his son-in-law
Henry Herbert, the second Earl of Pembroke (president 1586–
1601), though with greater firmness towards recusants. One of
the richest men in England, he made the court at Ludlow a
centre of lavish entertainment, pomp and ceremony. He too was
warm in his sympathies with the Welsh people, their language
and their literature. Thomas Wiliems, the contemporary commentator on the Welsh scene, calls him 'Llygad holl Gymru'—
the eye of all Wales. Unfortunately, periods of chronic illness
made him leave Ludlow more and more for his home in Wilton,
and at such times the hold of the Council on the government of
Wales and on its gentry slackened. It was immediately after his
death that Essex and Gelly Meyrick stirred up support for the
disastrous rebellion against the Queen that was to cost both their
lives.

Work in the Council as well as in Parliament gave many
lawyers the chance to rise to fame. Three such from South Wales
were David Lewis, William Aubrey and Sir John Herbert, all of
whom served as M.P.'s and became eminent civil lawyers and
heads of Oxford Colleges. Sir John was second secretary of state
for both Elizabeth and James, but resigned disappointed at not
being made principal secretary and died after fighting a duel in
Cardiff in 1617. All three maintained a connection with their
native Wales, though they worked mainly in England. Another
gifted Elizabethan lawyer was Simon Thelwall. Both he and
Herbert had a remarkable gift for languages. It was Thelwall
who sentenced the Catholic martyr Richard Gwyn in 1584; it
was Aubrey who helped condemn the Puritan John Penry in
1593.

SOCIAL LIFE

We can here attempt only a broad sketch of social life in
Elizabethan times.* The great majority of the people lived in the
countryside, and here life varied widely from that of the great
gentleman to that of the common labourer. The prosperous
gentleman now graced his expanding estate with a new house or
a new wing to an old one, built now in stone though with less
thought for defence than for comfort and appearance; with ceil-
ings and stair-cases of oak, glass windows instead of shutters,
panelled walls instead of tapestry, large fireplaces and exquisite
furniture and fabrics from abroad. Carew Castle, home of the
notorious Sir John Perrot, was a grand example. Here, among
the exquisitely furnished and decorated rooms, he had a large
library with books in many languages and a music room equipped
with all sorts of instruments.

Many yeomen too, as they prospered, modernized their homes:
the animals were moved to separate buildings, the living rooms
given a floor of stone flags instead of beaten earth, and the loft

* A full account packed with interest is given in *Elizabethan Wales* by Dyfnallt Owen.

By permission of the National Library of Wales

30. AN ELIZABETHAN HOUSE: PLAS LLANGWYFAN

and ladder replaced with a complete storey of bedrooms fitted
with a staircase. Upstairs straw mattresses gave way to proper
bedsteads or bunks with feather beds, sheets, blankets and quilts.
Downstairs the walls were lined with cupboards and coffers, and
rude makeshift trestle boards gave way to solid designed tables
adorned with linen cloths and pewter, or on occasion silver
dishes instead of wooden platters and mugs. At the other end of
the social scale however, the cottage of tenant farmer and
labourer remained, alas, a squalid and unhealthy hovel often
shared with his animals, with its earthen floor, and with holes in
the mud walls for windows and in the rotting thatch for chim-
neys. With only the rudest of furniture, fire and utensils it
offered little comfort save for some protection from the weather
during meal-times and a place to sleep in a life normally spent
out-of-doors.

Building materials varied according to the locality, and each
area had its distinctive feature—stone farmhouses in Pembrokeshire, houses of timber and plaster in Mid-Wales, and long low,
dwellings in North Wales roofed with good slate instead of the
thatch which was usual everywhere else. Wood was the chief
fuel except in a few areas like Cardiganshire, where peat was
more readily available. Coal was rapidly gaining favour, however,
in those counties such as Glamorgan where it was plentiful.

Greater contact with England resulted in Welsh men and
women of all levels abandoning the simplicity and modesty which
marked their clothes in medieval times. By Elizabeth's reign their
taste in dress was as lavish, colourful and expensive as their
English neighbours. All sorts of expensive fabrics were now
obtainable to make the tailored gowns, bodices, stomachers,
many petticoats and great hooped skirts with which the squire's
wife and daughter vied with their social equals.[3] Brooches and
other jewelry were, of course, no longer decorated with pictures of the Virgin Mary or sacred relics, but were even more
exquisitely and expensively made and set with precious stones
and pearls. Gentlemen often outdid their women folk in the
extravagance of their dress, with coats and doublets of velvet

and satin, ruffs at neck and wrist, silk stockings and shoes of Spanish leather, and all set off with a sword or rapier at the hip. The yeoman too—and even the tenant farmer—moved with the times in the matter of dress: he now sported stout leather shoes, stockings of wool and hose of frieze (rough woollen cloth) with a doublet of fustian or frieze and a felt cap. He too was as fond as his 'betters' of displaying a rich variety of colours. Even the lowliest labourer was no longer content to go about barefoot and tattered; his dress included stout boots, stockings of wool and a jerkin of coarse russet.

The food of Welshmen too was changing. From the tenant farmer up they began to vary the monotonous pastoral dishes of their forefathers with a choice of meats, mutton, pork, beef and veal, with pies and broths, often white bread and a variety of vegetables. The labourer's diet was simpler—cheese, *cawl,* oat-cake or black bread, mutton or goatsmeat. The common drink was sour milk or beer; but wine imported from France and Spain now appeared more and more often on the table of gentlefolk and well-to-do yeomen.

Life in Elizabethan Wales was not all hard work and feuding. Gentry, like the Stradlings and Bulkeleys, went hunting and hawking in their own deer parks. Archery was not only a sport but a regular exercise enforced on all able-bodied men by the government, who regarded bowmen as essential to the defence of the realm as musketeers. Fishing, legal or illegal, bowls and a very rough and tumble form of football were enjoyed by all classes. Pembrokeshire had its *knappan*, a sort of bloodthirsty rugby played with a wooden ball. The harp and crwth were appreciated not only in the drawing rooms of the great but on the village green and hill-common to stimulate the dancing and singing on festive days. Dicing and gambling were forbidden by law but universally indulged in by rich and poor alike. *Eistedd-fodau* were still popular, though held as much in order to license professional bards and wandering minstrels as for competition.

A characteristic common to almost all the great families was their patronage of literature in various forms. Many like Elis Prys, the Mostyns and the Salusburys supported Welsh bards and were prominent in the famous Caerwys *eisteddfodau* of 1523 and 1568. Some like John Salusbury and Simon Thelwall were themselves something of poets. The scholarly Sir Edward Stradling, was a patron of young men like Siôn Dafydd Rhys and was also the collector of a great library at St. Donat's. Nor had the Elizabethan gentry of Wales, close though their connection was with England, abandoned the Welsh language for English. William Herbert (1501–70) the first Earl of Pembroke, though President of the Council of Wales (1550–53 and 1555–58), always spoke Welsh in preference to English in spite of the ruling of the Act of Union.

Lords, esquires and gentlemen now travelled farther afield, often on official business. The state of the roads in fact discouraged travel. Roman roads were still the only good great roads. The others were little better than tracks, often stony and always dusty in summer and muddy in winter. An act of 1555 made all parishes responsible for the upkeep of their roads. They were to appoint a highway-surveyor annually who could demand six days' labour from every parishioner. The improvement in the roads as a result was definite but limited, as it relied on the industry of the surveyor and the willing co-operation of the parishioners. The common folk rarely moved out of their locality, so the weekly markets and the wider-ranging half-yearly fairs were still their great social occasions as well as their means of local and regional trade; here they exchanged not only goods but news, and received notice of the latest declarations of the Queen and her Council of Wales.

Town life improved under the Tudors as we have seen. Improved law and order gave them the security necessary for expansion, and attracted the trade on which they thrived. Towns like Caernarfon, Carmarthen and Cardiff were no longer the military bastions of the alien conqueror. By Elizabeth's day they had become centres of trade, crafts and other services, more Welsh in character and language and in friendly relation with the surrounding countryside. Townsfolk, however, still formed only a small part of the total population of Wales and even these were

still countrymen at heart; they still worked and grazed outside
the town walls, and had large gardens attached to their houses
within them. The fortunes of the towns varied. Many ancient
castle-towns like Hay in south Wales and Cricieth in the north
decayed while others like Denbigh (see the map on p. 131)
extended into sprawling suburbs which in time became new
towns themselves often larger than the old and better designed
and supplied with water, wider streets and other amenities.
Towns varied considerably in size accordingly. Denbigh, for
example, had a population of perhaps 3,000, Cardigan only 500
and Harlech even less.

It so happened that at the time towns in Wales grew, the
craft-guilds which had dominated town life in the Middle Ages
declined. They were robbed of much of their property and privileges in the reign of Edward VI and in any case their local
jealousies did not fit in with the ideas of free trade now popular
with the government and new capitalists. Nevertheless many
guilds lingered on in the towns such as Carmarthen, Cardiff and
Ruthin. Denbigh had thriving guilds of weavers, glovers, smiths
and many others. Between them they cornered all the trade of the
country from the Dee to the Conwy and even further. Little
wonder that it produced great merchants like Richard Clough
and the Myddeltons who defended the town against the many
domineering great families around.

Plague still attacked these towns from time to time— Carmarthen, Beaumaris, Conway and many others took steps to
lessen its toll by stringent regulations regarding sanitation. In
this respect Denbigh was backward. The other scourges of
poverty and vagrancy fortunately worried the smaller towns of
Wales less than the larger towns in England.

EDUCATION

Tudor Wales shared with England in the fresh interest in
education which the New Learning inevitably brought. Ideally
the great aim of schoolmasters now was to turn their pupils into
courteous, cultivated gentlemen; but there were more practical

reasons for sending the young to school. The Reformation and Counter-reformation brought a demand for better educated clergy, and the growth of commerce and industry presented new opportunities for young men with initiative and some learning. The Act of Union created offices in local and national government, and also by enforcing primogeniture deprived younger sons of a share in the family estates, and compelled them to train for careers as clergy, lawyers, doctors or merchants. Even eldest sons needed a smattering of legal knowledge in order to defend their estates and engage in the litigation that now seemed to become the hobby of the Welsh landowners.

All this the gentry and even the yeomen realized. They sent their sons to the best schools in England, old establishments such as Winchester and Westminster, newer ones like St. Paul's and, nearer home, Shrewsbury, or the many Edward VI grammar schools endowed by the 'conscience money' taken from the proceeds of dissolving monasteries and chantries.

Soon, however, the gentry were founding and supporting similar schools in Wales. Bishop Barlow in 1541 moved an old

By permission of the National Library of Wales

31. AN ELIZABETHAN GRAMMAR SCHOOL

church college from Abergwili to Brecon and gave it the name of Christ's College. Later he added a free grammar school to it. Geoffrey Glyn, brother to the Bishop of Bangor, established Friars' School there out of funds raised by closing the Dominican Friary. Gabriel Goodman supported Ruthin school in 1595 from the tithes of the dissolved church of St. Peter. Beaumaris Grammar School was built in 1602 by David Hughes, an Anglesey man who had risen to be steward of a Norfolk manor. Cowbridge Grammar School owes its foundation in James I's reign to the adopted heir of Edward Stradling. It became fashionable among the well-to-do to establish scholarships in schools like these. The Wynns of Gwydir gave one at Friars' School to support scholars from Beddgelert. However, it was probably John Williams,* James I's rich goldsmith, himself a Beddgelert boy, who endowed the free school at Llanrwst and not Sir John Wynn. Among many other grammar schools now established were Ruabon, Presteigne, Abergavenny and Carmarthen.

The aim of the founders was probably best expressed by Gabriel Goodman when he told Queen Elizabeth that the first purpose of Ruthin School was 'the virtuous and godly education of children in Their duties to God and Her Majesty'. The curriculum followed, however, was the study of Latin and little else, for it was thought that no career at the university or as priest, lawyer, diplomat or doctor would be possible without it. The use of Welsh by the pupils was discouraged and sometimes punished. But this did not mean that Welsh as such was belittled any more than English, which was similarly frowned upon in English schools.[4]

All in all, by the end of Elizabeth's reign the sons of the gentry had adequate opportunities near home of securing an education which would qualify them to proceed to Oxford (usually Jesus College) or Cambridge. There was provision too for a few bright

---

* 1584–1627? not to be confused with Archbishop John Williams (see chapters 12 and 13). An earlier John Williams (1500?–1559) was keeper of Henry VIII's jewels, and President of the Council of Wales in 1559.

boys from humbler homes. William Morgan is a good example: son of a tenant farmer, he received his first education as a companion to John Wynn at Gwydir, and was later supported at Cambridge partly by Maurice Wynn and partly by his own odd-jobbing for other students. But boys like him were an exception. There must have been schools for children of the lower classes: we know of such at Denbigh, Bangor-on-Dee, Montgomery and Llandinam, often supported by 'ordinary' benefactors. But few of these lasted long; the schooling of all boys and girls as a right was as yet the dream of a few, which would eventually come true in part in the eighteenth century and not fully until our own twentieth century.

ORIGINAL EXTRACTS

1   ST. DONAT'S CASTLE: A GREAT ESTATE
It stondith on a meane hille a quarter of a mile from the Severn Se. In the which space bytwixt the castelle and the Severn is a parke of falow dere. There is a nother park of redde deere more by northe west from the castelle. The parkes booth and the castelle long to Stradeling a gentilman of very fair landes in that countery.

(L. T. Smith: *Leland's Itinerary in Wales*, p. 27)

2   SIR HENRY SIDNEY'S PRIDE IN HIS PRESIDENCY OF THE COUNCIL OF WALES:
Great that it is that in some sort I govern the third part of this realm under her most gracious majesty; high it is for by that I have precedence of great personages and by far my betters; happy it is for the goodness of the people whom I govern; and most happy it is for the commodity I have, by the authority of that place, to do good every day.

(W.Ll. Williams: *The Making of Modern Wales*, pp. 95–6)

3   BLANCHE PARRY'S DRESS AT ELIZABETH'S CORONATION:
According to the royal accounts she was supplied with—

7 yds. of scarlet, 15 yds. of crimson velvet, 1¼ yds. of cloth of gold, yellow with work, and ¾ yd. cloth of gold, black with work.

(C. A. Bradford: *Blanche Parry*)

4   GRAMMAR SCHOOL REGULATIONS:

(Bangor) . . . in all things and at all times he (the master) shall use such mildness of countenance and such Gentleness in speech that he may influence the Dullards (if any such there be) to study.

(Ruthin) Boys shall not be struck (by a monitor) on the Ears, Noses, Eyes or faces

(G. Dyfnallt Owen: *Elizabethan Wales*, pp. 201–2)

CHAPTER XI

MEN AT WORK

As we have seen, both the manorial and kindred systems of the
early middle ages had gradually broken down. This process was
speeded up by the English conquest, the Black Death, the revolt
of Glyndŵr and the Wars of the Roses, and by 1500 had produced
a 'revolution' in land holding. Freemen thought of themselves
more as individual landowners and less as members of a community or kindred, and were anxious to make not only a living
but also a profit in money out of their holdings. Success in this
made them greedy for more land. The system of dividing an
inheritance in land among all the heirs known as *cyfran* (gavelkind) tended down the years in many cases so to reduce an
individual's share as to make it unworkable. Reluctantly he
would part with it at a price to a larger, luckier neighbour who,
as his lands and influence grew, could apply more and more
pressure on such less fortunate owners.[1]

War and plague had affected the medieval bond (serf) *trefi*
even more drastically so that by the end of the fifteenth century
much bond land lay unoccupied and abandoned. The land ex-
ploiters, many of them rich burgesses from the towns, again
competed fiercely with each other to obtain this former bond
land. In the Principality they were helped by the charter of 1507
which freed all the bondmen there, for no longer were they, the
buyers, afraid that in buying bond-land they would be burdened
with the duties of bondmen.

It was of course the dissolution of the monasteries in 1536–39
that brought about the greatest single transfer of land in our
history. In fact it created few new landowners; rather it swelled

the holding of existing large-scale and local landowners, such as
the Mansels at Margam or the Bulkeleys of Beaumaris.

After acquiring an individual holding, the next step was to
enclose it with fences, walls or ditches. When John Leland
came to Anglesey about 1537–8, he was told that within living
memory it was never the custom of men in Anglesey to separate
their holdings.

> 'but now still more and more they dig strong hillocks in their grounds and
> with the stones of them rudely congested they divide their grounds after
> Devonshire's fashion'.

This practice was as yet probably not widespread; nor were
such walls or fences, ditches or baulks necessarily permanent. It
must be remembered too that such enclosure at this time meant
the enclosing of a man's rightful holding of meadow and arable
land, and must be distinguished from the wholesale enclosing of
common and waste land that was to mark the end of the eighteenth
century. To rob a Welsh farmer, almost inevitably a small-holder,
of the common upon which he could graze his few cattle, and
feed his pigs and poultry was a very serious matter. But occasionally it did happen and was strenuously and violently resisted.
When the lessee of some common land formerly belonging to the
monastery of Strata Marcella enclosed it with a ditch, the local
inhabitants at once filled it up. When he persisted, the men
dressed up in women's clothes (like the nineteenth century
Rebbecaites), occupied the common, cut down some oaks to
show their right, and swore that if anyone tried to enclose the
common lands 'they (would) die upon them'.[2]

There was in Wales, however, no general uprising like Ket's
rebellion of 1549 in England. This was probably because one
type of enclosure was generally absent from Wales, namely the
enclosure of arable land in order to convert it to pasture for
sheep, with all the unemployment that this brought. Wales
already had ample natural sheep walks on its moorlands and
mountains. Rather, enclosure where it occurred was designed
to consolidate a holding with a view to better farming.

THE WOOL TRADE

Next to agriculture, the wool and woollen cloth industry still occupied the greatest number of people. But during the sixteenth century it declined, partly, because of the fall in demand during the long wars with Spain, but mainly due to the inferior quality of both the wool and its working as compared with the West of England. Cloth slowly took second place to raw wool in the exports from the ports of South Wales, notably Carmarthen which lost its own importance as a result. In the North, however, the trade continued to hold its own. Gradually the clothing industry in Wales, as in England, ceased to be concentrated in the towns and became largely a scattered cottage craft in which all the family shared as a sideline to farming.

INDUSTRY

Considerable though the changes in agriculture were in Tudor times, they do not compare with those in mining and metal working. Indeed, Professor William Rees has given the title 'The First Industrial Revolution' to the events of the sixteenth and seventeenth centuries.

Henry VII was naturally quick to recognize the value of his kingdom's mineral resources. Almost immediately after Bosworth he set up a commission, led by his uncle Jasper, to safeguard Crown rights with regard to the mining of precious metals. The king had the right within his domains to the ores of the precious metals—gold, silver, copper and tin—necessary for coinage, even when dug from land that was not his. Britain had no mines of pure gold or pure silver. But the presence of gold and silver in the ores of copper and lead respectively gave the king claim on these also. The Acts of Union extended this right to the whole of Wales at a critical time when timber for smelting was becoming drastically scarce in south-east England. Moreover, its new legal system offered to English capitalists the kind of security against lawlessness they needed before venturing their money in new enterprises in Wales.

The Tudor monarchs were no less interested in the heavier metals—iron and lead—for they provided the armaments now necessary for the defence of the realm. Wales was known to be rich in these; they had been worked fitfully as a 'sideline' by monks and others, mainly around the outcrops of the coal seams in north-east and south Wales. Henry VIII was the first to embark on an armaments programme of the modern kind. He equipped his navy with new vessels, armed them with newly-cast cannon and shot, and encouraged a variety of experiments in the working and testing of metals. He sent his Master of Mines and others prospecting in the Taff valley and nearby Llantrisant. In 1543 the royal gunsmith successfully produced the first iron guns to be made in one piece, to replace the expensive bronze castings then in use. This gave both the iron and ship-building industries a boost.

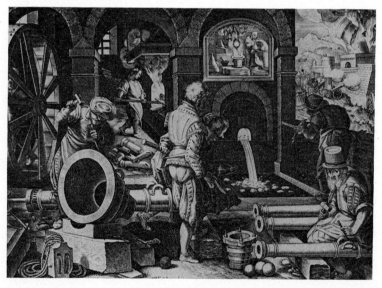

By permission of the Radio Times Hulton Picture Library

32. GUNSMITHS AT WORK

Nevertheless success was limited. The industry remained scattered and disorganized, and its product of doubtful quality because it lacked two things; large-scale capital and technical expertise. Merchants and smelters in Germany had both, and in 1564 Queen Elizabeth, urged no doubt by Cecil, invited their assistance. Joint-stock companies, that is companies whose working capital is provided in varying shares by a number of persons, had already operated successfully in foreign trade. Now they were applied to industry at home. In 1568 two joint-stock companies were set up under royal charter: the Society of Mines Royal, managed by a rich German merchant Daniel Hechstetter, to mine and smelt gold, silver, quicksilver and copper; and the Society of Mineral and Battery Works, directed by Christopher Schutz, a German brass founder, with the sole 'right of battery', i.e. the casting and forging of cannon and the making of brass sheet and wire. They were meant originally to have separate functions and to work in separate areas, the Society of Mines Royal in Wales and eight counties of England and the Society of Mineral and Battery Works in the remaining English counties (including Monmouthshire). But their operations soon overlapped and they continued to work as friendly sister-companies, safeguarding the royal monopoly. Cecil was a prominent shareholder in both.

On the whole the Mines Royal Society met with doubtful success. Disappointed with their large-scale ventures in copper mining in Cumberland and Cornwall, they turned to Wales in the 1580s. A scheme was begun of smelting copper at Neath. The site had many advantages: it had plentiful supplies of timber and of coal, now coming increasingly into use as a fuel; small ships could come right up the Neath estuary to the works, bringing copper ore from Cornwall and returning with timber or coal or the finished metal; and the fast-flowing tributary streams provided good water-power to work the bellows and the hammers. In spite of the hard work and skill of the German manager, Ulhrich Foss, however, the venture was never thriving, and after 1600 was dormant until it was revived a century later

by Humphrey Mackworth. Experiments in copper mining at
Parys Mountain, Anglesey met with a similar fate though supported by such eminent men as Sir Henry Sidney of the Council
of the Marches, the Earl of Leicester and the great William Cecil
himself.

Lead-mining too was revived in Cardiganshire at this time.
The workings once run by the monks of Strata Florida, and which
Leland noticed in 1538, were leased by the Mines Royal Company
to private 'adventurers' and re-opened with the help of German
engineers.[3] But success was fitful until 1617 when the Crown
leased the mines to Hugh (later Sir Hugh) Myddelton as a result
of his success eight years earlier in promoting the New River
Scheme for bringing fresh water to London. The old story that
the huge fortune he spent on the New River Project came from
the lead mines in Wales can therefore scarcely be true; but the
need for lead conduits in London may have spurred his interest
in the Cardiganshire lead mines. They were certainly highly
profitable. Up to 1631, when he died, Myddelton had sent
£50,000 worth of silver to the king's London mint. He was
followed in Cardiganshire by Thomas Bushell, an 'adventurer'
indeed, who persisted with the mining in spite of almost in-
superable difficulties of drainage and ventilation, of securing
labour and timber, and, most important of all, of defending the
works against the violent opposition of local landlords. These

By permission of the National Museum of Wales

33. COIN MINTED BY THOMAS BUSHELL

A shilling of Charles I, Aberystwyth mint, 1638-42. Note the plumes marking
Welsh silver, and the book which is the special mintmark of Aberystwyth.

naturally resented the Crown's right, in the search for precious silver, to destroy their land and woods without paying compensation. But, with the king's support and his own engineering skill, Bushell at last suceeded. His annual output of silver alone was said to be £40,000, and he was allowed to set up a mint in Aberystwyth Castle (See p. 154). He repaid his debt to the King handsomely with money and goods during the Civil War, until in 1646 the Cardiganshire mines fell into the hands of the Roundheads and Bushell fled to Lundy Island in the Bristol Channel, where he defied Cromwell's men for a considerable period until they came to terms with him and restored his mineral rights. But he never again took up mining in Wales.

The lead deposits of Denbighshire and Flintshire, unlike those of Cardiganshire, were not rich in silver, so the Society of Mines Royal was not greatly interested, and the local landlords, notably the Mostyn family, were free to work their own lands for their own profit. An erratic period in the sixteenth century was followed in Stuart days by considerable success especially in the area around Halkyn and Holywell, until the Civil War again brought the work to a halt. Lead was also worked on a small scale in the seventeenth century in the Conway valley by the Wynn family and in Pwllheli.

The iron industry in Wales was more successful, thanks to the need for armaments and the scarcity of timber for smelting in south-east England. By Elizabeth's reign England had won a name for ordnance; it was our cast-iron guns that in large measure defeated Spain both at sea at the time of the Armada and in the Netherlands. By the reign of James I the making of ordnance was being discouraged in order to prevent cannon being exported to the country's enemies.

In Sussex and Surrey the two vigorous industries of shipbuilding and iron-foundery were in conflict, for both made great demands on timber; for the navy it was a choice between ships or cannon. Abundant timber and iron-ore, together with secure working conditions, attracted English iron-masters into south-east Wales. In the sixties foundries were opened up here with the help of German workers by Sir Henry Sidney to support the iron works he already owned in Sussex. Bristol merchants too invested capital in the furnaces of Glamorgan and Monmouth, and in 1625 petitioned the king to allow a greater number of guns to be cast at Cardiff 'where the best iron ordnance is made'.

Iron was of special interest to the Mineral and Battery Company. The ventures at Pontypool of one of its members, Richard Hanbury, proved very profitable, in spite of strong local opposition because of the enormous destruction of the surrounding woodlands to provide the charcoal needed for smelting. It was with its wireworks on former monastic land at Tintern that the Company attained its greatest success. Iron wire was now greatly in demand; its uses ranged from making 'cards' for carding wool to supplying foundations for ladies' dresses and great hooped skirts. By 1603 some 10,000 people in England and Wales depended for a livelihood on the wire manufacturers at Tintern. The Queen herself, no less, shared in the profit from the holdings she took over from the Duke of Norfolk when she executed him for treason in 1572. The workers at the wireworks also shared in the venture in that there was set up for them a pioneer welfare scheme for sickness benefits, pensions and schooling for their children.

In spite of its marked success in the sixteenth and seventeenth centuries, the full development of the iron industry had to wait for the discoveries of the eighteenth century in using coal as a fuel for the furnaces and steam engines. There was a remarkable increase, however, during Tudor and Stuart times in the demand for coal. This was due firstly to the increase of population; secondly, to the growing scarcity of firewood caused by the clearance of woods to form arable land and pasture, and the insatiable appetite of the mineral workings for charcoal; and, thirdly, the realization of the value of coal for export. John Leland commented on coal workings in north-east Wales, in Pembrokeshire, and in east Carmarthenshire and west Glamorgan. Of these three regions it was the third, between Llanelli and Neath, that made the greatest progress in Elizabethan days. Here

the estuaries of the Burry, Tawe and Neath rivers ran deep into
the coal field, making easy both access to the coal and transport
away by sea. By 1688 coal formed 90 per cent of the Welsh
export trade, most of it coastwise traffic but a considerable
quantity going to Ireland, France and the Channel Islands. Swansea
was by far the greatest exporter.

Thus east Wales concentrated on iron and west Wales on coal,
while the wealth of the secluded wooded valleys deep in the
Glamorgan hills was as yet largely untapped. As mines grew
deeper the costs and hazards of working them increased, often
to a point where they were no longer profitable. Faced with
difficulties of drainage and ventilation, with dangers from flooding, roof-falls and fire-damp, the coal industry like the iron, had
to wait for the increased knowledge of engineering and chemistry
of the eighteenth and nineteenth centuries.

TRADE AND TRANSPORT

Trade, both home and foreign, certainly benefited from the
settled conditions in Wales and the protection afforded by the
Tudors. The cattle trade to England along the drover-tracks, the
'treasure fleet' of the Welsh, prospered. Exports and imports
still were channelled through a number of towns on the now
quiet border, such as Oswestry, Shrewsbury, Leominster and
Hereford. But overland trade in general was hampered by the
atrocious state of the roads. Coastwise traffic where possible was
much to be preferred.

The ports of South Wales grew very much busier in Elizabeth's
time, especially those of Glamorgan. This was largely due to the
contact with Bristol and the north Devon coast. Their ships
ventured farther afield too: ports from Neath to Milford specia-
lized in coal but Cardiff exported iron, munitions and much
agricultural produce, particularly butter, as well. The chief imports everywhere were wine, fine cloth, fruits, spices and sugar.
Fishing still maintained the little havens of the west coasts, but
the ports of north Wales and Beaumaris in particular slowly
declined.

34. ELIZABETHAN MERCHANT SHIP

Note the dress of the people shown in this sketch. Guess who they are and what they are doing.

Elizabeth and her ministers were concerned to build up the nation's capital and also ensure able-bodied mariners for the navy. So they gave vigorous support to the sea-going trade of Wales as of England, not only indirectly by encouraging its agricultural and mineral resources, but also by such direct methods as developing fisheries, by passing Navigation Acts confining trade to English and Welsh ships, and by strong measures to clamp down on piracy and smuggling especially in the Bristol Channel.

PIRACY AND SMUGGLING

Both smuggling and piracy were old crimes, as common as the plague and just as difficult to stamp out. Until the sixteenth century pirates had been most active in the narrow seas around south-eastern England. As the government became increasingly strict, however, they moved their haunts farther westward and particularly to South Wales. Here the broken coastline and the many creeks and inlets of the Bristol Channel and Milford Haven afforded them ideal hunting-grounds and hide-outs. Here too it was far more difficult for the arm of the law to reach them, partly because of poor communications and partly because the local people were still unaccustomed to taking orders from London or even Ludlow. By the 1570s these piratical 'Adventurers of the West Country' were more active in Wales than anywhere else in the British Isles.

Smuggling was inevitable where the customs officers were generally unpaid and relied on bribes and 'tips' and worse practices to make a living. Wheat, cheese and butter were regularly smuggled out, often in spite of the suffering of the local inhabitants because of the scarcity and consequent high prices of such essential food stuffs.

Smuggling more than anything proved old Rowland Lee right when he protested that to appoint Welsh gentry as J.P.s was merely setting one thief to catch another. The gentry were often in league with the very smugglers and pirates whom it was their duty to catch. John Vaughan, J.P., for example, mayor and customs officer at Carmarthen in 1572 protested so loudly against the illegal export of leather to Spain that the smugglers once marooned him on Caldy Island. But he himself at the same time smuggled shiploads of leather from Carmarthen to France in exchange for equally illicit French wine! By the end of Elizabeth's reign guns made in Glamorgan foundries were being smuggled out of Cardiff to enemy Spain, in spite of the very serious penalties the government naturally imposed.

The most outstanding of these 'secret' supporters of contraband traffic was probably Sir John Perrot of Carew (1530–92),

By permission of the National Museum of Wales

35. TWO DOUBTFUL ADVENTURERS
(a) Sir John Perrot;   (b) Sir John Wynn.

the most powerful of the Pembrokeshire squires. As flamboyant
and ruthless as his reputed royal father, Henry VIII, he played
fast and loose with the law in order to line his pockets and satisfy
his sense of dare-devil. The Privy Council complained repeatedly
that notorious pirates were allowed to escape justice because of
his negligence or connivance. Among them was John Callice the
master-pirate of south Wales. His flagrant robberies between
1575 and 1577 became such a national scandal that Elizabeth's
Council devoted one of its sessions in January 1577 entirely to
him, and ordered the Council of Wales to set up a commission
to investigate his piracies in Glamorgan and Monmouth. One of
the commissioners appointed was none other than John Perrot!
Callice was eventually caught, but, putting on an air of devout
repentance, he turned Queen's evidence, denouncing all his confederates, and was allowed to go free on payment of a paltry

£50. Hicks, Herbert, Ward and Tom Clarke, were other rascals who now lay in wait for defenceless vessels in the western approaches and the sea lanes which crowded into the Bristol Channel.

North Wales too had its share of illicit trading. Bardsey was now as much the haunt of pirates as it had once been of saints. And at Beaumaris Sir Richard Bulkeley was not above giving his support to Hugh Griffith, a native of Cefn Amwlch in Llŷn and perhaps the most cruel sea-robber of them all. Sir Richard's own younger brother Edward turned pirate, and like Callice and Griffith at last met his death on the pirate-infested Barbary coast of north Africa.

Many of those who turned to piracy were, like Edward Bulkeley, younger sons deprived by the new law of primogeniture of a share in the family fortune. A career on the land, in business or, if they had the education, in a profession was too lowly for their proud sense of family, or too humdrum for their sense of adventure. But there were others, who were elder sons, who went buccaneering just for the 'kicks'. Outstanding among them was Thomas Prys of Plas Iolyn whom we met earlier.

ORIGINAL EXTRACTS

1   LAND-GRABBING: AN ACTION IN THE COURT OF STAR CHAMBER, 1601:

Complainant: John Thomas of Llangatog, gent.

Defendant: Sir John Vaughan of Goldengrove, knight.

Indictment: That Vaughan invited Thomas to a feast, made him drunk, and then persuaded him, while drunk, to make over all his hereditary lands in Llangatog and Ellansowen to the defendant.

       (I. ap O. Edwards: *Star Chamber Proceedings relating to Wales*, p. 51)

2   A RIOT AGAINST ENCLOSURES AT NEATH, 1577:

(A London Welshman, John Price had leased and partly enclosed common-land at Cors y Felin formerly owned by Neath Abbey. A party of yeomen, however, had destroyed the hedges and—)

. . . did then and there make greatt rejoysinge and tryumphinge with greatt and lowde voyses sayinge that they would not decist from there saide Ryotous and wicked enterprise so longe as one hedge or mounde were there standinge.

(G. Dyfnallt Owen: *Elizabethan Wales*, p. 89)

A LEAD-MINER'S TALE: THE UNGRATEFUL CROW
(*Leland records finding many lead mines in Cardiganshire*)
I saw on the right hond on a hille side . . . wher hath bene great digging for leade, the melting whereof hath destroid the wooddes that sumtime grew plentifulli therabout. I hard a marvelus tale of a crow fedd by a digger there, that tooke away his fed(er's) pursse, and wille the digger folowid the crow for his purs, the residew of his felows were oppressid in the pitte with a ruin

(L. T. Smith: *Leland's Itinerary in Wales*, p. 124)

CHAPTER XII

THE FIRST STUARTS

THE story of Wales in the reigns of James I and Charles I is not marked by any great events distinctive to Wales alone. The main interest lies in the part that the Welsh gentry played on the national stage of England, Scotland and Wales, all now sharing the same monarch.

JAMES I AND THE WELSH GENTRY

The affection of Wales for the house of Tudor spilled over into early Stuart times. James I's accession on 24 March, 1603 was announced with enthusiasm in Denbigh Square, in Welsh by none other than Bishop Morgan, in English by Hugh Clough.[1] James too, for his part, was to show during his reign a soft spot for Wales, his new Celtic kingdom. The ministers, privy councillors, judges and ambassadors he chose included more than a fair share of Welshmen.

At the outset of his reign James had the solid backing of the Welsh gentry. Some, like Sir Bevis Thelwall of the Denbighshire family but now a rich London silk merchant, he knew before his accession. Sir William Maurice of Clenennau was such a staunch protector of James's interests that he was called in jest 'the King's godfather'. Before Parliament even met he had urged that Scotland should be legally united with England and Wales, believing in all sincerity that it was in this way that the interests of Wales would be best served. His unswerving loyalty to the Stuart cause was to be continued by his great-grandsons Sir John and Sir William Owen during the Civil War.

Even more than in Tudor times the 'great families' were dominant in Wales. To take one example alone, the whole history

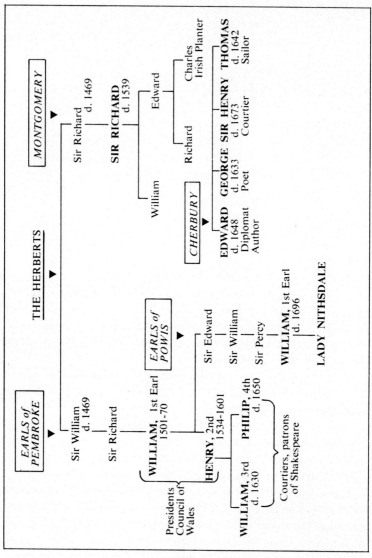

This chart shows only the main branches of this very widespread family

of England and Wales in the seventeenth century could be represented by one or other of the many branches of the Herbert
family. The main stock, made Earls of Pembroke, had won the
favour of every Tudor monarch, had served them well as Presidents of the Council of Wales, and grown very rich, not least
by joining in new industrial ventures. But they had remained
avowedly Welsh, speaking the language and patronizing its literature. Henry Herbert, who had died in 1601, was acclaimed
'llygad holl Gymru'. His sons William and Philip, the third and
fourth earls, found favour and high office with James (he visited
Wilton (Wilts.), now their main residence, immediately after
his accession) but won greater fame, perhaps, as the patrons of
Shakespeare, who dedicated his great first Folio to them in 1623.
Without being 'first favourites' they wielded very great power
behind the throne, and if the good advice they offered both James
and his son had been followed the course of Stuart history might
well have been different. But Charles I rejected them in favour
of Buckingham whom they much disliked. William died in 1630.
Not surprisingly, during the Civil War Philip gradually moved
to the side of Parliament. Yet, though deeply involved in national
events both brothers kept an interest in Welsh affairs during
James's reign. William was hailed as 'colofn y deyrnas' (the
pillar of the kingdom) and Philip as 'the Welsh lord'. Gradually,
however, these Herberts were drawn to London and Wilton,
and lost their Welsh influence and with it, their native language.

Four brothers of the Montgomery branch of the Herbert family
became famous in James's reign. Edward (1583–1648) wrote a
celebrated autobiography, one of the first in the English language,
describing particularly his journeys on the continent, many as
James's ambassador in Paris. Another was the saintly, devout poet
George Herbert (1593–1633). A third, Sir Henry (1595–1673),
served as Master of King's Revels to James I, his son and grandson,
while the fourth, Thomas Herbert (1597–1642?), won fame as
a seaman serving in many expeditions such as that of Sir Robert
Mansel to Algiers in 1620–21. These Montgomery Herberts were
of course strongly royalist and Protestant. A third branch, the

Welshpool Herberts, while equally true in their support of the
Stuarts, were however, staunch Catholics. One of its members,
the Earl of Powis, chose in 1688 to go into exile with the last of
the Stuart kings.

ˈIn North Wales the family that rose now to greatest prominence was that of the Wynns of Gwydir, near Llanrwst. They
had been steadily accumulating lands over a wide area of Caernarfonshire for a century before the coming of John (Wyn) ap
Maredudd in Henry VIII's reign. His son Maurice was the
first to adopt the surname Wynn after the new English fashion.
Maurice's son, Sir John (1553–1627), is the best known of the
clan, which he 'glorified' in his famous History of the Gwydir Family,
a manuscript (eventually printed in 1770) which is a most valuable document of the times. After spending some time at Oxford
and the London law schools, and possibly abroad, he settled to a
vigorous public life. He was determined to make his family
predominant in Caernarfonshire, which he, like his father and
grandfather served as sheriff and M.P.[3]

Sir John was the very prototype of an 'adventurer', perhaps
in the worst sense of the word. In his greed for possessions and
power, he was ruthless both within and without the law. At
times, however, he met his match; Bishop William Morgan for
example, who Sir John claimed, owed his education to the Wynn
family, nevertheless steadfastly refused to sell him church lands
around Llanrwst. The Court of the Marches too, of which he
himself was a member, ordered him to cease persecuting his
tenants at Dolwyddelan, and, when he tried to defy them, called
his bluff. Only a bribe to a groom of King James narrowly saved
the wily knight.

Sir John 'adventured' in other, less doubtful, ways, in the
manufacture of cloth in the Conway valley, in copper mining in
Anglesey and in an ambitious project for draining Traeth Mawr,
Porthmadoc, which in fact was not realized until two centuries
later. By the next reign the ascendancy in Caernarfonshire had
passed to the Griffiths of Cefn Amwlch in Llŷn. But tradition in
the Conway valley remembers Sir John as a man of oppression,

for the legend lingers here that his spirit is condemned to lie trapped under the Swallow Falls, some five miles from Gwydir, where it is hoped it may be purified.

Space forbids us to detail all the families on which the life of Wales was now centred. Collectively they would almost all be found not only at Westminster as M.P.'s representing shire or county town, but also at Ludlow at the Council of Wales and the Marches.

THE COUNCIL OF WALES

The Council continued to be the administrative centre for Wales under the Stuarts. Just as James found it difficult to succeed Elizabeth, so the four presidents who now followed each other in quick succession found it impossible to emulate the halcyon days of Sir Henry Sidney. The authority of the Council no less than that of the King was now to be challenged. The new presidents—Lords Zouche, Eure, Gerard and Northampton were not great magnates with local ties like Henry Herbert, Earl of Pembroke, but rather officials of good family but no great standing. Under them the Council lost its brilliance and much of its reputation as a prince's court. Even as a court of law it declined, its important cases being taken (by Sir John Wynn for example) to the jealous courts at Westminster.

Reasons for its decline are not difficult to find. Common lawyers had always resented and envied its prerogative powers. Many of the Welsh gentry too had always disliked the authority of the Council, but the firm tolerance and general sympathy of Sidney and Herbert had quenched their fire. Now they were ready to challenge it again in much the same spirit as Parliament was ready to question the new king. Moreover, the long peace that the first Stuart gave lost the presidents their importance as lord-lieutenants responsible for the defence of the realm. A long-standing weakness of the Council too had been the independence enjoyed by the earls of Worcester of Raglan since the Act of 1543. In 1601, at the death of Pembroke, Edward Somerset, the fourth earl, succeeded in making Monmouthshire and Glamorgan independent of the Council under his own lord-lieutenancy, and so it remained for thirty years.

The authority of the Council was also challenged early in James's reign by the English border-counties. Cheshire and the city of Bristol had succeeded in breaking free from the Council's authority in Elizabeth's reign. Now the remaining four shires of Salop, Hereford, Worcester and Gloucester tried to do so. The matter was argued out by the King's judges, between Justice Coke for the shires and Sir Francis Bacon for the Council, and in the House of Commons. It was only the King's insistence on his own prerogative that saved the Council's authority. James might well say 'no Council, no King' as he had already said 'no Bishop, no King'.

WALES, JAMES I AND PARLIAMENT

By 1603 Welsh M.P.s had served their apprenticeship in government. They had also become a largely united body who were to pursue for the next fifty years certain agreed lines of policy. First of these was support for the Crown and all it had stood for in the best years of Elizabeth. This was not a mere sentimental 'hiraeth' for the Tudors, for they were quite ready to question, if necessary, the actions of both James I and certainly his son. Secondly they were firmly on the side of the Established Church. Thirdly they defended the Council at Ludlow which, with the Welsh language, gave them a distinctive place in the new Britain. Lastly, they were very sensitive about the defence of the coasts of Wales against invasion, and especially in the early years of the century when Catholic Spain and Ireland were seen as the national enemies.

Parliament had been used by the Tudors to rubber-stamp their policies and to provide the money to carry them out. Use had made it important and led its members to think, rightly or wrongly, that they had certain privileges. While the old Queen lived, they had played down their demands. But under James they took the initiative in the struggle to assert their privileges as against the King's Prerogative or his 'right' to overrule privilege and previous practice where necessary. To the King who had been bullied by Scots lords and Presbyters his Prerogative was the brightest jewel in his Crown, and he would defend it in religion, in the appointment of ministers, in raising finances, and in foreign policy—everywhere. We must now study these aspects in turn.

Religion was the King's immediate problem. In this, James like Elizabeth chose the middle way of Anglicanism and toleration. So he disappointed both pressure-groups of Catholics and Puritans. Unlike Elizabeth, however, he early showed that uncertainty of touch in dealing with people and affairs which was the besetting sin of the Stuarts and ultimately the cause of their downfall. The extreme Catholics turned to violence. The famous Gunpowder Plotters of 1605 had their contacts in both south and north Wales, among them Hugh Owen the master conspirator from Llŷn.* Inevitably there followed a further period of persecution, especially of the Jesuits. The result was that the Catholics went 'underground'. Outwardly they conformed but held secret sessions in some great house, where often in a 'priest's hole' lay hid a hunted Jesuit. The records of those who paid fines for recusancy show that it was the same great families, and especially their womenfolk, that clung stubbornly to the old faith—the Edwardses of Plas Newydd near Chirk, the Pennants of Brynford, the Mostyns of Greenfield, the Pughs of Creuddyn (Llandudno) and the Herberts of Welshpool. The Earl of Worcester, for example, conformed to all outward appearance while remaining at heart a Papist. He even served as a judge in the trial of the Gunpowder Plotters, while all the time his wife at Raglan, almost openly, sheltered Jesuits like John Salusbury the confirmed 'superior' of the order in Wales and the founder in 1622 of their seminary at Cwm. All in all, however, the Catholics were becoming a small minority.

* Sir John Wynn is said to have been warned not to attend the 'Gunpowder' Parliament by his kinsman Thomas Wiliems the lexicographer.

The Puritan element in Parliament, on the other hand, was growing in size, activity and power. James had hardly arrived in England before the Puritans thrust their Millenary Petition at him, seeking simpler cermonies and better ministry in the church, and were backed by the House of Commons. The King rudely rejected their pleas at the Hampton Court Conference in 1604, but he made one outstanding contribution to religion: he ordered a new version of the Scriptures which eventually appeared as the Authorized Bible in 1611, and which has remained the standard version down to our own day. Dr. John Davies largely relied on it in compiling the new Welsh Bible, which appeared as Bishop Parry's Bible in 1620, and which again has remained the basic form until the publication of the New Welsh Testament in 1975.

In Wales, however, the Puritans do not seem to have been any more popular under James than under Elizabeth. Doubtless there were many like Sir Thomas Myddelton, who gradually became more and more a Puritan as he became more and more a successful merchant. But then he also became more and more a Londoner, not immediately in touch with Welsh life, though it was to be he who, with Rowland Heylyn, financed the sudden spate of Welsh devotional books that appeared around 1630, including the pocket Bible of that date and the Welsh translation of Lewis Bayly's *Practice of Piety*.

The second challenge to James's Prerogative came through his ministers and his need for money. James had a particular fondness for favourites, who not only influenced him on matters of state but encouraged his own natural extravagance, and so added to the burden of debt left him by Elizabeth. Fortunately, he also inherited her wise secretary of state and lord-treasurer, Robert Cecil, son of old Burghley, and with him, as second-secretary another Welshman Sir John Herbert (of a south Wales branch) a distinguished lawyer and diplomat. Their main task was to justify his ways of raising funds. The money from certain feudal dues, tonnage and poundage, or customs, he could well regard as his own by right. But these were not enough, and James also imposed new taxes, such as that on currants, claimed benevolences or 'gifts' and fixed loans, and sold offices and new peerages (Sir John Wynn became a baronet in this way). But Parliament objected most of all to 'purveyance' or the right to take at will goods and services for the royal use, and to the sale of monopolies or patents. In 1611 James, finally exasperated by their haggling, dissolved Parliament. Apart from one equally futile Parliament, the 'Addled', called and dismissed in the one year, 1614, he ruled alone for the next ten years. Now his favourites had free reign. The two Herbert brothers, William and Philip, had to yield first place to the Howards (and their hangers-on, the Trevors of Trevalun) and later to the Duke of Buckingham. It was a change for the worse; Buckingham not only ruled the court and all its intrigue, but intervened in matters of state—a field in which he had little ability. Remarkably, the Herberts remained in favour although they openly criticized him.

The question of the king's prerogative was taken up at this time by perhaps the two ablest men of the day, Francis Bacon, now Lord Chancellor and Sir Edward Coke, the Lord Chief Justice. Bacon claimed that the King was above the law and the judges were his servants, while Coke held the common law to be above both King and Parliment. The authority of the Council of Wales over the Border counties was a case in point, as we have seen.

Events took a new turn in 1621. Bacon fell from power, accused of taking bribes. One who had bribed him was Sir John Trevor. But bribery was almost an accepted practice of political life; Sir John Wynn had saved himself from imprisonment by a bribe. So too were sinecures or 'soft jobs' for favourites; Trevor, again, as part of his job as naval surveyor, shared in the very lucrative duties on sweet wines and Newcastle coal. Monopolies, or the sole right of selling certain goods, though condemned in Elizabeth's reign, still flourished. Philip Herbert had a share in the monopoly for glass-making, with works at Milford Haven. This he sold to Sir Robert Mansel, the admiral, who tried to defend his monopoly as a genuine patent when monopolies were again attacked by Parliament in 1624 and finally made illegal.

The Habbit of no
Other, then A prop
of Heresie, A full
substanc, of a faire
pretender, but a
damnable deceiuer
Worthie of all that
is befalne him, a pro
test against God and
all christianety

As blowes the wind
My mill shall grind.

37. ARCHBISHOP JOHN WILLIAMS
Three items here accuse him of being a turncoat. Guess the earliest date of the
portrait.

It was foreign affairs that had made James recall Parliament in 1621. Hitherto his policy of peace towards England's neighbours had paid off; war was a luxury the king could not afford. Then in 1618 the Thirty Years' War broke out. Now James had to choose between his son-in-law, the Protestant Elector Frederick, and Catholic Spain. He still hoped that a Spanish marriage for his son Charles would enable him to persuade Spain to withdraw support from the Emperor; but meantime he must find money to support Frederick. So Parliament had to be called. Immediately the strongly Protestant Commons called for war against Spain and the persecution of Catholics at home. To these new claims of the right to interfere in foreign policy and religion they added freedom of speech and freedom from arrest. Now for the first time the Lords joined them, and, by condemning Bacon, claimed the right to control the King's ministers. These claims made up the political gunpowder which, fused by Charles I, would explode in civil war.

Bacon was replaced as Lord Keeper of the Great Seal by John Williams of Conway. A member of the Wynn family he had risen in the church after his schooling at Ruthin and Cambridge. Able, shrewd, he had risen in James's favour. He was to play a major role in the struggle between King and Parliament.

In 1623 Prince Charles with Buckingham went incognito to Spain to woo the Infanta in a vessel commanded by Thomas Herbert of the Montgomery branch. With him too as his groom went Richard Wynn of Gwydir. But it was another Welshman, his naval escort Sir Sackville Trevor of Trevalun, who rescued the prince from drowning when he fell into Cadiz harbour. The incident was in keeping with the whole farcical expedition which ended in failure. Charles and Buckingham returned repulsed and furious. James reluctantly gave up his Spanish policy and, for once in complete agreement with Parliament, was given funds to support the Protestant cause abroad in return for an act condemning monopolies.

WELSH SEAMEN AND COLONIZERS

James's policy of peace with Spain 'put a damper' on the activities of the English and Welsh seamen accustomed to the roistering days of Elizabeth. It also gave pirates and privateers a grand opportunity to terrorize the seas from the English Channel to the coast of North Africa. Corsairs from Barbary were now so bold as to land on Lundy Isle and the west coast, and kidnap and enslave the inhabitants. Two Welsh captains, both Glamorgan men, had the unenviable task of hunting them down. They were Sir Thomas Button and Sir Robert Mansel. Both had been trained to the sea in the last years of the old Queen, and had won profit by attacking Spanish vessels. But now that sport was finished. Mansel turned to politics, and to industrial 'adventures'. Button, however, stuck to the sea and during 1612–13 made a remarkable Arctic voyage. He failed to find the north-west passage, the first object of the expedition, but succeeded in exploring the west coast of the great Bay which Hudson had found a few years earlier. In 1620 the two friends, now both admirals, were given the task of destroying the Algerian lairs of the Barbary corsairs. But for some strange reason Mansel, leading the expedition, held off attacking Algiers until it was too late, and the ships returned to England with the pirates little daunted.

James's reign, however, was remarkable for pioneer ventures in colonization. In 1606 the London Company in Virginia, and in 1620 the famous Pilgrim Fathers to the north established settlements on the eastern seaboard of North America which, added to in the reign of Charles I, formed the nucleus of New England and eventually of the United States. But the reign of James I saw the making not only of New England and of New Scotland (Nova Scotia) but also of Cambriol or New Wales on the easternmost tip of Newfoundland (see map, p. 175). The founder was William Vaughan, an eccentric and deeply religious scholar of Llangyndeyrn in Carmarthenshire, who saw in settlements overseas a chance to save some of his countrymen at least from the dire poverty and lack of initiative which they suffered in Wales. He felt very bitter towards the uncaring gentry of his

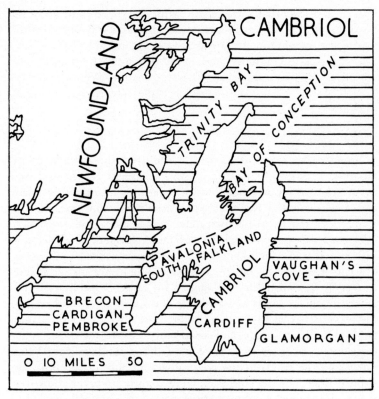

38. CAMBRIOL
Note the place-names.

day: 'our stock is decayed', he said, 'and nowadays we rear up two-legged asses which do nothing but wrangle in law'. But in Cambriol there was opportunity in plenty for farming, fruit growing, lumbering, fishing and even, it was said, gold-mining. In 1617 and again in 1619 he financed companies of Welshmen to sail out to Cambriol and settle. Vaughan himself may have voyaged in 1622 and again in 1628. To judge from the names—Cardiff, Pembroke, Cardigan, Carmarthen, Brecon—which they gave their little settlements almost all the colonists came from South

Wales. But eventually the arctic winters, disease, pirates, the hostility of the lawless fishermen of the Grand Banks, and not least their own indolence and shiftlessness, and indeed Vaughan's lack of practical common sense, were all too much for the Welsh colonists. By 1637 they had all left. So after twenty years the dream of the earnest visionary of Llangyndeyrn had come to nought.

CHARLES I AND WALES

Broadly the reign of Charles I repeated the pattern of his father's. A period of working with Parliament is followed by a period of working without, but eventually events outside England and Wales compel the recall of Parliament. But there is this difference; thanks to his own defects as a king, and the truculence of his opponents, Charles further experienced a period of bitter civil war which ended in his own execution.

Charles, unlike his father, was handsome of person and blameless in his personal life. He lacked his father's intelligence but shared his many faults as a king: he was unreliable, blinkered by his utter belief in his Divine Right, entirely lacking the Tudor flair for handling people, and remarkably unfortunate in his choice of friends. He showed none of his father's fondness for Wales, nor would he listen to the good advice of able counsellors like John Williams or the Herberts. He was quite prepared, however, to use Welshmen as soldiers and sailors in the expeditions led by Buckingham against France and Spain in support of the Protestants in the Thirty Years' War. They were as costly as they were disastrous. The three Parliaments which he now called were led by a growing and truculent Puritan element and refused him money until he attended to their grievances—the repression of free speech, arrest without trial, martial law and illegal taxation. These they expressed in the famous Petition of Right of 1628. Soon after, Buckingham was assassinated and in 1629 Charles dissolved Parliament.

For eleven years the stubborn King ruled without Parliament, raising money by whatever means he could, lawful or unlawful.

He was helped by two men whose mark was 'thorough': in 1633 William Laud became his Archbishop of Canterbury and Wentworth (later Earl of Strafford) his governor of Ireland. John Williams he fined and later imprisoned. Laud, once Bishop of St. David's, genuinely set about to rid the Anglican church of laxity in worship and in living. He was so strongly anti-Puritan that he was suspected of being a Catholic. Wentworth, in Ireland, was equally firm in insisting on the supremacy of the English King and the English Church, and in confiscating Irish land in order to grant it to English settlers. Nevertheless he also did a great deal of good, checking corruption, organizing a disciplined army, and encouraging trade.

His poverty made Charles keep out of the Thirty Years' War, which was now at its height. England, as a result, knew a period of prosperity when trade flourished, the navy was reformed, piracy put down, and the poor protected against enclosures and unemployment.

Ship-money was the worst of the many devices that Charles now used in order to finance his absolute rule.[2] While this was presented as an emergency measure for coastal defence, Wales could not complain, for the old fear of invasion still lingered in spite of the reassurance of Wentworth's strong rule in Ireland. Charles in fact did embark on a programme of shipbuilding, helped by his Welsh captains Mansel, Trevor and Button. Nor did his extension of the tax to inland areas much affect Wales with her eleven seaboard counties. The difficulty here was the collection of the tax. Welshmen relied for ready cash on the cattle trade, which John Williams called 'The Spanish Fleet of Wales which brings hither the little gold and silver we have'. There were 'dead' times between the cattle sales when no cash was available. Yet the desperate king could not wait for a convenient annual payment, but insisted on payment by instalments from each county. Distance from London and the difficulty and danger of carrying the payments in coin made matters worse. So did the epidemics that repeatedly made chaos of all arrangements.

Wales now joined mildly in the protest against ship-money which was loud in England, especially when it became clear that Charles intended it as a permanent tax. One by one the Welsh counties defaulted or delayed. Yet Wales in the end did better for the King than her larger neighbour; four Welsh counties (one of them being inland Radnor) are among the nine counties of England and Wales that best met his demands.

Charles' attempt with Laud to impose the English Prayer Book on the Scots now led to the Bishops' War of 1639 and 1640. He again made over-large demands upon Wales for soldiers. The 2,000 required, the largest army gathered in Wales since the Act of Union, were eventually mustered, but not without grumbling. When the Catholic Earl of Worcester was put in charge of south Wales, rumour began that a papist plot on behalf of the King was afoot. The rumour was no doubt spread by a growing Puritan element in the very same counties of Monmouth and Glamorgan.

Events now moved quickly. The Scots defeated Charles. He failed to raise funds from the Short Parliament. The Scots invaded the north of England, and refused to retreat until a new parliament was called and they had been paid £850 per day. The baffled King was forced to call the Long Parliament, probably the most famous in our history. This immediately attacked the King's ministers. Wentworth, now Earl of Strafford, who had been brought back from Ireland, was meanly abandoned by the King and executed. Laud was imprisoned. Next, Parliament made itself permanent, condemned all Charles's devices for raising money, and abolished all his arbitrary courts including the Court of the Council of Wales.

Even now it was not too late to avoid a clash. The country at large felt the Puritans had gone too far; the Welsh M.P.s resented the recent pressure on the King and his ministers. John Williams, released from prison, was now made Archbishop of York, and offered the King good advice. Had Charles accepted it there is room to believe that the Civil War might have been averted.

But again, as with James I, an overseas event intervened and forced the King's hand. With Strafford's strong rule removed, the Irish in the autumn of 1641 broke out in savage rebellion. The old fear of invasion was revived in Welsh breasts, and the Welsh M.P.s again hardened against Charles. There were fears generally that the King might use the army raised to put down the Irish in order to suppress Protestantism in this island. Parliament voted to abolish all bishops and presented the King with the Grand Remonstrance, setting out all his misdoings. Charles, incensed by the attack of the London mob upon the queen, broke into the Commons to arrest its five ringleaders but was too late. Only armed force could now decide between King and Commons and both sides prepared for war.

Welsh M.P.s had now to think hard about their loyalties. In April Parliament seized Hull. In June the Commons counted their supporters: twenty of the twenty-seven Welsh members were on their side. But by August when Charles raised his standard at Nottingham they had dwindled to a mere seven. Soon they would be only five, four of them from the counties of Pembroke and Denbigh where the Puritans were strongest. Loyalty to the Crown, ingrained since Tudor days, had triumphed. Wales in the Civil War would be overwhelmingly Royalist.

ORIGINAL EXTRACTS

1 THE DIARY OF ROBERT PARRY: PROCLAMATION AND TRAGEDY: (*Parry records the proclamation of the accession of James I at Denbigh.*)

On Wensday folowinge Doctor Morgan then bushop of Sct Assaphe & Sr. John Salusburie knight Will' Myddelton esqr accompenyed wth the Aldermen & other the officers of the towne made the like p'clamacon in the towne of Denbighe in Northwales. And hughe Cloughe beinge there Alderman p'nownced the same a loude in Englishe & the Bushoppe deliv' the same in Welshe to the people whoe well applauded the same.

That night the sayde Hughe Cloughe was founde drowned in a lyttle well wthin his own backeside, in wch well there was not water to cov' half his bodye; but he fallinge upon his head therein was nev' harde of before he was myssed an howre or two wthin night.

(*Arch. Camb.*, xv, 1915, p. 128)

2   THE DIARY OF WILLIAM BULKELEY OF DRONWY:
    RURAL LIFE IN ANGLESEY:

(17 February, 1631) I writ letters for Tho: lewis thence to ye cocke fight at llanllibio.

(4 July, 1631) I rid to the race at Malltraeth . . . thence to Jane whites and dranke beere there a while . . . thence to ye race Rees lloyds horse got ye race . . . home before sunrising.

(28 October, 1635) I pd. yestday X^s mise (ship-money) towards ye king's ship.

(Anglesey Antiquarian Soc. Trans., 1937)

3   SIR JOHN WYNN REJOICES:

(a) Yet a great temporall blessinge yt is, and a great harts ease to a man to finde that he is well dissended . . .

(b) This worthy prelate Rich: Davies was a poor Curate's son . . . In Queen Marie's time he was fain to flee with his wife to Geneva, where . . . he was so industrious yt in 3 years or somewhat more he attain'd ye Country language spoken in Geneva, wch I think to be French;—Oh! how my heart doth warm in recording ye memory of so worthy a man—He dyed poor having never had regard to Riches.

(Sir John Wynn: *History of the Gwydir Family*, pp. 36, 64–5)

CHAPTER XIII

ADVENTURERS AT WAR 1642–49

THE CONTESTANTS

THE events leading up to the Civil War had been political and religious. Yet fundamentally the struggle was also, in large part, an economic and social one. Broadly speaking, it was fought between those elements which had been dominant before the Renaissance and those which had risen to power after it. When then they took sides in the summer of 1642, the aristocracy and landed gentry of the countryside were generally for the king, the middle class, merchants and industrialists of the towns for Parliament. Peasants and artisans in country or town dutifully lined up with their local 'betters' to provide footsoldiers. Even the religious difference was basically economic; there were good Anglicans of the 'centre' in both camps, but the Catholics of the 'right' were definitely in the king's and the Puritans of the 'left' in Parliament's. Again, the immediate advantage in resources lay with the royalists, in money, valuable gold and silver plate; but this capital was limited and largely irreplaceable. In the long term the reproductive capital of industry and commerce was bound to be more valuable.

These economic and social factors were reflected in the geographical distribution of the two forces in England; the conservative and rural north and west generally supporting Charles, and the south and east with its many towns, thriving commerce and Puritanism, declaring for Parliament.

Parliament's early seizure of the navy was to prove a distinct boon to it. As to the land-forces, the immediate advantage in captains, swordsmen and cavalry lay presumably with the King. But the infantry of both sides, recruited by Charles through Commissions of Array, and by Parliament through Militia Acts,

proved equally bad. Apart from brief expeditions to France, the
Netherlands or Spain, the country had known peace for a
century, and the average Englishman or Welshman had grown
unused to arms, unless he had been a professional soldier. So in
the early years of the Civil War both armies showed themselves
disorganized and undisciplined and generally unwilling to march
beyond their own district.

In Wales the advantage lay clearly with the King. Here the
towns were small and the merchant class, Parliament's most
vigorous supporters, few. Here, even more than in England, the
peasants would follow the lead of the land-owning gentry, the
mainstay of the King. So, as in the Hundred Years' War and
the Wars of the Roses, Wales was again 'the nursery of the
King's infantry'. The King too held the castles except for Chirk
in the north, which he quickly won from Sir Thomas Myddelton
anyway, and Pembroke and Tenby in the south. War now gave
them a new lease of life, and their crumbling walls and towers
were suddenly put into good repair, often entirely at the expense
of royalists such as Archbishop John Williams at Conway. Econo-
mically, however, Wales was a comparatively poor country and
the help it could provide in money, munitions and food was
limited, particularly as war quickly disturbed its main trade in
wool and especially cattle. But Wales supplied the King with a
road to Ireland whence he might expect support. These four
factors: the footsoldiers, the repaired castles, the available but
limited wealth, and the Irish traffic were to be for Wales the
key factors in the struggle.

Wales was overwhelmingly royalist but active support varied
markedly from area to area. In North Wales the gentry were
staunchly royalist, though there were pockets of sympathy with
Parliament especially in Llŷn in the far west and around Wrexham and the Chirk estates of the Myddeltons. Here the castles
formed three almost parallel lines of defence strung along the
rivers Dee, Clwyd and Conway upon which the King was to fall
back as the war wore on. Chester and the Dee crossings were

the vital features and the scene of the most active and prolonged fighting.

The farther west from this area lay the estates of the gentry, the less active their interest in the struggle and the more difficult the King's commissioners of array, or recruiting officers, found it to raise troops. Flintshire and Denbighshire provided over 2,000 of the Welshmen who fought at Edgehill in 1642, whereas not even John Owen, the King's best soldier in North Wales, nor Archbishop Williams, his ablest adviser, could persuade the men of Caernarfonshire to march there.

Broadly, the position was the same in south Wales. In the east, around the estates of the enormously wealthy Marquis of Worcester at Raglan, the King found his most loyal support throughout the war. Here again the action centred on the crossings of the Severn at Gloucester, Worcester and Hereford. Westward the royalists were increasingly lukewarm, while in the far west, in English Pembrokeshire, Parliament found its strongest support in Wales. Here lay the estates of the Earl of Essex, Parliament's commander-in-chief. Here too was a merchant tradition. Above all, here in Milford Haven the navy, seized by Parliament at the outbreak of war, could freely operate in its support. This area was to be of vital importance during the Second Civil War. In all, interest centres on the extreme north-east, south-east and south-west corners of Wales. Not until the end of the first war did the north-west really experience the clash. Large areas of central Wales were completely untouched throughout.

Wales had always provided more than her fair share of professional soldiers. Many of these now came home to serve as 'ready-made' captains in the rival forces. Sir Charles Lloyd of Montgomeryshire had learned the art of fortification as a soldier in Holland and now became Charles's engineer-in-chief. Robert Ellice of Denbighshire had served under Gustavus Adolphus before he returned to capture Chirk Castle for Charles early in 1643. But there were others who declared for Parliament, notably the greatest veteran of them all Sir Thomas Morgan

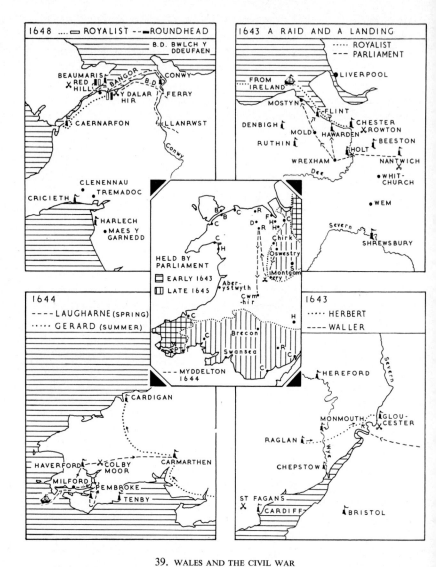

39. WALES AND THE CIVIL WAR

The map is designed to show that the action was almost entirely confined to the four corners of Wales.

(1604–79) who, like his Elizabethan namesake, spent a generation
abroad fighting for the Protestant cause in the Thirty Years' War
before serving Parliament as commander-in-chief in south-east
Wales under Fairfax, his old comrade-in-arms. The rival cavalry
commanders John Owen for the King and Michael Jones for
Parliament had also served abroad.

THE FIRST CIVIL WAR 1642–47

A feature, particularly of the First Civil War, is the almost
complete lack of connection between north and south Wales in
the strategy of either side. Geography probably provides the
explanation. This feature certainly makes it difficult to find a
pattern in describing the events of the struggle. It must, however, be attempted year by year.

In 1642 at the outset of war the initiative lay with the King.
His aim was to quell his rebellious Parliament and to take their
main stronghold, London. From Nottingham Charles marched
to Shrewsbury and north-east Wales to muster an army. Meanwhile the Earl of Hertford, who had been made commander-in-
chief in the south, had failed to find support in Devon and
Somerset and had crossed in coal boats to Glamorgan. But the
troops he then mustered were too late to join the King, who
had already set out for London. So badly organized were the
King's army and that of Essex which came to meet him that they
passed each other en route! Then, on 23 October, they turned
and faced each other at Edgehill. The battle was indecisive but
it halted Charles long enough for the Londoners to organize their
defences, meet the King at Turnham Green, and send him back
to Oxford, which became his headquarters for the rest of the war.

In 1643 it was still up to the King to carry the fight to the
enemy and to win London. But first he must take strong points
like Hull, Bristol, Gloucester and Plymouth, which still held out
for Parliament. The royal troops, always reluctant to fight far
afield, were doubly so when there was a chance that the enemy
might sally out from these strong points in their rear and attack
their homes. Clearly the immediate concern of the royalists of

south Wales was to take Gloucester. Lord Hertford had again failed in November to bring a force of thousands across the Severn at Tewkesbury. So Charles gave the command in south Wales to the young Lord Herbert of Raglan, son of the Earl of Worcester who had poured out wealth in the King's cause. But he proved no better general. In March he gathered an army of 2,000 to lay siege to Gloucester but foolishly omitted to seal the crossings of the Severn as he came and as a result Waller, for Parliament, crossed behind him and captured the surprised royalist army. In July Prince Rupert took Bristol with the help of a Welsh Regiment led by Colonel John Owen, who was wounded in the assault but survived. In August Herbert again mustered 4,000 foot and 800 horse and again laid siege to Gloucester. That city was now in desperate straits. But Essex made a dramatic forced-march from London and compelled the royalists to withdraw. The relief of Gloucester was decisive. It cancelled out the royalist capture of Bristol and meant that the wealthiest part of Wales was cut off from the main body of the king's forces.

Meanwhile, in the north, in Shropshire and Cheshire the forces of Parliament were establishing themselves, in spite of early set-backs such as the loss of Chirk Castle. In June 1643 its late owner, Sir Thomas Myddelton, became the Parliamentary commander for the six counties of north Wales, and in spite of his age proved himself a most capable general. Ably assisted by his lieutenants, Sir William Brereton and Colonel Thomas Mytton, he established salients at Beeston, Nantwich and Wem facing Chester and held them in spite of fierce resistance. On November 9th his forces broke out, crossed the Dee at Holt Bridge by a ruse, occupied Wrexham (where they quartered in the famous parish church) and Mold, seized Hawarden Castle and laid siege to Flint. Now Chester could be threatened on the Welsh as well as the English side. By the 18th they were at Mostyn but here they met a dramatic check from Ireland.

In spite of royalist victories in the north and south-west of England, the campaigns of 1643 had ended in stalemate and

Charles had failed in his broad plan of taking London. In the autumn both sides sought help. Parliament came to terms with the Presbyterians in Scotland and the King with the Catholics in Ireland. As a result a Scots army marched into England, and an army of Englishmen, sent to Ireland after the rebellion of 1641, was released to sail to Wales. Archbishop Williams in Conway anxiously awaited the coming of his 'English-Irish'. Would they come before the Roundhead raiders, already at Flint? At last they arrived, 2,500 of them, in sixteen ships which dropped anchor in Mostyn harbour a mere six miles away from the enemy. Nothing could have been more timely! The dismayed Parliamentary invaders retreated in haste, abandoning Flint and Hawarden as they went.

The arrival of the 'Irish' army could have been a decisive factor in the war. It certainly made a difference. Chester, to which the bulk of the army was marched, was relieved. Beeston Castle was captured and the Roundheads driven behind the

By permission of the National Museum of Wales

40. RIVAL COMMANDERS
(a) Sir Thomas Myddelton (b) Sir John Owen.

defences of Nantwich. But now the fighting tended to become more savage and brutal.

Archbishop Williams now felt the position sufficiently secure for him to journey in December/January to Oxford and there take stock of the situation with Charles and his counsellors. His opinion was outspoken and statesmanlike. The royalists had reached the limit of their resources while those of Parliament in men and money multiplied. The king's men too were badly behaved and losing him the sympathy of the countryside. So, he declared 'I know no better course than to struggle no further'. Yet if His Majesty chose to go on with the war, 'I am ready to live and die in your service'.

The new year, 1644 proved the Archbishop right in the north. The King had lost the initiative and the arrival of the Scots at his back put him on the defensive. In spite of additions to their number, the Irish proved a broken reed. Led by Lord Byron, the arrogant governor of Chester, they were decisively beaten at Nantwich in January. The King attempted to remedy matters by making Prince Rupert commander of all his forces in Wales. The dynamic Prince hurried hither and thither along the border, organizing the defences of Shrewsbury and Chester and making constant demands on the reluctant countryside for men and supplies. But Myddelton and Mytton more than held both him and Byron.

Meanwhile in south-west Wales, the tide of war ebbed and flowed. In 1643, the royalist Earl of Carbery had won all the area except Pembroke, stubbornly defended by John Poyer its mayor. But then emerged a young and vigorous leader for the Parliamentary army, Rowland Laugharne, who early in 1644, aided by the fleet in Milford Haven, cleared Carbery out of Pembrokeshire and Carmarthenshire. Rupert's reply was to appoint Sir Charles Gerard to replace Carbery. Gerard, a very able professional soldier, again drove Laugharne back into south Pembrokeshire in the summer. The appointment of this professional, however, affronted the gentry, while the unruly conduct of his soldiers offended the local inhabitants. Everywhere the opposition to the King was hardening.

Now the Scots invaded the north, and Rupert and Gerard had
to withdraw to meet them at the battle of Marston Moor on
2 July, where the Royalists were defeated. Back in Wales the
pendulum of fortune swung again; Laugharne broke out of
Pembroke, and Myddelton and Mytton took Oswestry, the gateway to the upper Severn Valley and Mid-Wales. Rupert returned
furious from the battlefield and again scoured Denbighshire and
Flintshire for men and money, giving offence by his arrogance.
Then he galloped away to Bristol. This was Myddelton's opportunity. During the night of 3 September he marched his men out
of Oswestry and at dawn surprised the royalist garrison at Newtown, capturing a large store of munitions. Next he took
Montgomery and stored the powder in the Castle. Hurriedly the
forces of King and of Parliament converged on the town. Here
was fought the greatest battle of the first Civil War on Welsh
soil. It was a decisive victory for Parliament, and, according to

By permission of the Radio Times Hulton Picture Library

41. RIVAL SOLDIERS
(a) A Roundhead   (b) A Cavalier.

Archbishop Williams, a greater defeat for the King than Marston Moor.

Myddelton was now master of mid Wales. During the autumn he took royalist strongholds at Powis Castle, and Abbey Cwm Hir. In the north he found resistance toughened and he failed to capture Ruthin Castle and his own home at Chirk. But, in review, 1644 had been a good year for the Roundhead cause. The Irish troops had been wasted. The Royalists were in retreat.

January 1645 saw Parliament really take up the offensive. Their noose about Chester tightened and they made determined attacks on Beeston and Hawarden castles, the city's defensive outposts on the east and west respectively. Both besiegers and besieged now suffered from a shortage of food, and their forays for sheep and cattle brought bitter complaints from the inhabitants. In February Princes Rupert and Maurice brought relief to Chester, but only at the expense of losing Shrewsbury, which Mytton captured by night. When urgent business called the princes away, the besiegers closed on Chester again.

The raids into north-east Wales of Michael Jones, a dashing colonel of cavalry and veteran of the Irish wars, kept the royalists in a constant state of alarm. Now too they fell to quarrelling amongst themselves. Colonel Roger Mostyn withdrew his men from the defence of Chester because of the arrogance of Lord Byron, its governor. In Conway too Colonel John Owen, who had been given command of the town, took the castle also by violence from his fellow-royalist John Williams, who had repaired, supplied and armed it at his own expense. The King rebuked Owen; nevertheless he remained in the castle, and the Archbishop retired to his family house at Penrhyn near Bangor, hurt but still loyal.

There had been disagreements too in the enemy ranks: between Parliament and the Army, between Presbyters and Independents, between the older, moderate generals like the Earl of Manchester and younger, utterly committed commanders like Cromwell. In 1645, however, Parliament put its house in order.

A New Model Army was created of paid, uniformed* and trained men, who, unlike the county levies, would fight anywhere. Secondly the 'Self-denying Ordinance' gave the Army new, keen and efficient generals by compelling all commanders who were also members of either House of Parliament to resign (Cromwell was made an exception).

In June the Self-Denying Ordinance compelled Myddelton to yield his command to Mytton. On the 14th the King's defeat at Naseby robbed him of the Midlands. Now only Wales was left to him. He moved to south Wales—to Raglan and then to Cardiff. But his hopes of support there were quickly dashed, largely because Gerard had offended both gentry and peasantry by his demands. In August Laugharne defeated Gerard's men at Colby Moor and in September Rupert surrendered Bristol. Soon all the counties of south Wales had declared for Parliament. Some spirited gentry of Glamorgan still tried to revive the King's cause, but all in vain. With the surrender of Raglan Castle in August 1646 the war in South Wales was over.

Meantime Charles wearily marched north, hoping to join Montrose who was still successful in Scotland. He was attended by his faithful lifeguards (among them a trooper Richard Symonds, who has left a remarkable diary of this period).[1] Shadowed all the way by a detachment of Roundhead cavalry, he moved over the hills to Presteigne—Newtown—Llanfyllin—Llangollen—Chirk —Chester. There from the castle tower on 24 September he saw his men defeated at the battle of Rowton Heath nearby.[2] Chester was no longer safe for its royal master and he fell back into the next line of defence at Denbigh stoutly held by Colonel William Salusbury (known as *Hen Hosanau Gleision*—Old Blue Stockings) who said he would never yield the castle unless ordered by the King. Charles now took counsel with Colonel John Owen and Archbishop Williams who, we assume, had patched up their quarrel. Then he marched away, only to learn that Montrose in Scotland had at last been defeated, and surrendered himself to

* These were the first English soldiers to wear red tunics.

the victorious Scots at Newark. Never again was Charles to see Wales.

All the Royalist forces in north Wales now concentrated on helping Chester, tightly invested by the Roundheads. Troops from distant Caernarfonshire and Montgomeryshire rendezvoused at Denbigh Green. But on 1 November, 1645 Mytton and Jones fell on them and routed them. A fortnight later Beeston Castle too had to yield to the Roundheads. Now the state of the beleaguered city of Chester, beset by famine, constant bombardment and the cold of winter, was desperate. The Royalists tried by every ruse to get supplies in through the Roundhead cordon but rarely succeeded. On one occasion a 100 cavaliers dared to gallop pell-mell through the besiegers' lines, each carrying 7 stone of meat, some oatmeal and some gunpowder to bring welcome relief to the defenders in the city. But for Chester to hold out any longer was folly. On 3 February, 1646 the city surrendered and the gallant defenders were allowed to march out with honour.

Everywhere in 1646 the war became one of sieges. Chester gone, Byron and his royalists retreated into north Wales to Caernarfon, ravaging as they went, and giving the western counties their first real taste of war. The Roundheads hurried after them to attack the great castles which alone could hope to hold out for the King. Chirk, Hawarden and Ruthin all fell in turn. Denbigh was too strong to be taken quickly, and after entrenching it around securely, Mytton left it for constant bombardment and hunger to reduce. Then, by-passing the great coastal castles of Flint, Rhuddlan and Conway, he marched via Llanrwst Bridge and the old Roman Road through Bwlch y Ddeufaen to Llandegai. Here he was welcomed by none other than Archbishop Williams who had decided to change sides! For years he had been foretelling failure; he had been affronted at Conway; but it was the arrogance of Byron and the vandalism of his troops that finally made him a turncoat. Mytton continued to Caernarfon finding much support as he went. Five weeks later on 4 June the great castle, attacked by land and cut off by sea,

surrendered, and soon Beaumaris and all Anglesey followed suit.
Six castles remained. Rhuddlan surrendered in July and Flint in
August. Their captors then joined those troops already en-
trenched around Denbigh, which finally yielded on 14 October.
Conway town in the meantime had been taken with the Archbishop's help. He himself was wounded in the attack, but the
castle, which he, ironically, had strengthened, held out until
18 November when John Owen marched out, colours flying, to
retire to Clenennau to await another chance to draw sword for
his King. Holt Castle, on the Dee, small but immensely strong,
had been at the centre of continual warfare; but it held out
until January 1647. True to form, remote Harlech held out for
King Charles longest of any, as it had for Glyndŵr and Jasper
Tudor. It finally yielded on 15 March.

Orders were given for the castles to be 'slighted', or damaged
beyond use. Small garrisons were to be left in Conway, Caernarfon, Beaumaris and Denbigh and the remaining troops, idle
and often undisciplined, disbanded. But revolts in Caernarfonshire warned Parliament that they might suddenly need to be
recalled. And the Cavalier gentry of Glamorgan were known to
be restless.

THE SECOND CIVIL WAR 1648

The uneasy peace of 1646–7 was broken in 1648 by a series of
local rebellions against the authority of Parliament which, co-
inciding as they did with an invasion of England by the Scots,
might have led to a general war again and possibly to a restoration
of the King. In this Second Civil War Wales played a distinctive
part.

Public sympathy had moved in favour of the King and against
growing extremism in the ranks of Parliament and the Army,
who now held Charles prisoner. Active royalists too were glad
to stir up trouble; Lord Byron informed the Scots, who were
now in secret negotiation with the King, that North Wales was

ready to revolt the moment they marched south. But it was dis-
satisfaction over the payment and disbanding of the victorious
soldiery that brought matters to a head.

It all began in Pembroke. Here, in January 1648, the mayor,
John Poyer, a merchant who had held the town for Parliament
in the first war, refused to yield the town and castle to Colonel
Fleming, sent by Parliament to replace him. He insisted that his
officers and men be first given their arrears of pay. He repulsed
all attempts to remove him by land and by a naval force in
Milford Haven. Soon he was joined by large numbers of rebellious
soldiers, led by Colonel Rice Powell in the absence of Rowland
Laugharne, who was in London to answer accusations of Royalist
plotting.

In April Poyer and Powell declared for the King. Parliament
ordered Colonel Horton to south Wales to restore order. But he
found the area very disturbed and hostile. Repulsed by Powell,

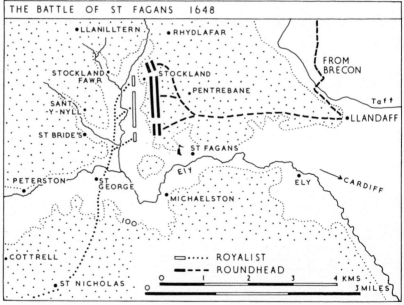

42. THE BATTLE OF ST. FAGANS 1648.

he fell back on Brecon. When news came that Powell had taken the initiative and was marching into Glamorgan, Horton made a desperate forced-march southwards in bad weather and succeeded in cutting him off near St. Fagans before he reached Cardiff. Now Laugharne fled from London, joined Powell and took command of the rebels. For four days the two armies faced each other. On Monday 8 May, hearing that the great Cromwell himself was marching to meet him and had already reached Gloucester, Laugharne attacked. His men outnumbered Horton's, by more than two-to-one, but they were mostly ill-armed foot soldiers. After a desperate struggle, Horton's seasoned troops from the New Model Army won the day. Laugharne fled to Pembroke to join Poyer, and Powell to Tenby. This battle of St. Fagans was the greatest of the war in Wales.*

The pattern of the first war was now repeated in South Wales. The royalists could not take the field again and the struggle had become one of sieges. The situation was nevertheless serious for Parliament. Throughout England and Wales sympathy for Charles smouldered, and burst into flame in riots in the city of London and open rebellion in Kent and Essex. On the very day of the battle of St. Fagan's Mytton was refused entry to Beaumaris castle and returned to Caernarfon for safety. It is now clear that the revolts in the west occurred by prearranged plan between south Wales and north Wales and, through Byron, with the Scots, who were massing to cross the border. Little wonder that Cromwell, furious, hurried through a hostile south Wales to undertake the siege of the immensely strong castle of Pembroke.

In north Wales, Sir John Owen of Clenennau rose in open revolt and collected royalist forces. Mytton, besieged in Caernarfon sent to Twisleton, the governor of Denbigh, for help. Twisleton, collecting what forces he could, marched towards Caernarfon but Owen decided to intercept him. On 5 June at *Y Dalar Hir*, along the shore of the Menai Straits between Bangor and Aber, they met. Again the experienced Roundheads won.

* See extract 1, chapter 14.

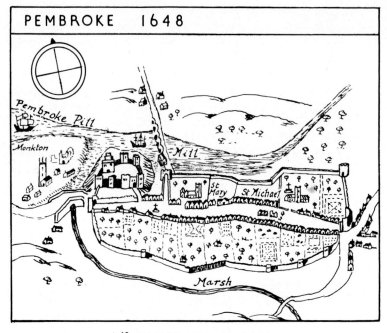

PEMBROKE 1648

43. PEMBROKE TOWN AND CASTLE

Sir John Owen was wounded, captured, and imprisoned in Denbigh, where he remained in spite of dramatic attempts to rescue him.[3]

Meantime far south, Powell had surrendered Tenby to Horton, but Laugharne and Poyer in mighty Pembroke castle still kept Cromwell at bay even outside the town. Until he could bring up great cannon by sea, starvation was his only weapon, but his own men were almost as hungry as the townsfolk and garrison, and he himself helpless with an attack of gout. The weeks dragged by, still the guns had not arrived and news came that the Scots were marching down. At last the guns did come and were trained on the great walls.[4] A week later on the 11 July Pembroke surrendered, having defied Cromwell for nearly two months. Three days earlier the Scots had crossed the border into England.

Now Cromwell hurried north through the midlands to York-shire, then struck westward across the Pennines to put himself between the invading army and Scotland. At Preston he an-nihilated the Scots in a three-day fight in atrocious weather. Meanwhile the coming of the Scots was the signal for Byron to gather again a Royalist force in north Wales. News of the defeat at Preston made him retreat to Anglesey and Beaumaris castle. Here, however, the royalists insisted that their own young Richard Bulkeley should lead them, and Byron fled to the Isle of Man. Mytton now gathered his Roundhead force at Bangor. There he waited for two weeks for a fleet of small boats from Conway. Then, under the cover of night, he quietly floated his men across the Straits to Anglesey. Through Bulkeley's neglect, they landed without opposition. At Red Hill above Beaumaris next day, October 1st, his cavalry broke the royalists who fell back on the great castle and soon surrendered. The rebellion in Wales was over.

Sir John Owen was tried and condemned to death, but for some reason, reprieved and lived until 1666 at Clenennau. His old rival in arms, Archbishop John Williams died in March 1650. Laugharne, Poyer and Powell were court-martialled and con-demned to death. The court decided, however, that only one should die. A child was used to choose the victim. Two pieces of paper bore the words 'Life given of God', a third was blank. The boy drew the blank for Poyer. The blustering merchant who had held Pembroke for Parliament in the first war and for the King in the second died a brave man. Young Bulkeley was killed in 1650 in a duel on Lavan Sands (between Beaumaris and the mainland) with Richard Cheadle, the man accused of providing Mytton with the all-important boats. One by one the royalist adventurers had left the stage of war and its lime-light.

Their royal leader had gone before. Parliament had wanted to re-negotiate with the King, but the Army, now the real power, had had enough. It removed 143 members from the Commons. It was the remainder, the 'Rump', which was responsible for putting the King of England on trial, for his condemnation by a

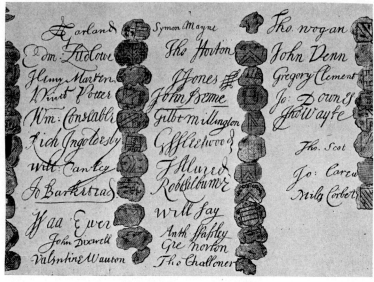

44. A KING'S DEATH WARRANT
The signatures of the regicides. Find the two Welsh ones.

minority of the court, and for his execution on 30 January, 1649.
Two Welsh regicides were amongst those who signed his death
warrant: John Jones of Maesygarnedd, M.P. for Merioneth, and
Thomas Wogan, M.P. for Cardigan boroughs.

ORIGINAL EXTRACTS

1   TROOPER SYMONDS'S DIARY:
     THE KING'S LAST MARCH IN WALES:
     Munday 22, 1645—to Chirk. Newes this day . . . that part of the outworkes
     at Chester was betrayed to the enemy by a Captain and Leiftenant, both
     apprehended. The King sent . . . to Lord Byron to Chester to hold out
     twenty-four hours.
     Tuesday—The King went into Chester.
     Wednesday 24 September—(*Battle of Rowton Heath*) They beat us agen for't.
     Thursday 25. This night I saw a rainbow within a myle of Denbigh at five
     in the morning, and the moone shined bright; twas just against the moone.
                    (Richard Symonds: *Diary of the Marches of the Royal Army*, p. 241)

2 A RESOURCEFUL CAVALIER: (*A royalist colonel is ordered by his commander on Rowton Heath to get an urgent message to the King in Chester. But first he must cross the River Dee*)

The Colonel executed his orders with better speed than could be expected; for he galloped directly to the river Dee, under Huntingdon house, got a wooden tub (used for slaughtering of swine) and a batting staff (used for batting coarse linen) for an oar, put a servant into the tub with him, and in this desperate manner swam over the river, his horse swimming by him, ordered his servant to stay there with the tub for his return, and was with the king in little more than a quarter of an hour. . . .

(Quoted in N. Tucker: *North Wales in the Civil War*, p. 77)

3 AN ATTEMPT TO RESCUE SIR JOHN OWEN FROM DENBIGH CASTLE, 1648:

On Monday night last, the captaine of the guard being gone to bed, . . . a party of the cavilliers came . . . with scaling ladders . . . privily to the walls without giving any alarm at all, the corporall and the two sentinels of guard being privy to their design. And about some 60 of the cavalliers had scaled the walls, and had got over without any opposition at all, and were within the walls at least an hour before any alarm was given, and it was a hundred to one that we had not been all surprized and ruined, but we were miraculously delivered. . . .

It so pleased God that the captain of the guard could not sleep in his bed, but was much troubled, tho' he knew not for what, and at last he resolved to rise and to walk the rounds with his souldiers . . . at last he espied a party got over the walls, and scaling ladders upon the walls, whereupon the alarum was given to the castle, and the towne also by these means took the alarm. But they all yeilded themselves prisoners at mercy.

(*ibid*, pp. 148–9)

4 CROMWELL'S LAST SUMMONS TO POYER IN PEMBROKE, 10 July, 1648:

Sir,—I have considered your condition and my own duty; and (without threatening) must tell you that if (for the sake of some) this offer be refused, and thereby misery and ruin befall the poor soldiers and people with you, I know where to charge the blood you spill. I expect your answer within these two hours. In case this offer be refused, send no more to me about the subject. I rest your servant—Ol. Cromwell.

(J. R. Phillips: *Civil War in Wales*, 2nd edn., pp. 414–5)

CHAPTER XIV

PURITANS IN POWER

THE brief period of the Interregnum or Commonwealth 1649–60 is one of the most important in our history. In the end the monarchy was restored; yet, it would be wrong to regard the Commonwealth as a failure. It restored the life of the nation after the chaos of the Civil War, and its prestige abroad. At perhaps no time in their history were the people of Britain more compelled to think of great issues in church and state and in life generally. It gave Wales more benefits than most—an early taste of state education, for example—and prepared the climate in which the great religious revival of the next century would transform the nation.

For eleven years there was no king. Parliament ruled in name, but the army in fact; the Independents in religion ruled the army; and the greatest Independent was Cromwell. The Commonwealth was thus a theocracy, government by men of religion. The Puritans saw their task as twofold: to govern Wales and to convert it to their creed.[1]

THE COUNTY COMMITTEES

Local government was the immediate problem even before Charles was executed, for the First War ended not in a national truce and a treaty but piecemeal, area by area. During the war Parliament had successfully used committees to raise troops on a county basis. These were now employed to restore law and order, to guard against rebellion and to raise funds by fining the losers, by sequestration, that is taking their lands, and by diverting the stipends and tithes of the clergy towards preaching and teaching. The committee members were nominated by Parliament, not elected, and numbered as many as thirty or forty. They

45. THE PURITAN
Note the Bible and the sword.

included men of standing in the county who had been keen
Parliamentarians during the war and some 'neutrals' previously
accustomed to local government, together with a few Roundhead soldiers as a safety measure.

There were special difficulties in Wales, however. It was a
comparatively poor country, with fewer men of substance able
to serve; those that could were almost certain to be Royalists
and not to be trusted; in any case the Welsh gentry were too
fond of family feuding to be honest counsellors. The Second Civil
War gave Cromwell a sharp reminder of the overwhelming
royalist sympathies of the Welsh. In all, Wales presented a
special problem, to be solved in the end by special means, as we
shall see.

Committees were quickly working in some counties—Pembroke which had been strongly Parliamentarian from the start,
Montgomery because of its early 'conquest' in 1644, Radnor
owing to the influence of Vavasor Powell, and Denbigh due to the
power of the Myddeltons. But all the other counties of the west
and south remained difficult. This had three important results.
It meant, firstly that the same man had to serve on more than one
county committee; Colonel Mytton, a Shropshire man, for
example, was included in the committees of Montgomery,
Merioneth, Caernarfon, Anglesey and Flint. Secondly, 'outsiders', Englishmen from far across the border were nominated
to make up the numbers; Cromwell himself and his son Richard
were listed on the Glamorgan committee. Thus the Commonwealth government, like Puritanism, was largely an English
imposition on Wales.

Thirdly, authority in actual practice came to rest finally on
outstanding individuals. This led inevitably to accusations of corruption from their enemies, many of which were only too well
founded. Examples of such 'adventurers' who now rose to power
and wealth were Edward Vaughan in Montgomeryshire, and
Colonel John Carter and Thomas Madryn in Caernarfonshire.

Two men in particular now came to the fore and need special
note. A Parliamentary soldier from the beginning, Philip Jones

had risen to the rank of colonel by 1646, and was Horton's second in command at his victory at St. Fagans. He now showed great ability as a member of at least five of the county committees, and by 1655 was the dominant figure in south Wales. Meantime he had amassed a considerable fortune and an estate at Fonmon, but he successfully defended himself against charges of corruption. In time he moved into a wider sphere of national influence, valued by Cromwell for his moderation and loyalty. He became a member of the Protector's Council of State and later of his 'other House' as Philip, Lord Jones. He supervised Cromwell's household and even pressed him to become king. It was he, in fact, who supervised Cromwell's funeral arrangements. After the downfall of Richard Cromwell he came to terms with the royalists and retired to his Fonmon estates.

Equally eminent in North Wales was John Jones, Maesygarnedd, the Regicide. Born in Merioneth, he was brought up in London in the service of the Myddeltons and became a deeply sincere Puritan. He rose to be Colonel of the Horse in the Civil War and M.P. for Merioneth. He, too, gained Cromwell's favour. During 1650–54 he, together with two others, governed Ireland. In 1656 he married Cromwell's sister. He too became a member of his brother-in-law's Council of State and of his 'other House', again with the title John, Lord Jones. After Cromwell's death he tried to stem the tide of returning royalist sympathy but in vain. Unlike the other Lord Jones, he was arrested at the Restoration, tried and condemned as a regicide, and died with great dignity in October 1660. He shared much of Cromwell's spirit; he was a devout Puritan, a family man, a tireless and honest administrator who remained a countryman at heart —compassionate, fearing extremism, and above all dreading anarchy.

THE PURITANS

There were few Puritans in Wales before the Civil War. John Penry, the herald-martyr of the movement, had sounded his trumpet-call on behalf of good preaching and good living fifty years too early. But eventually small groups appeared, particularly along the border lands and in those new shires created by the Act of Union, and curiously in localities where Catholic recusancy had been strongest, such as east Denbighshire around Wrexham, and especially in Monmouthshire.

Puritanism was an English product which penetrated into the Welsh border lands during the 1630's. It took root first in the south-east, thanks to the work of three clergymen all of whom had been to Oxford and possibly imbibed the new ideas there: William Wroth (1576–1641) a Monmouthshire man and now rector of Llanfaches; William Erbery (1604–54) the rector of St. Mary's in his native Cardiff; and his curate Walter Cadoc (1610-1659), originally a native of Llangwm (Mons.)—also strangely a Jesuit centre. About 1634-5 all fell foul of Archbishop Laud for their Puritan ideas and eventually lost their livings. Wroth, now in his sixties, remained at Llanfaches preaching to a congregation outside his old church. Cradoc went north to Wrexham where his sermons won many converts, among them Morgan Llwyd (1619–59), a Merioneth lad, then scarcely more than a schoolboy.

Within a year persecution drove Cradoc south to Brampton Bryan in the valley of the Teme where Radnorshire, Herefordshire and Salop meet. Here another Puritan congregation had gathered. Now he gained another convert in Vavasor Powell, a young schoolmaster from nearby Knucklas. Cradoc was also in touch with Puritans in London whence he had to flee to avoid a summons of the Court of High Commission. Wroth too had contact with English Puritans in London and Bristol. It was a London Puritan, lately returned from New England, who helped Wroth, Cradoc and Llwyd in 1639 set up the Llanfaches congregation as Wales's first Independent Church, though as yet without a building of their own.

When the Civil War broke out the Puritans in royalist Wales were clearly at a disadvantage. The saintly parson, William Wroth had died just before the fighting began. Erbury became a chaplain in the Parliamentary forces and Llwyd a soldier. The Llanfaches congregation fled first to Bristol, then, when that city fell to Rupert, to London. Here they absorbed many of the new ideas and strange doctrines that flooded into the capital from Holland and New England. Cradoc and Powell were with them there, and for the next few years these two were busy urging Parliament to provide Wales with a better ministry. They were to be in the forefront of all Puritan activities up to the Restoration.

As early as 1623, Dr. Lewis Bayly, Bishop of Bangor and author of a 'best-seller', *The Practice of Piety*, had given a very gloomy picture of the spiritual apathy of the Welsh people. Like John Penry he blamed the lack of preaching and the neglect of their pastoral duties by the clergy, many of whom were Englishmen out of touch with their flocks. Vavasor Powell declared in 1641 that there were fewer conscientious preachers in Wales than there were counties. Rhys Prichard, vicar of Llandovery an author of the celebrated *Welshman's Candle*, had described Wales as a land of crowded alehouses and empty churches. These statements were probably exaggerated. Nevertheless Wales offered the Puritans a very fruitful field of labour. But the ministers had to wait for the victories of the soldiers.

By 1645 victory was sufficiently sure for Parliament to dispatch Cradoc and two other genuine Puritans to South Wales as itinerant ministers to preach the Gospel in the Welsh language. Gradually Puritanism 'ran over the mountains between Brecknock and Monmouth like fire in the thatch', and up the river valleys to places as remote as Llangurig. By 1650 there were approximately 130 clergy in Wales 'preaching the Word' in Puritan fashion, about seventy-five in the south and fifty-five in the north. Many of these, it is true, would be 'trimmers', fairweather friends of the now victorious sect. We must remember too that the great majority of the clergy remained Anglicans. But the seed had been sown.

THE ACT FOR THE PROPAGATION

The second Civil War in 1648 warned Parliament that Wales needed special treatment of the kind already given northern

England and now being prepared for Ireland and New England. In July 1649 they took the first step of putting South Wales in charge of Major General Thomas Harrison, one of Cromwell's most zealous officers, and adding him to all the county committees. In February 1650 they passed 'a most momentous Act:' 'An Act for the Better Propagation and Preaching of the Gospel in Wales'. Though apparently concerned only with religion, this famous act was an outstanding milestone in the history of government and education in Wales. Its purpose was to ensure fit ministers and schoolmasters who would preach and teach according to Puritan tenets, based solely on the authority of the Bible. Belief in kings and bishops, the practice of pluralism, and the use of Anglican ritual and the Prayer Book were all to be condemned, as well as negligence and 'scandalous' living. Those approved would be state-supported out of money got from fining proven royalists and selling their lands.

The 'Propagation' Act appointed seventy-one secular persons as Commissioners to hear charges of 'delinquency, scandal, malignancy (supporting king and bishop) or non-residency' against any cleric or schoolmaster, and if the charges were proved, to dismiss them, subject to an appeal. The first three names on the list of commissioners significantly were General Harrison, Colonel Philip Jones and Colonel John Jones. Twenty-five ministers, further, were to act as Approvers, deciding to whom the Commissioners should grant certificates of fitness as preachers and teachers. Cradoc and Powell are among those listed. Ministers were to be paid up to £100 a year and schoolmasters £40, and provision was also made for their families. The Act was to remain in force until March 1653 only.

Examination of their names shows that the Commissioners were appointed generally as a reward for previous services, generally military service. Hence there was a marked absence of members of old Welsh families. A large number of the seventy-one were not Welshmen, and came from counties as far afield as Buckinghamshire, Cornwall and Yorkshire. Eleven hailed from

English border counties and thirteen from the vicinity of Wrexham, one only from Carmarthenshire and Cardiganshire, and not
one from Anglesey, Caernarfon and Merioneth. The list of
Approvers shows largely the same imbalanced distribution, and
proves the same point that the Propagation was an imposition by
Puritan England and the border upon a royalist and anglican west.
'Wales during the Propagation was ruled by a military middle
class'.

The Commissioners and Approvers got to work at once, and
by the end of 1650 some 280 clergy had been ejected from their
livings, over two-thirds of them from southern counties; mainly
for pluralism in the north but also for drunken-ness, using the
Prayer Book, and 'malignancy' in the south. To eject ministers
was an easy matter; to replace them a much more difficult one.
The Propagators' only answer was to appoint itinerant ministers
who journeyed from parish to parish. Many of these, among
them, of course, several of the Approvers themselves, covered
wide areas. Walter Cradoc ranged from Monmouthshire to
Presteigne. But the king of itinerants was the tireless Baptist
Vavasor Powell, who travelled over Brecknock, Radnorshire and
Montgomeryshire, often preaching in three places on the same
day and riding 100 miles a week. Roving ministers could never
be satisfactory, however. Most of them were unlearned men and
often ridiculed. In any case they were in a sense pluralists, with
too many churches to give immediate and satisfactory pastoral
care to any.

Nearly all the congregations now set up were Independents,
owning direct allegiance to Jesus Christ and to no other person,
body or government; concerned only with the reading and
preaching of 'the Word'; worshipping without ritual or adorn-
ment or even a set building; sober in dress and way of life, and
observing the Sabbath day strictly. Within the freedom and
tolerance afforded by this broad interpretation, and influenced
by the new ideas flooding through London from the Continent
and America, there now sprang up a bewildering variety of sects
differing from each other in matters of doctrine and church

government—Seekers, Ranters, Fifth Monarchy Men, Baptists, Quakers and many more. Erbury joined the Seekers, waiting patiently for God to grant them new commissions as apostles. Vavasor Powell and Morgan Llwyd were Fifth Monarchists, believing that Christ was about to come in person to establish his own fifth monarchy or empire which would last for 1,000 years (the previous four empires were Assyria, Persia, Greece and Rome). The confusion of sects, with the bewilderment they must have caused to an uneducated peasantry, is nowhere better brought out than in a remarkable book written by Morgan Llwyd in 1653, *Llyfr y Tri Aderyn*. It takes the form of conversations between three birds: the Eagle (Cromwell), the Raven (Royalists and the Established Church) and the Dove (Puritans).[2] Finally, of course, it is the Dove who has the truth. It is not a well planned work, but Llwyd is at his best when he writes as he would preach:

'O people of Wales! To you my voice doth come. O Dwellers in Gwynedd and Deheubarth, Unto you do I call. The dawn has broken, and the sun is rising upon you. The birds are singing: Awake (O Welshman) Awake!'

Listed among the Approvers too was John Miles (1621–83). Another native of the Herefordshire border, he had served as a Roundhead chaplain during the war. During a visit to London in 1649 he was baptized and commissioned to spread Baptist principles in Wales. With his headquarters at Ilston in Gower, he now became an itinerant, setting up churches at Llanharan, Carmarthen, Hay and Abergavenny. With a genius for organization, he bound these individual congregations into a circuit or union, with a general assembly to make regulations that would be binding on all. In this he was approaching Presbyterianism, a creed that took little root in Wales at this time. His Welsh Baptist sect was known as the Particular (or 'Closed) Baptists, believing that only those adult believers who had been fully immersed at Baptism should share in holy communion and other sacraments. In this they differed from the 'Open' Baptists of Radnorshire led by Vavasor Powell. Gradually, under Miles's

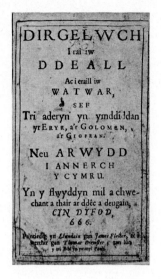
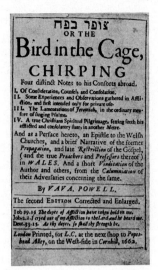

By permission of the National Library of Wales

46. TWO 'BIRD' BOOKS

(a) *Llyfr y Tri Aderyn* (Morgan Llwyd);
(b) *A Bird in a Cage, Chirping* (Vavasor Powell)

guidance, there emerged a form of the Baptist sect that had its own distinctively Welsh characteristics with its tight organization and exclusive communion.

The Propagation's unique contribution was in the field of education. The Parliamentarians appreciated the need for literacy both in order to understand the Scriptures and to cope with the multiplicity of doctrines. Thus they did not interfere with the existing grammar schools nor take away any funds from a school endowed by a royalist whose estate was otherwise forfeited. Now they set up over sixty schools mainly in the larger towns of Wales. Inevitably, as the map on p. 278 shows, the schools were most numerous in those areas where the Commissioners and Approvers were strongest, namely in the border counties, with half as many more in the south than the north. Parliament provided the funds to equip the schools and pay the schoolmasters.

Tuition was free, and both sexes were often educated together. The curriculum was similar to that of the grammar school but of course with a strong Puritan bias centring on the Bible and other religious works. Welsh, one would guess, was frequently used as the language of instruction, but there is no sure evidence of this.

The Act for the Propagation, to Cromwell's regret, was not renewed in 1653. The itinerants settled (Llwyd in Wrexham, Cradoc in Usk, and Miles in Llanelli) and the schools dwindled, and disappeared altogether soon after the Restoration. The 'Propagation' had failed to convert the great mass of Welshmen, who remained royalist and Anglican at heart, worshipping in secret after the manner of the Prayer Book. It had in any case been limited to the eastern fringes of Wales. Nevertheless this remarkable experiment had achieved much for Wales. It had given her a form of government all her own for the first time since the Act of Union. It had undoubtedly improved standards of preaching and of morality, and recognized the use of the Welsh language. It had, moreover, pointed the way for future progress. The private meeting-places, the open-air itinerant preaching, the intense studying of the Scriptures were all features taken up by the great revivalists of the next century. Propagation paved the way for Methodism. Finally, it had made Wales the scene of the first state provision of free schooling in Britain. With it began a series of charitable experiments in education that was to last for two centuries. 'God', said Cromwell, 'had kindled a seed there (in Wales) hardly to be paralleled'.

THE PROTECTORATE

Soon after the end of 'Propagation' Cromwell expelled the Rump and replaced it with 'Barebones' Parliament. It was neither elected nor representative but a collection of 140 picked Puritans or 'Saints'. In Wales it was a victory for the Fifth Monarchists. The six members for Wales, three for the north and three for the south, were chosen by Harrison and Vavasor Powell. Under them Puritan power reached its high-water mark.

But in five months the impractical visionary 'Parliament of the Saints' had been replaced perforce by the Protectorate. Cromwell, now ruling alone, valued moderation and religious toleration for all sects, even, within limits, for Catholics and Jews. In March 1654 he appointed Triers who would examine ministers and schoolmasters for their fitness, thus continuing in Wales the work of the Propagation. The Triers were capable, moderate men but they found their task of filling the empty churches with preachers and hearers a most difficult one. No longer could they pay itinerant ministers: the best among them had already settled in fixed livings anyway. More churches closed. In desperation they joined adjacent parishes or, reluctantly allowed a sort of pluralism. Worst of all they found it necessary to send English-speaking ministers to essentially Welsh parishes, which only emphasized that Puritanism in Wales was an English imposition. The schools too declined and at the Restoration only a third of them flourished.

Walter Cradoc and the majority of Welsh Puritans were firm in their support of Cromwell. But the disappointed Fifth Monarchy men, led by the tireless, fanatical Powell, attacked Cromwell, 'the perjured villain', bitterly. In one violent sermon in London Powell declaimed: 'Let us go home and pray and say "Lord, wilt thou have Oliver Cromwell or Jesus Christ to reign over us?" ' For this insult he was given the first of his many stints in prison.

In spite of the failure of his first Parliament in 1654–55, the Protector still hoped that all parties would work with him to obtain settled government, and in February 1655 issued a proclamation promising pardon 'to all persons fearing God, though of different judgments, by protecting them in the sober and quiet exercise and profession of religion'. This was to be the finest declaration in support of religious toleration for many years.

During the royalist rebellion of Penruddock in the next month, the Welsh Puritans, including Vavasor, closed their ranks in support of Cromwell. But the rising, although quickly stamped out, convinced the Protector that national security, not toleration, must come first. He now divided the land into eleven areas and put each in charge of a major-general. Wales and Hereford were put in charge of Major-general James Berry, once a clerk in a Shropshire ironworks, now a most efficient soldier-administrator and an utterly sincere Puritan. He soon found his task well-nigh impossible. On the one hand he was faced with the great weight of discontent among the royalists, owing to their loss of lands and money, and among the people in general because of Cromwell's restriction on festivities and sports. On the other hand he was needled by the bitter attacks of fanatics such as Powell. In December 1655 Powell published his manifesto 'A Word for God . . . against Wickedness in High Places', a violent condemnation of the Protector backed by 322 signatures. But Berry remained patient, not wanting by punishing him to give Powell the chance to set himself up as a martyr. It was the right policy: the Puritan moderates, led by Cradoc, now openly abandoned Powell.

Meantime a new sect, the Friends or, to give them their better-known nickname, the Quakers, had been introduced to Wales from England. These were the most extreme Puritans, believing only in the spiritual life, the daily self-denial and thrift of the individual, and denying all need for priests, ceremonies, vestments, oaths and tithes. In 1653 John ap John (1625?–97), a Ruabon man and a member of Morgan Llwyd's congregation at Wrexham, heard George Fox, the 'apostle' of the Quakers, preach in Lancashire and was 'convinced'. He journeyed tirelessly around Wales, at times with Fox himself, and was repeatedly imprisoned, mainly for interrupting services in 'the steeple-houses', as the Quakers quaintly called the churches. Many of the disillusioned Fifth Monarchists, probably Llwyd himself, joined them. Other Puritans, however, Vavasor Powell among them, opposed them. Because of their persistence and certain eccentricities, such as refusing to remove their hats in church, the Quakers suffered ridicule and persecution. Their womenfolk, who were as active as the men, were beaten and stoned and stripped of their clothing. Still, by 1660 a line of little Quaker groups or 'conventicles' stretched from Chester to Cardiff and westward to Swansea, while another branched up the Severn Valley into Montgomeryshire and Merioneth.

In Autumn 1656 Cromwell called another Parliament. At their request the unpopular system of the Major-Generals was abandoned, a second house (of Lords) was nominated—two of its members being Colonels John and Philip Jones—and Cromwell, having refused the Crown, was named Lord Protector. But by February 1658 this Parliament too had proved useless in the task of governing in practice and was dissolved. The ageing Lord Protector wearily ruled alone until his death on 3 September, which had always been a fateful date in his career.

For almost two years there was confusion. Richard Cromwell, named Protector after his father's death, failed to rule; so too did the Army and the Rump, which they restored. Eventually the moderate men of action had had enough. Among them was the veteran Roundhead general, Thomas Myddelton, who had been ejected from the Commons by Pride's 'Purge' and had retired to develop his estates at Chirk. In the summer of 1659 he joined a rising in Cheshire under Sir George Booth and at Wrexham proclaimed Prince Charles king. The rebellion failed but Myddelton escaped. Before he could be captured, General Monk and his veteran Welsh lieutenant, Sir Thomas Morgan, with their crack Scottish regiment had crossed the Tweed at Coldstream (hence the Coldstream Guards) and marched to London. There Monk restored the Presbyterians, including Myddelton, to Parliament and negotiated with Prince Charles. On 12 May Myddelton again declared Charles at Wrexham. On 25 May the new king landed.

It was the end of Puritan rule, but not of Puritan faith. Wales for the very great part returned with relief to royalism and anglicanism. Cradoc and Llwyd had already died in 1659 within months of each other, Powell was in prison. But Wales had experienced a way of life that, stripped of its fanaticism, was robust and wholesome. The seed had been sown more plentifully in south Wales than in north, in Gwent than Dyfed, in

Powys than Gwynedd. Even Anglesey, which could scarcely boast a single sincere Puritan, had felt this 'wind of change' which one day would blow as the trumpet call of Methodism.

ORIGINAL EXTRACTS

1 COLONEL HORTON REPORTS VICTORY AT ST. FAGANS:

. . . after a sharpe dispute for near two hours, it pleased the Lord mightily to appeare for us in giving the enemy a totall rout, the perticulars thereof I shall within short time at large present you with. . . . Our word was 'God is our strength', and truly we found Him so to be; and desire the sole glory may be given to Him, and ourselves looked upon as weak instruments in his hands, and amongst whom as I am, so I desire to be accounted, who am, Sir,

In the field,
May 8, 1648

Your most humble and faithfull servant,
Tho. Horton

(Quoted in Hugh Thomas: *Cyfnod y Rhyfel Cartref*, p. 42)

2 THE THREE BIRDS DEBATE:

Raven (*Royalist*)—They (the Puritans) are a deceitful people; they speak fairly, and offer long prayers that avail nothing after all.

Eagle (*Cromwell*)—Let us ask the Dove to answer for herself. What say you to this?

Dove (*Puritans*)—It is better to say nothing to unreasonable folk: but the truth is that we meet frequently, that we speak fairly, that we try to do good to everybody, and that we would wish to do better. And if it can be proved that we have willed to hurt anyone, take thou O! Eagle revenge upon us. . . . And as to the long prayers, you yourself realize that we receive almost every thing for which we ask.

Eagle—Name one thing that the Doves received.

Dove—We prayed that the Doves should have the upper hand in the war, and for many other things, and they were given us.

Raven—Were you doves in the time of war? More akin to devils by far.

Dove—It is true that some unruly birds joined our party, and it was they who did wrongfully through the lands.

Raven—Croak! I have it in my heart to kill this smooth-tongued Dove.

Eagle—Enough. I see you would wish to start a fresh war if you could. Enough of fighting; you have been defeated often enough.

Raven—Let be; my day will come yet.

(Translated from Morgan Llwyd: *Llyfr y Tri Aderyn*, ed. Anthropos, pp. 28–9)

CHAPTER XV

THE AGE OF LOUIS XIV AND LOUIS XV

WHILE Oliver Cromwell fought and finally executed his king, and then struggled to rule without one, the great continental countries were being taken over by kings determined to rule as despots. Thus while England was moving away from absolute monarchy, the other great countries of Europe moved powerfully towards it. Cromwell was an autocrat by circumstance, Louis XIV by choice.

The seventeenth century is undoubtedly the century of France as the sixteenth had been that of Spain. The reign of Louis XIV 1643–1715—the longest in the history of Europe—saw her become the dominant country of the continent in power, in force of arms, in culture and in fashion.

We saw earlier that, thanks to Richelieu and Mazarin, Louis XIV was handed a 'going concern' when in 1661 he personally took over the reins of government. At home every element that might challenge his kingship—nobles, Huguenots, the mob, the States General, the church—had all been subdued. He was blessed with ample resources, with devoted ministers like Colbert, and with brilliant generals like Turenne. France not only towered over her neighbours, all of them either in decline like Spain, or distracted like England and Sweden, or ruined like Germany, but bade fair to win a flourishing empire in Canada, India and the West Indies. Louis took full advantage of his good fortune. Looking 'every inch a king', he worked hard and continued the wise policies of his mentors. So this 'professional king' became the very pattern of autocracy for all despots, and his brilliant court the centre of culture and fashion for all Europe.

The main lines of Louis's conduct of home affairs were laid down by Jean Colbert in the first half of the reign. The nobles he rendered harmless by frittering away their best energies in the showy, frivolous, costly life of the court at Versailles. The king's council was made up of middle class men, and the actual work of administration throughout the country conducted by civil servants or *intendants*. To Colbert the wealth of his country was everything, and wealth depended on work. So he encouraged agriculture, manufactures and commerce, and made roads and cut canals in order to stimulate them. He promoted French trade and colonies, and built merchant ships and a royal navy in order to strengthen and protect them. Wealth too he saved by insisting on the honest collecting of the taxes that drained and, for the moment, cowed the peasantry who did the work. Unfortunately Colbert made two major errors. Firstly, he overdid his supervision; trade was stifled by his tolls and tariffs, and the development of colonies by excessive 'red tape'. Secondly, he misguidedly accepted the current Mercantilist theory that the wealth of Europe was a fixed quantity, and any additional share of it for France must mean so much less for her neighbours. It must, therefore, be taken away from Spain or England or the United Provinces by war.

Louis needed no prompting in order to go to war and violate the international agreements made at the Treaty of Westphalia. The main aspiration of the kings of France had long been to win the Spanish and German lands between her and the Rhine, and so make of the river a 'natural boundary'. This was the policy that set Louis thinking or making war for almost the whole of his reign. He fought four wars, each successive one greater and longer than the last and involving more and more countries. In all four the constant enemy of France was the little republic that lived by its own industry and commerce, its own dogged courage and its water-defences—the United Provinces (Holland).

England's role in these wars was at first uncertain. At sea, in commerce, and in the Far East, Holland was her obvious rival. This rivalry had led to two indecisive Dutch Wars. In the first

(1652–54) she regained under Cromwell and Admiral Blake most of her lost prestige at sea, only to lose it again in the second (1665–67), thanks to the mismanagement of Charles II. Then came the first of Louis's wars against the Dutch (1667–8). Now England joined with Sweden to defend her old rival and Louis made peace. By 1670, however, Charles, faced with the restraints of Parliament, and impoverished, had accepted subsidies from Louis and changed sides. England played an important part in the war which followed. Louis's great army raged down the Rhineland, and the Dutch, abandoned by both England and Sweden, were saved only by again cutting the dykes and flooding the land. To their rescue came William of Orange, who possessed all the dogged perseverance and patriotism of his great ancestor of a century before, William the Silent. He won Spain, Denmark and the German states to his aid, and Louis made peace in 1678, having gained much of the Rhineland but nothing of Holland.

For ten years there was peace. In 1685 Louis, now at the peak of his power, committed his supreme blunder. He revoked the Edict of Nantes and robbed the Huguenots, whom he had always hated, of their freedom of worship. As a result, France's neighbours not only gained by immigration some 200,000 of her best craftsmen, but realized that it was time that the Protestant countries should join against the common enemy. In 1685 too, James II succeeded to the throne of England, and tried openly to restore Catholicism and rule without Parliament. Louis hoped that her internal quarrels would weaken England. But by 1688 all parties there had had enough of James. They quietly agreed to the remarkable 'Revolution' whereby Parliament became dominant in government, and offered the throne to none other than Louis's arch-enemy, William. England and Holland were irrevocably joined against France.

Hereafter, England was France's rival on land and sea and in colonies overseas for more than a century, and her avowed enemy in seven bitter wars. The first two occupied almost all Louis's remaining years. The War of the League of Augsburg (1689–97) with Spain and Austria in alliance with England and Holland, saw

France dominant on land but England on sea. William died in 1702 and was succeeded by his sister-in-law Anne, but the struggle went on. The War of Spanish Succession (1702–13) was a tremendous conflict, with France and Spain opposed to almost every other country in Europe. In it England not only won greater renown at sea, but, thanks to the Duke of Marlborough, probably her greatest soldier ever, showed in great victories, such as Blenheim (1704), fought at the heart of Europe, that she could also win on land. In 1713, Louis, old and tired, signed the Treaty of Utrecht. From it England gained new footholds of empire in Newfoundland and Nova Scotia, dominance in the Mediterranean with Gibraltar and Minorca, and valuable trading concessions with Spanish America.

Louis XIV died in 1715 whispering to the little great-grandson of five years who was to succeed him as Louis XV, 'I have been too fond of war: do not imitate me in that'. Indeed for twenty-six years there was peace. George I, prince of the German state of Hanover, duly succeeded Anne in 1714. But this new continental connection did not at once involve England in fresh wars, in spite of the Jacobite rebellion in the next year. Walpole, George's Prime Minister for twenty years, studiously kept the peace while England grew in prosperity.

In 1739 conflict broke out again, over much the same issues in Europe and overseas, and continued over three wars almost continuously to 1763. In the first two, ending in 1748, England won little renown in battles on the continent and little gain in America and India. But from the third, the Seven Years' War (1756–63), England after a bad start emerged victorious, thanks to the strategies of William Pitt who subsidized Frederick the Great, king of Prussia, to occupy the French on the continent, while the English forces were employed at sea and in battles in North America and India. By the Treaty of Paris of 1763 England gained Canada and other French possessions in North America, a dominant position in India, and other rich concessions in the West Indies. France was well-nigh exhausted. The wars of

Louis XIV and Louis XV had shown clearly that a small parliamentary democracy like England could marshal the means to outbid the enormous resources of a great despotism like France.

But her wars must not blind us to the great achievements of France in other fields. During this 'grand siècle' she dominated Europe in every aspect of civilized living. French became the language of fashion and diplomacy, and the brilliant court at Versailles the model of courtliness and elegance. In spite of the censorship that Louis imposed on all works that might criticize his kingship, there flourished great dramatists like Molière, philosophers like Descartes, Voltaire and Rousseau, and theologians like Fénelon. Science too was directly encouraged by Louis who set up the Institute of France. The culture of France had great effect upon Britain. During the period of the Restoration appeared great poets like Milton, notable playwrights like Dryden, an eminent philosopher in Locke and an outstanding architect in Wren, and brilliant scientists in Newton, Boyle and Halley. Charles II, imitating his cousin Louis, founded the Royal Society, our premier institute of science. Welshmen, like Edward Lhuyd the antiquary and William Jones the mathematician, were to make their own contribution to the new enthusiasm for scientific enquiry.

Western Europe was imitated too by the rising states of the north and east. Sweden, highlighted in the Thirty Years' War, had developed a parliamentary system and a national church similar to England's. But she had reached her zenith by 1660, and thereafter gradually yielded her supremacy in the Baltic to Russia and Prussia, two states as absolute as France, set up by the Romanoff and Hohenzollern families respectively. Peter the Great and Catherine the Great turned Russia's face to the west, setting up a despotism, a tax system, and fashions in dress and architecture similar to Louis's, but imitating England and Holland in promoting the practical arts such as ship-building and engineering. Catherine sent a commission to Wales to inquire into the extraordinary success of Griffith Jones' schools. A succession of despots between 1640 and 1786 hammered the scattered possessions of the Hohenzollerns in ruined Germany into the despotic kingdom of Prussia. The most notable of them, Frederick the Great (1740–86), began by imitating French ways and using the French language as if it were his mother tongue. But he outdid Louis's policy of attacking his weaker neighbours when he seized Silesia from Maria Theresa, who was trying with far less success to govern despotically over the hotch-potch of nations under Austrian rule.

Germany was to make her own distinctive contribution to culture, not in imitation of France but along the traditional lines of the Northern Renaissance in theology and philosophy, in science, in music and in education. The new university of Halle set up in Prussian Saxony in 1694 made an outstanding contribution to German culture and to European thought generally. It was the ideas of its great Pietist professor of theology, Hermann Francke, which inspired the S.P.C.K. and Griffith Jones Llanddowror to embark on their great work of charity and education. It was in Saxony too that the Moravians found a base for their missionary work of salvation and education. It was in a Moravian meeting in London in 1738 that John Wesley 'saw the light' and began his great work of convincing the affluent England of Walpole and Pitt of their sin and of the means of salvation. Moreover, following the great Luther two centuries earlier, they taught Europe the value of congregational singing. So there was a direct line between Saxony and Charles Wesley and Williams Pantycelyn, the 'sweet singer of Wales'.

During the century we have surveyed here England had moved towards free institutions, France away from them. In so doing England in the end had won an empire and France a revolution. In the sixteenth century Erasmus by suggestion and Luther by intent had brought about the Reformation. In the same way Voltaire and Rousseau in the eighteenth fathered the French Revolution and changed the whole political temper of Europe.

CHAPTER XVI

CAVALIERS IN CONTROL 1660-1688

THE Restoration of 1660 meant the return of the Monarchy, but now limited; of Parliament, but now stripped of Cromwell's experiments; and of the Anglican church, but now reduced by the loss of a great body of nonconformists.

The reigns of Charles II and James II which followed, though outwardly gay, were marked by much intrigue, deceit and cruelty, and by a general lowering of the tone of national life. The people of England and Wales, reacting to the restrictions of the puritan Commonwealth, were glad in 1660 to see Charles come; they were even more glad in 1688 to see his brother James go. Yet, during these twenty-eight years much was achieved in politics, in religion, in colonial development and not least in literature and science. It is a good period of preparation.

CHARLES II AND JAMES II

We cannot here attempt to follow in detail the tortuous course of events of Cavalier rule. It will be enough to trace how by 1688 these major features emerged: the domination of Parliament, party politics, religious toleration, and the acceptance of France as the national enemy.

The key question was religion. Parliament was strongly Anglican and persecuted both Puritans and Catholics in four Acts 1661–65, known by the name of Charles's chief minister as the Clarendon Code. In all they decreed that Puritans and Catholics who refused to conform with the rites of the Church of England could not take part in public life, act as clergymen or schoolmasters, hold a religious meeting (conventicle) or even come within five miles of a corporate town. The penalties for

breaking these laws were savage, and included fine, imprisonment and even transportation. As the reign wore on Parliament
became increasingly anti-Catholic. The King, however, was at
heart, if not openly, a Catholic and tried in 1662 and again in 1672
to declare toleration for all, provided the Catholics were included. Parliament retaliated with the Test Act of 1673 which
compelled anyone holding office in the Government or the army
to conform as an Anglican.

Charles could and repeatedly did dissolve a difficult or dis-
obedient Parliament. Equally, if he did so, he would have to
forego the supplies which only they could vote him. His expenses
were mounting because of his own extravagance and the increas-
ing cost of government, and especially because of the unnecessary
and unprofitable wars against the Dutch in 1664–68 and 1772–74.
Accordingly, after 1670 he accepted bribes from the French
King Louis XIV in return for a promise firstly to help Louis fight
the Dutch abroad, and secondly to restore Catholicism at home
in England, if necessary with the help of French soldiers. The
second promise was secret and known only to the two Catholic
members of Charles's five-man ministry, the 'Cabal', which had
replaced Clarendon. It was the discovery of this secret alliance by
Shaftesbury, one of its Protestant members in 1673 that led to
the Test Act, which of course automatically broke up the 'Cabal'.
Danby now became Charles's chief minister.

Two parties were now emerging from the welter of political
intrigue: the Court Party, led by Danby, which aimed to keep
the authority of the crown and the Anglican church, refusing
toleration to all non-conformists; and the Country Party led by
Shaftesbury, which sought to limit the royal power and favoured
toleration for Puritans, but certainly not for Catholics. Both
parties agreed that France and not Holland was the national
enemy. Danby was hampered because his royal master was fickle,
in sympathy with Catholics, and in the pay of France. He turned
accordingly to using bribery to get his way with the Commons
and so set the fashion for wholesale corruption that was to damn
British politics for at least a century and a half.

Shaftesbury was no less unscrupulous, and at one point he, too, accepted bribes from Louis! In 1678 a lying, unfrocked priest named Titus Oates declared that the Jesuits were planning to kill the King. This 'Popish Plot' was a tissue of lies, but Shaftesbury used it to the full to whip up anti-Catholic feeling to a frenzy. This led to the downfall of Danby and to the death of hundreds of innocent Catholics. Shaftesbury now proposed that the King's brother James, Duke of York, an avowed Catholic, should be excluded from succession to the throne in favour of the Duke of Monmouth, Charles's illegitimate son by a Welsh mother, Lucy Walter. But the King stuck at last on a point of principle: his brother, not his son, must succeed him. The Exclusion was fought out over three brief Parliaments, until in 1681 Charles dissolved the last and ruled alone until his death in 1685, again financed by Louis. One permanent feature emerged from this wrangling. Into common use now came the nicknames 'Whig' (literally a Scottish outlaw) for the exclusionist Country party and 'Tory' (an Irish robber) for the non-exclusionist Court party.

In the last years of Charles's reign the Tories came into their own. Shaftesbury was discredited and died in exile. As a result James II when he came to the throne was in a strong position. When the Duke of Monmouth rebelled in the West Country, he was defeated and executed and his followers condemned to death or transportation in their hundreds by Wrexham-born Judge Jeffreys, whose name has become a byword for cruelty.

But James quickly forfeited all support. He soon got rid of Parliament and appointed Catholics to all important posts, over-riding the penal laws by two Declarations of Indulgence. Seven bishops, including William Lloyd of St. Asaph, were imprisoned for pronouncing his action illegal but were acquitted at their trial, although James tried with his standing army to over-awe the judges and jury. Just before the trial James's second and Catholic wife gave birth to a son who was to be known as the 'Old Pretender'. It was now clear that the King would attempt to establish a Catholic dynasty similar to that of Louis XIV, who in 1685 had banned Protestantism in France. Not only the Whigs and the Nonconformists, but the Tories, the church and the universities were now ranged against James. Jointly they invited the great Dutch protestant William, husband of Mary, James's Protestant daughter by his first marriage, to come to England and restore national liberty and the Protestant religion. On 5 November he landed in Torbay and James fled. The whole nation was glad to see the last of the Stuarts.

WALES AND RESTORATION POLITICS

Wales even more than England gave a great welcome to the return of Charles and the Church. The old pre-war families returned to political power. But not quite as before. The war and the Commonwealth had begun a process of radical social change in England and Wales that was to continue for the rest of the seventeenth century and the early eighteenth. Increasingly over a period a gulf widens between the greater landlords and the lesser squires and freeholders. Since Wales was a land of smaller landlords the effect was greater here, and had far-spreading political and cultural implications. Almost all the gentry, great or small, had supported the king and had suffered very great losses in land and money both during the war and under the Commonwealth. The greater landlords had sufficient capital or influence left to help them recover; they could afford the best lawyers to plead for them, marry their children to well-off families, or strike out into new and profitable ventures in industry or overseas trade. The squires, on the other hand, tended to decline into yeoman or even tenant farmer status. As such they could not afford to take part in political life, certainly not as M.P.s in London. Parliamentary representation became in Wales the preserve of an exclusive group of great families. Thus the Bulkeleys represented Anglesey in Parliament unbroken for fifty-three years after 1660, and the Vaughans of Golden Grove stood for Carmarthen town for sixty-two years—to take only two examples.

Now Wales was to feel the full impact of one unfortunate result of the Act of Union, that the great gentry abandoned their interest in Welsh affairs in favour of those of England, and Wales was left comparatively leaderless. No longer did Welsh M.P.s band together to form a 'Welsh Interest' as they often did before the war. Instead they became mere hangers-on at court, or political adventurers, concerned with English party politics and with their social equals in London rather than their tenants at home. The corrupt practices they learnt at Westminster were matched by the political apathy of the squirearchy at home. Not even the old fear of invasion from Spain was present any longer to stir interest and unite the Welsh members in a common cause, for France was clearly now the enemy and the Channel coast of southern England, and not the shores of Wales, was the front line.

The Restoration also meant the revival of the Council of Wales and the March which had been disbanded in 1642. But it too had lost much of its old authority, its work now being confined almost entirely to civil actions. The Earl of Carbery who had made such a poor show as the King's general in west Wales, was the first restored president. Carbery was corrupt and self-seeking and rarely went to Ludlow. Henry Somerset, Third Marquis of Worcester, who replaced him in 1672 went there even more infrequently. He is, in fact, a good example of the absentee great lord, for although nine-tenths of his estates and three of his seats were in south-east Wales he chose to live at Badminton in Gloucestershire. Nevertheless, within the limits now imposed on him he served Wales and the King well, remaining loyal to the Stuarts, even when their Catholic tendencies threatened the Protestantism to which he was a convert. He saw it as his own particular task to ensure that Wales remained loyal and did not side with the Exclusionists.

In 1682 he had his reward: he was made Duke of Beaufort. In the summer of 1684 he celebrated by making a 'progress' or triumphal tour round all the counties of Wales. His servant Thomas Dineley has left a remarkable record of the itinerary, interspersed with notes and sketches about the places visited

47. THE DUKE VISITS PRESTEIGNE

A typical page from Thomas Dineley's *The Progress of the Duke of Beaufort.*

which gives us a useful picture of Wales of the day. The Duke traversed each county, escorted by the local gentry amid great pomp and feasting, and reviewed the county militia to satisfy himself that they had firearms and had been properly trained.[2]

But the Duke's triumphal 'progress' was the last dying spasm of the Council of Wales. When in 1688, at James II's order, Beaufort summoned the chief gentry of Wales to Ludlow, more than half of them made some excuse not to attend, and those who came decided nothing. The days of Ludlow as the capital for Wales were over. A few months later, in 1689 the Council was disbanded for ever. Welshmen hereafter must look to Westminster not Ludlow for their politics. Wales had lost a mark of her separate identity as a nation.

Wales, in fact, now sent more than her fair share of outstanding lawyers and politicians to London. Six of these legal 'adventurers' who attained fame or notoriety deserve mention. Sir John Vaughan (1603–74) of Trawsgoed in Cardiganshire rose to be a judge and an eloquent member of the 'Country' Party. He is famous for his ruling that jurors should be free to give their own verdict even against the direction of the judge. He also defended the independence of the Welsh courts. An even more famous judge was Sir Leoline Jenkins (1625–85). Unlike Vaughan he came of a humble family in Cowbridge, Glamorgan, and rose by his own talent and hard work to be principal of Jesus College, Oxford, and Secretary of State and diplomat for Charles II. Conscientious and incorruptible, he proposed a great number of reforms many of which were not adopted until long after his own day. An earlier secretary of state and diplomat for Charles was Sir John Trevor of Trevalun (1626–72). All these three were public servants of integrity and principle. This can scarcely be said of the remaining group of three who rose to fame under James II. George Jeffreys was the infamous hanging judge of the 'Bloody Assizes' of 1685. His reward was to be made Lord Chancellor and henchman to James. Jeffreys at least was an unswerving Anglican and royalist, remaining true to the foolish king and dying in prison in 1689. But Sir William Williams (1634–1700) son of an Anglesey parson apparently knew no such loyalty. He came to notice as a prominent member of the Country party and Speaker of the House of Commons. But in 1686 he suddenly changed sides (apparently in order to avoid

By permission of the National Museum of Wales

48. A CONTRAST IN RESTORATION JUDGES
(a) Sir John Vaughan   (b) Baron George Jeffreys.

a heavy fine for libel imposed on him by Jeffreys, who was his
bitter enemy) and supported James, whom he had previously
condemned for his popery. At the Revolution he changed again
and helped to draft the Declaration of Rights! Sir John Trevor
of Brynkynallt (1638–1717) was a similar political chameleon.
He was largely responsible for the martyrdom of the Monmouthshire Papists after the Popish Plot scare, yet rose to be Speaker
and privy councillor under James. Dismissed at the Revolution,
he quickly regained his offices under William III, but was finally
sent packing for bribery!

The careers of these last three 'adventurers' show the
deterioration both in political morals at the end of the seventeenth century, and in the Welsh 'interest', for none of the
group had much concern for the affairs of Wales.

The gradual divorce of Wales and her greater landlords
showed even more in culture. Increasingly they ceased to speak
Welsh or to support its literature. It became accepted by their
tenants, the great majority of whom clung to the vernacular, that

English was after all the language of society and advancement, a process to be greatly accelerated by the Industrial Revolution. Education, too, suffered with the decline of the lesser land-owners. Far fewer could now afford to send their sons to universities. Those who entered the Inns of Court to train as lawyers at the beginning of the eighteenth century numbered only a quarter of the entrants in the middle of the seventeenth century. The education of the ordinary people had been promoted by philanthropists of a Puritan bent and from London. The Anglican gentry at home in Wales accordingly felt little desire to support them.

PURITANS AND PAPISTS IN PERSECUTION

With the Restoration in favour of the Anglicans the tide of religion in Wales turned. Immediate action was taken against the openly extremist Puritans. Vavasor Powell was clapped in Welsh-pool gaol a month before Charles landed in Dover, and was not freed until his coronation in 1661. By the summer of 1660 there were forty Quakers in prison in Cardiff and another twenty-eight in the gaols of Denbigh and Flint. As early as September 1660 an Act of Parliament resulted in scores of Welsh Puritan clergy losing their livings to make way for Anglicans, many of whom had themselves been ousted under the Commonwealth, though they were not always returned to their former parishes. Many of the Puritan ministers conformed. Some of these honestly believed that toleration would soon come anyway; others, of course, were fairweather friends and not sincere Puritans at all. In the Welsh livings there was again chaos; hasty appointments were made and just as hurriedly cancelled. But the returning wave of Anglicanism was irresistible. At first the Presbyterians hoped at least for toleration, but soon it became clear after a conference held at the Savoy in 1661 that they too would be engulfed in the headlong wave of returning Anglicanism which was nowhere stronger than in Wales. The Presbyterians became the 'right wing' of the Puritan movement just as the

Quakers were its 'left wing'. The addition of the Presbyterians greatly strengthened the cause of Non-conformity.

The Cavalier Parliament when it met in May 1661 was fervently Anglican, and particularly its Welsh members who were Cavaliers to a man. Charles in his easy-going way favoured toleration, if only to relieve his Catholic friends. But Parliament would have none of this. 'More loyal than the King and more Anglican than the Bishops themselves', it insisted on complete conformity and ruthless revenge on the Puritans.

Soon came the Clarendon Code. First in 1661 the Corporation Act required all members of corporations to conform to the rites of the Anglican Church. This was designed to weaken the Presbyterians who were strong in the towns. As such it did not greatly affect Wales which had comparatively few towns and few Presbyterians.

The Act of Uniformity of 1662 certainly affected Wales. It was a harsh law, rigorously enforced. Every clergyman, school-master and fellow of a college must accept the Book of Common Prayer by 24 May, 1662 (St. Bartholomew's Day; hence the Act was known as 'Black Bartholomew') or be ejected. The Welsh bishops and the bishop of Hereford were charged with seeing that, by the 1 May 1665, the Prayer Book was translated afresh into Welsh and a copy provided in every church where Welsh was usually spoken. The Welsh version actually appeared in 1664. Reluctantly numbers of dissenters fell in line, but scores of Puritan ministers and schoolmasters refused to conform and lost their livings or closed their schools. Thus were finally lost to the Church some of its most devout, high-principled and learned servants.

The Puritans now, like the Papists long since, continued everywhere to meet in the privacy of their own homes, or in secret out-of-the-way places. One large congregation met in a cave near Llandysul. The authorities feared that such gatherings or 'conventicles' would be used for political purposes, to plot against the government and stir up treason and riot. So they replied with three measures that brought the most savage persecution. The first Conventicle Act of 1664 defined as illegal any meeting in a house where there were gathered for worship more than four people over sixteen years of age in addition to the normal family. Those caught could be fined, imprisoned and, for the third offence, transported overseas. The second Conventicle Act of 1669 removed the barbaric threat of transportation, which was almost tantamount to slavery, but made illegal any meeting of five persons, even in the open air. The Five-Mile Act of 1665, like the Corporation Act, was designed to drive Puritans out of the towns where their cause flourished best, and ruled that no ejected minister was to come within five miles of any town or any parish where he had formerly conducted a meeting.

The suffering of all non-Anglicans under these acts has its own special place in our history of heroism. The annals of the nonconformist churches are full of the distress, loss and cruelty that members of all their denominations now endured. The suffering of the gentle Free-Baptist, Henry Williams, Ysgafell—to take only one example—has remained a byword in Montgomeryshire. He was in and out of prison for a period of over nine years for holding conventicles; on one occasion at least he was battered almost to death, on another his house was burnt down and his cattle taken away while he was in prison. On yet another occasion it was his family who suffered; on seeing the militia gallop up to raid his home once again, he escaped through the back door to hide some of his papers. His old father, however, tried to resist but was brutally struck down and killed while William's pregnant wife escaping across the Severn with her children, was saved from a similar fate only by the intervention of an officer kinder than his brutal soldiery. Yet Williams and his fellow dissenters continued cheerfully to believe in the workings of a kindly Providence. The story was told for two centuries and more how one year, when the harvest failed for all around, his field of wheat ripened miraculously and repaid more than double his loss from yet another raid on his property.

One of the worst features of the persecution was the use of spies who were to be paid under the terms of the acts for informing the justices of any conventicles. Llangybi, for example, in remote Llŷn, then 'a desolate uncleaned land of marsh and brushwood' was a centre for illegal meetings. To a house there on a Sunday morning in 1676 thirteen men came to hear James Owen, a noted South Wales dissenter, preach. But two of them were informers who reported the matter to the J.P.s forthwith. The preacher fled to the next county, beyond the authority of the magistrates, but the others were taken after much violent resistance and were fined. But this was only one case; the spies were everywhere.

Fortunately for the dissenters, there were periods when the laws were not strictly enforced and persecution died down. It was such lulls in the storm that enabled the dissenter to hold out, men such as Edward Lawrence who, as he said, pointing to his wife and ten children, had eleven good reasons for giving in! It must be remembered too that the rugged countryside of Wales on the whole offered plenty of opportunity for concealment. Many magistrates were themselves unwilling to undertake the unpleasant duty of hunting and convicting offenders. In time the dissenters found all sorts of legal loopholes, such as living near the county boundary, and in an emergency escaping across it beyond the grasp of the local J.P.s. Preachers resorted to all sorts of 'dodges' so that the 'Word' should be heard. One preached through the window of his prison cell to a large crowd outside; another preached at the open window of his house while his neighbours opened theirs to hear him!

Vavasor Powell certainly could not be silenced. After only a month's freedom he was back in Fleet prison in 1661. Here he spent two years, his health suffering because of his close confinement in a cell which had a 'stinking dung-heap' immediately under the window. Yet it was here he wrote his little book with the cheerful title, *A Bird in the Cage, Chirping*! At the end of 1662 he was moved to Southsea prison. From his cell there he witnessed the Dutch Fleet assembling off the Isle of Wight in 1665 ready to attack the English coast. But he missed the great Plague of London in that year and in 1666 the Great Fire, which burned down his old prison in Fleet. No sooner had he been released in 1667 than this tough little man was away to London, then Montgomeryshire, Bristol, Bath, Newport and finally Merthyr Tydfil 'chirping' to large crowds. At last he was arrested on the false evidence of a rector, who claimed that his last congregation at Merthyr had carried arms. Brought to trial at Cowbridge and Cardiff, Powell repeatedly outwitted his questioners as nimbly as ever. Nevertheless he was committed to prison on some trivial count. When a request was made that he should be released on bail, the prosecuting counsel begged the judge to forbid it. 'No, my lord (because) he will then go preach'. And indeed preach he did, both in prison and when his gaoler allowed him out on parole, according to the report of a spy in 1669. Perhaps he now met Thomas Gouge, who was reported by the same spy for preaching to a large company in the same area. Vavasor would certainly have persuaded him of the extreme need for schools in Wales, as in 1650 he had persuaded Parliament to set up the Propagation. A year later, 27 October, 1670 he fell ill in prison and died.

Prison had matured Vavasor Powell; he was no longer the rash, quick-tempered, bigoted fanatic that he certainly had been. But prison did not conquer him; he still began each day cheerfully singing a hymn of his own composing, and ended it by recording his inmost thoughts in a diary. He was no great mystic like Llwyd, no great organizer like Miles. It has been said that 'in an age of protesters he was the arch-protester'. Yet he was more. By his preaching and his fortitude, and by his faithfulness to the vision given him, this most colourful of the early Puritans was in direct line between John Penry and Howell Harris. Between them they held the lifeline that was to save a whole nation in the eighteenth century.

The Papists were hated by Parliament even more than the Puritans. So, at the Restoration, rather than have the relief they expected, they fell out of the frying pan of the Commonwealth into the fire of the Clarendon Code. Charles tried to bring them relief under cover of his Indulgences in 1672. Parliament replied with the Test Act in 1673 which excluded Catholics from all offices civil and military. Their numbers in Wales had dropped considerably since the Civil War. In 1676 it would be roughly true to say that for every one Welsh Catholic there were four other non-conformists and 140 Anglicans.

They were grouped almost wholly into three pockets: one in Flintshire, another around Brecon, and a third in north-east Monmouthshire. More than half of the Welsh Catholics lived and worshipped in this third area, thanks mainly to the influence of the Marquis of Worcester at Raglan, although in fact he (soon to be Duke of Beaufort, as we have seen) was a convert to the Anglican faith and the castle itself in ruins after the War. At Cwm, remote in a rugged, wooded valley just over the Hereford border, the Jesuits had in 1622 established a 'college' or headquarters. It remained the Papist mission centre for all Wales until 1670 when a separate mission for North Wales and Shropshire was set up at Holywell. Apart from those periods when the heat of the penal laws was on, the Jesuit fathers, most of them trained on the Continent, moved about freely from their centre at Cwm, visiting the faithful in their homes and preaching openly in Welsh and English in places like Abergavenny to larger congregations than those in the Anglican Church nearby. In this they were defying not only the penal code but also laws passed in Elizabeth's reign.*

Just north of Abergavenny, at Llanfihangel Crucorney, lived John Arnold, a rabid Anglican and Whig whose family had done well out of the lands of nearby Llanthony Abbey. He and the Tory Marquis of Worcester had long been enemies. Early in 1678 Worcester, now president of the Council of Wales, dismissed Arnold as a J.P. Arnold immediately retaliated by sending an alarming report to the House of Commons about the activities of the Catholics in Monmouthshire. A few weeks later came the

* See p. 100.

infamous Popish Plot and the frenzied hysteria against all
Catholics that it deliberately provoked. Titus Oates, the infamous author of the 'plot' claimed that, as part of it, Dr. Herbert
Croft, a former Catholic but now the Anglican bishop of Hereford, was to be murdered. Bedloe, Oates's associate and an even
greater rogue, was Monmouthshire born. He asserted that two
great Catholic armies were to assemble, one in Radnor and
another in Cardigan, and with Spanish help were to capture all
south Wales.

This was Arnold's opportunity. He embarked with glee on a
vicious campaign of priest-hunting. Forewarned, the brethren
fled from Cwm. Of some thirty-four priests known to have been
in the area, eleven were captured, three died of privation while
trying to escape in the depths of winter, two died in prison and
four were martyred. All four were local men; all had been
trained in local seminaries; all disclaimed any knowledge of the
'plot'. In fact they were condemned under the Elizabethan Act
of 1585 as priests of a foreign order and therefore traitors. John
Lloyd had been a diligent, itinerant priest in Monmouthshire and
Glamorgan for twenty-five years, but Philip Evans, a much
younger man, for only three years. Both were captured in
different houses of the Turberville family in the Vale of Glamorgan, betrayed to the magistrates by a young ne'er-do-well son
of the same family. Both were tried and condemned in Cardiff in
May but not executed until 22 July, 1679. Evans behaved with
singular cheerfulness and fortitude, singing to the harp in his cell
to console his visitors. When his gaoler eventually brought him
notice of his immediate execution he was playing tennis. 'What
hurry is there?', he joked. 'Let me first play out my game'.
Next day the two were taken in a cart to the city limits. Evans
was the first to die. 'Sure this is the best pulpit a man can have
to preach in', he declared from the gallows, adding that he was
happy to die in such an honourable cause and that he forgave and
even thanked his executors. The quiet, elderly John Lloyd had
to watch while his young friend was hanged, disembowelled,
and quartered; then he took his turn in the same heroic way.

David Lewis (alias Charles Baker) a Jesuit had ministered to Catholics in Monmouth for thirty years, always travelling on foot and generally under cover of night, and named for his charity 'Tad y Tlodion' (Father of the Poor). He was now the Superior of the college at Cwm. He was arrested at Llantarnam in November, and then moved from one Monmouthshire gaol to another until he was convicted in March 1679. Meantime, just before Christmas 1678, Bishop Croft raided and ransacked Cwm. He reported to the House of Lords that he found the two houses most cunningly equipped with escape routes, secret passages and hidden rooms in which had been left a store of vestments, crosses, incense, relics and, most incriminating of all, a fine collection of Papist books.* [1]

In April Lewis was sent to London. He was confronted with Oates, Bedloe and probably Shaftesbury and promised his pardon if he would give them information about the plot or conform as an Anglican. 'Discover a Plot I could not, because I know of none', he declared, and 'Conform I would not, because against my conscience it was'. He was eventually executed at Usk on 27 August. The fourth martyr was John Kemble, a kindly old man of eighty years. He was hanged outside Hereford on 22 August and buried at Welsh Newton where he had ministered as a Catholic priest for fifty-three years. All four were canonized i.e. made saints of the Roman Catholic church in 1970. They were not so much martyrs in a religious cause as the victims of unscrupulous party politics and a petty feud between local gentry. This was surely the most scandalous episode of a corrupt age.

The persecution of the Quakers too was stepped up after the Restoration. Certainly in terms of numbers, of brutal treatment, of long periods in prison, and of loss of property, they undoubtedly suffered more than any for their faith. This was largely because of their refusal to swear any oath, or pay tithes, and because of their passive resistance to persecution. Yet they flourished, and particularly in counties like Monmouthshire,

---

* Part of which is now in the Cathedral Library of Hereford.

Glamorgan, Pembrokeshire and Montgomeryshire which were becoming more industrialized and where more English was spoken. Rural and Welsh-speaking Merioneth was the exception; for its population it had more Quakers than any other county and sent abroad more emigrants, whereas Montgomeryshire provided sixteen Friends with some of their most ardent supporters. Richard Davies, teacher, preacher and traveller became the 'apostle' and mediator for the Quakers in mid-Wales and his home at Cloddiau Cochion near Welshpool their headquarters. He suffered almost continuous imprisonment without bitterness. The two brothers Charles and Thomas Lloyd were the first of an outstanding family of Quakers. 'Convinced' in 1662–63, both suffered ten years 'open' confinement in Welshpool, strictly forbidden to visit their old ancestral home at Dolobran near Meifod. The Quaker sons of Charles Lloyd became leaders in industry and banking (founding Lloyd's Bank) and were prominent in humanitarian movements in the Birmingham area. Thomas emigrated to Pennsylvania and became its most powerful statesman. All in all, however, the Quakers had but limited success in Wales. The very success of the Lloyd brothers suggests the reason: worldly ambition probably clouded their spiritual vision, emigration reduced their numbers, and their failure to use the Welsh language stamped the Quakers as strangers.

THE RESULTS OF PERSECUTION

The persecution of non-Anglicans in part achieved its aim. Hundreds of dissenters abandoned their sects and conformed. The militant Catholics, such as those of Monmouthshire, were finally stamped out. In general, however, their suffering only hardened the determination of the nonconformists to hold fast to their beliefs in whatever way they could. Common suffering too drew the Puritan sects together, and, where it helped. Independents and Baptists and Presbyterians united for worship. A great many bravely defied the authorities. Others went underground or abandoned their accustomed haunts only to spring up openly or in secret elsewhere. With the Restoration, for example, the cause of the Strict Baptists, with their headquarters at Ilston and their general meetings, became impossible, and in 1663 their leader John Miles emigrated to America, as we shall see. The Conventicle Act of 1664 dashed the hopes of those remaining. But in 1666 a new leader appeared. William Jones possibly a Cardiganshire or Carmarthenshire man, an ejected Puritan minister, journeyed to Olchon the outlying unit of the Baptists in the hills of west Herefordshire, and was baptized. In 1668 two elders of Olchon returned the visit, and with Jones established a new congregation named 'Rhydwilym' on the upper valley of the Eastern Cleddau. The site was admirably suited for the secret meetings and marriages and burials that were now necessary, and became a centre for all west Wales. Thus Rhydwilym took the place of Ilston, and Jones replaced Miles. So were kept alive the strict beliefs of closed communion and adult immersion that still mark the Welsh Baptists today.

Religious persecution had, however, three other important long-term results: it promoted schools, developed industry at home, and encouraged colonization overseas. The thrilling story of the schools is told in a separate chapter. Industry profited not only because hardship sharpened the nonconformist belief in hard work and enterprise, but also because the Test and Corporation Acts compulsorily diverted their energies from working in government or the armed forces to manufacturing, trade and banking. This position remained unchanged even after the Toleration Act of 1689 allowed them freedom to worship. The Quakers, the most persecuted, provide the best examples. Industrious, shrewd, reserved, and united by close bonds of inter-marriage they worked as family groups to win outstanding success in business in Wales as well as England. The Lloyds of mid-Wales and Birmingham pioneered ironworking, and gave their name to one of today's largest clearing banks. At Pontypool the Hanburys pioneered wire-drawing, while their Quaker friends, the Allgoods, discovered a unique means of japanning or lacquering which remained a very profitable and close-guarded family secret for 150 years. Another group concentrated in the

Neath-Swansea area in the eighteenth century, and enterprised in coal, iron, engineering, leather. Quakers too became makers of the exquisite Swansea and Nantgarw china. Nor did they forget their social and humanitarian duties, but contributed largely to education and a host of good works. It is not surprising that the Industrial Revolution in Wales like its Quakerism was mainly an import from England.

Emigration from Wales to the New World, which had been a trickle under the first Stuarts, became a constant stream after 1660. Persecution does not account for all those who went; there were other important factors such as poverty at home, land-hunger, missionary zeal, and of course the call of adventure. Nevertheless it was the desire to be rid of restraints on religious worship that accounts for the spasmodic mass migrations of the period. John Miles, his little 'empire' of Close Baptists shattered by the penal laws, set sail with a small company in 1663. They landed in Massachusetts and settled in the little town of Rehoboth. Soon they found the Puritans there as intolerant as the Anglicans at home. They were fined for worshipping as Baptists and ordered to meet no more. So in 1667 the little company moved again, south-westwards to the limits of the colony, where, in the wooded wilderness, there was none to challenge them but the Red Indian tribes. They called their new settlement of log cabins Swanzey, in memory of their mother church back home in Glamorgan. Here they prospered in spite of tremendous hardships and of a war with the Indians in 1675, which compelled them to find shelter in Boston for a while. Suffering made Miles more tolerant, and gradually he and his Welsh Baptists were accepted by the rest of the colony.

Miles's difficulties showed that the northern New England states did not offer the complete freedom that the persecuted sects hoped for. By the time of the Popish Plot, the Catholic state of Maryland offered little attraction even for the viciously persecuted Papists at home in England. Not unnaturally therefore, it was to the undeveloped middle states, rich in soil and minerals, that William Penn chose to take his Quakers in the

By permission of the Radio Times Hulton Picture Library

49. SETTLERS GOING TO CHURCH
What defensive measures have they taken? Why?

largest surge of migration at this time. They were a strongly, if
not predominantly, Welsh contingent. In 1681, Penn, a devout
Quaker preacher and writer, bought by charter from the government a great tract of land west of the state of New Jersey and
around present-day Philadelphia. This he sold at about 7d. per
acre to all who sought religious freedom 'that an example may
be set up to the nations, there may be room there not here
(England) for such a Holy Experiment'. Welshmen were amongst
his earliest and biggest customers for the vast, fertile tracts.
John ap John, Richard Davies and Charles Lloyd bought thousands
of acres apiece and then sold them in smaller lots to Welsh
emigrants, although they did not emigrate themselves. Penn himself claimed to be of Welsh descent and had planned to call the
colony 'New Wales'. Many Welshmen went as doctors. Thomas
Lloyd of Dolobran was one. He emigrated as early as 1682,
quickly rose to prominence and eventually became deputy-
governor.

Bad weather, bad feeding and disease made a voyage to America
both arduous and dangerous. Penn first sailed in September 1681
with 100 others. A third of them died on the crossing from an

outbreak of smallpox, in spite of the attentions of a Dr. Wynne, one of the many Welshmen in the party. The peak year for emigrants from Wales seems to have been 1683. John ap Thomas, a gentleman of substance and a Quaker leader in Merionethshire, bought 5,000 acres but died in 1683 before he could emigrate. Nevertheless his widow went, with her many children. Thomas, the eldest boy, kept a record of their suffering during their stormy passage of twelve weeks. Here is one poignant entry:

'Our dear sister, Sydney, died today, 29th, 7mo, 1683. Mary, our dear sister, departed from this world on 18th, 8mo, 1683, at sea'

The Welsh emigrants came mostly from the counties of Glamorgan, Pembroke, Radnor, Montgomery and particularly Merioneth. At first certainly they were mainly men of substance, gentlemen and yeomen moving in family parties from the same congregation. But there were others, as the following selection of those who went in 1683 shows:

John Bevan of Treferig (Glamorgan), gentleman, with Barbara his wife and several children.

Florence Jones, relative of John Bevan.

John Lewis of Treferig, labourer in the employ of John Bevan.

William Edwards, yeoman.

George Painter, Haverfordwest, with wife and two children.

Jane Humphries, Haverfordwest, maid, in service of George Painter.

Edward Evans of Nantmel (Radnorshire) gentleman, wife and one daughter.

David Kinsey of Nantmel parish, carpenter.

David Davies, son of Richard Davies, Cloddiau Cochion (Mont.).

Thomas Morris of Mochnant Isa (Mont.) yeoman.

Katherine Robert, widow and two children.*

The clear intention was that the emigrants from Wales should live together in a compact area, known as the Welsh Tract. They would still be subject to the king and parliament at home, and enjoy their protection. In return, they would pay customs (duties) and taxes. They would still speak Welsh and cherish their Welsh traditions and ancestry—in fact be a part of Wales overseas, with this difference that they had freedom both to worship and to take part in the government and defence of the colony. The Welsh names they at once gave their settlements—Merion, Haverford, Radnor, Brynmawr, St. David's, Narberth, still remain in the suburbs of Philadelphia, but their Welsh identity was quickly lost. Dutch, Swedish and Finnish settlers soon settled among them, and the Welsh Tract was split up between two counties. Moreover, they ceased gradually to speak Welsh; to resort to the common language of English was the great temptation for the gentry among them, already accustomed to speaking English back in Wales, and became a necessity for the monoglot Welsh servants and labourers who had to scatter westwards to claim holdings of their own.

Emigration from Europe generally to America slackened off after about 1690, but continued rather longer in Wales. Radnorshire 'Open' Baptists, followers originally of Vavasor Powell, emigrated to Pennsylvania in a body in 1686. Another batch of the Rhydwilym 'Closed' Baptists of West Wales joined them in 1701, but because of religious disagreement soon moved southward on to Delaware and even Carolina. Then for three-quarters of the eighteenth century emigration again became a trickle. The sting of persecution had passed, and in any case the great Methodist Revival provided the faithful with the new hope of a Paradise at home.

* The terms of passage on the *William Galley* sailing from Carmarthen to Pennsylvania in 1698 were: adults £5 each, children under 12, half-price, suckling babies free; twenty tons of luggage free of charge. The ship's doctor to be paid 5/- by a man with a family, and 1/- by every single person.

ORIGINAL EXTRACTS

1   THE SECRET LIBRARY AT CWM, LLANROTHAL (HEREFORDS.):

(Bishop Croft, following his raid on Cwm in 1678, reports)

In one of these houses there was a study found, the door thereof very hardly to be discovered, being placed behind a bed and plastered over like the wall adjoining, in which was found great store of divinity books . . . several horse-loads . . . many whereof are written by the principal learned Jesuits . . . There are several books writen and printed against the Protestant religion, and many small Popish catechisms.

(Journ. Welsh Bib. Soc., December, 1962)

2   THE DUKE OF BEAUFORT'S PROGRESS, 1684:

(BEAUMARIS FERRY) The passengers being on board, those ferrymen who drive in the horses stand in the water up to the middle, and those within the boat lift up one of the horse's forelegs into the boat.

(MOSTYN) The melting houses belonging to the lead-mines of Sr. Roger Mostyn are sayd each to have a large Water Wheel giving motion to the forge bellows to melt and refine ye Lead-Oare in ye Pans.

(LUDLOW) Saterday August the second . . . the Duke of Beaufort . . . arrived here att Ludlow expressing a great deal of satisfaction of the Good Order in which he found the Militia of the severall Counties, and with his Reception and Entertainment in all places of North-Wales, the Gentry having everywhere mett and attended his Grace with Expression of a most loyall zeale and dutifull affection to his Sacred Matie. and the establisht Government.

(PRESTEIGN) . . . which Radnorshire Militia after his Grace in person had scann'd, by rideing through the ranks of each company a good volley being given, he entred the Town. The magistrates in their formalities stood ready to receive his Grace, the streets windows Trees and tops of the Houses abounding with spectators giving shout, acclamations and expressions of Joy

(T. Dineley: *The account of the official progress of the first Duke of Beaufort through Wales, 1684,* pp. 127, 96, 168, 176)

CHAPTER XVII

LIFE IN WALES 1688-1760

THE 'GLORIOUS REVOLUTION'

WITH James II gone, the Parliament of William and Mary hastened to restore the affairs of the nation to good order. By a series of great measures they had in a few years settled the political, religious and financial structure of England and Wales (and after 1707 largely of Scotland too) for at least a century and a half.

The Bill of Rights of 1689 and the Act of Settlement of 1701 finally established the principle of constututional or limited monarchy—of kingship dependent upon Parliament and the Protestant (Anglican) church. The Toleration Act of 1689 allowed freedom of worship to all Dissenters, and, in practice, to all Catholics; both were still barred, however, from taking office in government or the armed forces. The establishment of the National Debt in 1692 and of the Bank of England in 1694 put the nation's finances on a sound basis and gave a broad band of its citizens a vested interest in maintaining them. This quiet, bloodless Revolution thus enabled the people of England and Wales to embark with confidence on other enterprises at home and abroad that would in time put them a century ahead of most other European nations.

Yet, though 'settled', the first half of the eighteenth century is by no means a stagnant period; it witnessed important developments in economic, religious and cultural life. The remarkable movements in education and religion, of particular importance to Wales, will warrant separate chapters. The other aspects of the period we shall cover broadly here.

POLITICS IN THE EIGHTEENTH CENTURY

The system of two parties, Whigs and Tories, which had evolved during Charles II's reign now became permanent. Apart from two short periods under William III (1688–1702) and his sister-in-law Anne, (1702–14) government remained in the hands of the Whigs for almost eighty years. Unfortunately, the other Cavalier legacy of bribery, jobbery and intrigue also became accepted practice in the power-struggle, and degraded the national life. This was especially the case during the ministries of Robert Walpole (1721–42) and the Duke of Newcastle (1754–61). It is against the background of this degenerate 'gin-drinking period' that we must see the work of the revivalists in both England and Wales.

Abroad, the record is one of action, success and prosperity. From 1689 the country fought the 'Second Hundred Years War' with France, almost unbroken except for the period of Walpole. Eventually this brought victory and wide possessions and privileges overseas. This colonial empire ensured wealth, new markets and ample raw materials. These in turn stimulated manufacture and mining and gave birth to the Industrial Revolution.

In Wales the period saw the acceleration of those political tendencies which we noticed in the previous chapter. The smaller squires fell out in the race for power, and left the field clear for the great landed gentry who, here, were not challenged, as they were in England, by the aristocracy on the one hand and a vigorous commercial middle class on the other. Thus Wales was represented at Westminster by an increasingly restricted circle of county families; the Bulkeleys in Anglesey, the Williams-Wynns in Denbighshire, the Morgans in Monmouth and Brecon, and the Mansels in Glamorgan. These and others were the great families that were to represent county and borough often for a whole century and almost unchallenged. They were almost inevitably Tories and, because of that, often suspected of Jacobitism; the Vaughans of Golden Grove in Carmarthenshire and the Wynns of Glynllifon in Caernarfonshire were the Whig exceptions. But then Whig and Tory meant little more than a name or a colour. In standing for Parliament the average Welsh M.P. sought a chance not so much to declare on a point of political and religious principle, or on a matter of importance to Wales, but rather to enhance the prestige of his family and to win honours or offices or 'perks'.

Merioneth provides a good example. It was represented by the Vaughans of Corsygedol for almost a century without challenge. The first of them, Richard Vaughan, was always in opposition to the government, made no speeches and was noticeable only by his frequent absence from the sittings of the House. The story goes that after an unusually long absence the Serjeant-at-Arms was sent to Merioneth to bring Squire Vaughan to London. When he arrived at Dolgellau, however, the Serjeant was told that at that time of year Corsygedol was inaccessible over the mountains and unapproachable by sea because of impassable bogs! So the baffled officer returned to London alone.

Vaughan's stubborn independence was typical of the Welsh M.P.s of the day. Those who did attend Westminster showed little of national character to distinguish them from the English members. They became immersed in English politics without interest in the affairs of Wales.

Family rivalry was their main activity. It made elections long, exciting, often violent and certainly costly. Sometimes rival families agreed amongst themselves to take turn in representing their county. Viscount Bulkeley declined to stand for Beaumaris in the election of 1715 because, as a Jacobite, he resented the accession of George I. Instead he arranged with Meyrick of Bodorgan to replace him on the understanding that he could have the seat back when he wished. But at the election of 1722 Meyrick refused to stand down, and it cost Bulkeley over £10,000, it is said, to regain the seat. Beaumaris, with its mere twenty-four voters, remained a pocket borough of the family until 1832. Early in the new century Sir Watkin Williams Wynn ousted the Myddeltons from the Denbighshire seat. In the election of 1741, Wynn again easily defeated John Myddelton, but the sheriff, another Myddelton, declared 600 of Wynn's votes invalid and his own kinsman duly elected! Unfortunately for him, Walpole's ministry was now defeated and the tables turned. The sheriff was imprisoned and Wynn given the seat, which his family then held for over a hundred years. But victory cost Wynn £20,000.

The one eminent Welsh member was Robert Harley, the Tory M.P. for Radnor. In 1693 he fought a sword-duel with two of the rival family of Lewis in the streets of New Radnor. Able but lazy, he headed Anne's Tory government after 1710 as Earl of Oxford. But in 1714 as a result of a quarrel in the Tory ranks, he was dismissed. Two days later Queen Anne fell seriously ill and in three days she died. The Whigs took advantage of the split among the Tories and quickly declared George of Hanover King. If Harley had only held his office for one week longer the whole course of English political history might have been changed. As it is, Harley's fame rests not on his political career but on his great collection of manuscripts (the Harleian Collection) now in the British Museum. To it the study of Welsh history and literature owes a great deal.

JACOBITISM

Some interest and colour is given to the drab politics of the period by the story of the Jacobites ('Jacobus' is Latin for James), the name given to those who worked for the return of the exiled Stuart claimants (James II; his son, the Old Pretender; and grandson, the Young Pretender.) In Wales the story was one of considerable, if decreasing, sentiment but no action. There were plenty of individual would-be 'adventurers' among the Tory lords and squires, and a number of secret societies with all the paraphernalia of badges, tokens, passwords, songs and drinking toasts. But there was no popular movement, no marching, no clash.

The Stuarts had done little for Wales; Charles II had never set foot there, and when James II paid his only visit in 1686 it was to St. Winifred's shrine at Holywell, which only emphasized the fact that he was a fervent Catholic. Nor was the personal reputation of either likely to endear them to the Welsh people.

Yet immediately after the Revolution there was considerable Jacobite feeling in Wales, probably stronger than in England though less so than in Scotland. The out-and-out devotees had gone into exile with James II, men like the Marquis of Powis and many sons of leading families, who kept in touch with relatives at home and were, in themselves, Jacobite agents. Like Papism—with which it was inevitably associated—Jacobitism lingered unevenly in pockets here and there, nourished by some prominent local Tory landowner who could still influence and indeed compel his tenants to his point of view. Such leaders were the Dukes of Beaufort in Monmouthshire, Sir Charles Kemeys of Cefn Mably in Glamorgan, Colonel William Barlow of Slebech in Pembrokeshire, Lewis Pryce of Gogerddan in Cardiganshire and Viscount Bulkeley in Anglesey. It was in north-east Wales, in Flintshire and Denbighshire, however, that Stuart sentiment was strongest. In 1696 William III granted the lordships of Denbigh, Bromfield and Yale to a Dutch favourite. All Welsh M.P.s joined together—a unique occasion—to protest and the grant was revoked. But the resentment lingered on.

Towards the end of Anne's reign there was a revival of enthusiasm for the Jacobite cause, and plans were made to force the succession of the Old Pretender. But they came to naught. Queen Anne died suddenly, the Whigs acted quickly, and George I quietly took the throne. But in Wrexham on his coronation day no church bells rang and no bonfire was lighted; instead bands brawled through the streets singing Jacobite songs.

In the next year came the abortive 'Fifteen' Rebellion. But it brought no activity of note in Wales apart from a riot, again in Wrexham, when a mob, assisted by colliers from the nearby pits, wrecked two chapels of the Dissenters. Next year on Oak Apple Day (29 May) and again on White Rose Day (10 June, the birthday of James Stuart) Wrexham bells rang all day and the Jacobites sported 'feathers in their hats and oak boughs and openly blessed the Pretender'. The Earl of Nithsdale was among those condemned to death after the 'Fifteen'. But he escaped from the Tower of London thanks to the heroism of his Welsh wife

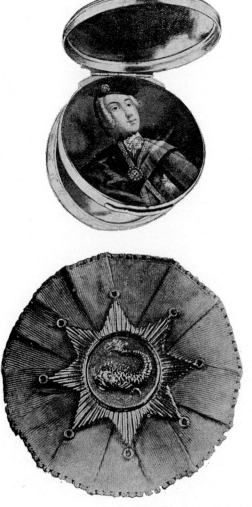

By permission of the Honourable Society of Cymmrodorion

50. JACOBITE RELICS IN WALES

(a) A double-lidded snuff-box with a secret portrait of the Pretender.
(b) The badge — star and dolphin — of the Society of Sea Serjeants.

Winifred, daughter of the Marquis of Powis who followed James II into exile. Attended by her maids, 'Mistress Evans and Mistress Morgan', she visited him in his prison and passed him out dressed as one of them.

The were many rumours of Jacobite plots after this, including a plan to land in Wales in 1717, but in 1722 Walpole magnified one such plot in order to justify his clamping down on them once and for all.[1] Gradually memory of the Stuarts faded, though it was kept alive for another half-century by many secret societies. Montgomeryshire had two such societies. William Bulkeley of Brynddu in the far north of Anglesey too noted in his famous diary under 3 May, 1738, a meeting 'of ye Jacobite Club at Llannerchymedd for this year, where all the noted Tories and Jacobites of this Country have constantly met once a month these 2 years'. Better known was the Society of Sea Serjeants, meeting in the far south of Wales. Established, or perhaps revived, in 1726, its members always affirmed that it was merely an association of Tory squires, mainly M.P.s, restricted to twenty-five members who spent a week together each year at one of the south Wales ports 'in innocent mirth and recreation' with processions, feasts, dances, etc. Contemporary public opinion, however, accepted all this as so much cover for Jacobite activities, and little wonder, since the Society badge was a Jacobite eight-point star with a dolphin in the middle, and since the leaders were in other ways known Jacobites. But no traitorous act could be pinned on them and the society remained in being until at least 1763.

The 'premier Jacobite club' of England and Wales, however, was 'The Cycle of the White Rose' of Denbighshire. It began as early as White Rose Day 1710. Again ostensibly a club for Tory squires of the county around Wrexham, meeting once a month at the home of each member in turn (or cycle), there can be no doubt about its Jacobite intentions. Its badge was the white rose and its password 'fiat' (Let it be done). At dinner the members solemnly drank toasts from specially engraved glasses standing over bowls of water to signify the Jacobite 'King' and his family in exile 'over the water'. Members' names were not listed in the normal way but in a circle with the word 'cycle' at its centre, an attempt presumably to disguise the name of the leader. But there is no doubt as to the moving spirit behind the Cycle. It was that Sir Watkin Williams Wynn, Tory M.P. for Denbighshire 1716–49 who by 1740 had won a veritable empire in north-east Wales. He, it is said, was the founder of the Club when a very young man. In the years after the 'fifteen' he was in constant touch with the exiled Stuarts, and by 1745 was accepted as the leading Jacobite figure south of the Scottish border.

Now came the 'Forty-five' and another sad tale of Stuart mismanagement. Wales, as a whole, played no part in it and Sir Watkin's contribution remains a mystery, largely because his wife burnt all his papers lest they might incriminate him. It seems clear that Charles Edward's landing in Scotland took the

By permission of the National Museum of Wales

51. SIR WATKIN WILLIAMS WYNN (d. 1749)

The leading Welsh Jacobite who amassed vast estates in North Wales through his family connections.

knight by surprise (and with only £200 in ready money), particularly as he expected a whole French army and not merely seven men. News came that the dashing Young Pretender had at once won all the Highlands to his standard, defeated an English army at Prestonpans and marched quickly south to Derby and the heart of England. Yet Sir Watkin stayed put. He would only move, it appears, if the Prince would first come to him and march through Wales.

Three Welshmen, however, went to the Prince. Two were brothers, William and Richard Vaughan of Courtfield in the border corner of Monmouthshire and Herefordshire, a family which had always remained resolutely Catholic. The third, David Morgan, was a London lawyer, but it was from his ancestral home at Penygraig (near Quaker's Yard) in Glamorgan that, with William Vaughan, he set out to join the rebel army. He rose quickly to favour with the Pretender and was called 'the Prince's Counsellor'. He was at the fateful council for war at Derby, arguing like the Prince that they should advance southwards, but through Wales where, Morgan declared, a great force was waiting to join them. But the highland chiefs, aghast at the lack of support in England, were set on retreat. Two days later a message is said to have come from Sir Watkin, offering to do anything the Prince wished. But it came too late. The rebel army had turned north. With them went the Vaughan brothers to fight bravely in the slaughter of the Jacobites at Culloden, and to live to win fame as generals in the army of Spain. But David Morgan went south, was captured in Staffordshire and suffered the brutal death of a traitor.

Sir Watkin and many other North Wales squires are said to have started out for Derby. But it is all so much hearsay, possibly invented at the time as a sop to conscience. The fact remains that, in spite of all the letters, promises and toasts, only three Welshmen actively supported the last desperate fling of the Jacobites.[2] The memory lingered on; the Cycle, for example, remained in being until 1869. But as an active force Jacobitism was as dead as a doornail. In the long term it had in any case been doomed to failure in Wales. Tactically the growing strength of the British fleet dashed the hopes of any successful landing, and, as Sir Watkin realized, without outside help there was little hope. The Whigs grew more and more powerful, and the rewards from land-owning and especially from commerce were too rewarding to be readily forfeited in a lost cause. By 1766 when George III, born and bred in England, came to the throne, all but the most obstinate Jacobites were ready to accept him as their rightful King. Above all the great mass of Welshmen, long indifferent to politics, now had all their interest and energy channelled into the great educational and religious movements that had swept the country. Little wonder that Sir Watkin hated the Methodists; did not William Williams, Pantycelyn, offer fervent prayer for the success of King George?

SOCIAL LIFE AND LABOUR

The seventeenth century brought no marked change in the daily life and work of the average Welshman. In the main, the description given in Chapters 10 and 11 for 1600 remains true for 1700.

Of a total population of around 400,000, the great majority lived in the country and worked on the land. Farms were still small, and farming relied on custom and rule-of-thumb, on com-munal help and on antiquated equipment. Even in the mid-eighteenth century Wales was still a country of scattered peasant holdings loosely centred on a small hamlet and/or church. (The large, tightly-knit village of England was unknown here except in the rich 'anglicized' valleys and on the coastal strips of the south). These groups were largely independent and self-sufficient. Local craftsmen and the weekly market supplied their essential needs, and the annual fair, the pedlar and the drover their 'luxury' goods and their contacts with the wider world.

The countryman's typical daily food was meagre and monoton-ous: barley bread, jellied oatmeal (or 'flummery'—one of the very few English words derived from the Welsh), cawl or thin broth and occasionally bacon. The labourer could still rely on his

52. COCKFIGHTING
The cockpit from Denbigh now restored in the Folk Museum at St. Fagans
(*above*).
A fight in progress (*below*).

family's spinning and weaving in their crowded cottage home to
eke out the sixpence or so he earned as a day's wage; and his
relations still accepted the old family responsibility of helping him
out in lean or troubled times. So, though poor, he was rarely
destitute and there was little call for the help of the Poor Law
in the parishes of Wales. His little leisure he spent indoors in
the *cyfarfod gwau* (the 'knit-in'), the Bible class, the circulatory
school or the noson lawen, or out-of-doors in the secretive cock-
fight or the bruising game of football.[4]

The towns though growing were still few and small; we remember that the Commonwealth had found only eighty towns
large enough to warrant a school. Carmarthen in the south and
Wrexham in the north were the largest of them. Of the industrial cities of the future, Swansea alone was of any size. The port
of Cardiff was small as yet, and its exports were chiefly wool and
corn. Bristol was already the metropolis of South Wales and
Chester of the North.

The cattle trade still prospered. The drovers provided yeoman
and squire with his 'fluid' capital, with news of events outside
Wales, and with a sort of parcel-service from London and other
large towns along their route. They still kept open the soft,
upland trackways favoured of old by pilgrim, pedlar and poet.
It was as well they did, else the roads, still very bad in spite of
the parish act of 1555, would have become impassable. In 1670
Charles II made John Ogilby his 'King's Cosmographer', with a
commission to survey all the great roads of England and Wales.
The result was his great *Britannia* of 1675 which depicts the
roads in sets of ingenious strip-maps (see page 256). Ogilby in-
cludes thirteen main roads in Wales, but their quality we can
only guess.

During the seventeenth century the great industries of the
future in south and north-east were still dormant. Iron working
was small, fitful and scattered, and copper-smelting and coal-
mining equally thin but localized. This was inevitable while the
capital was provided by individual local landlords with, of course,

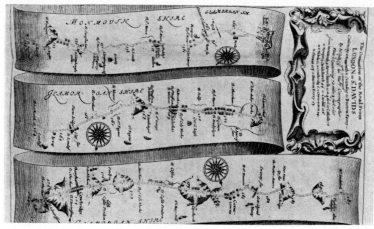

53. AN OGILBY STRIP-MAP

Part of the high road through Glamorgan. Compare it with today's A48 on a
1 inch O.S. map.

limited funds. In any case industrial enterprises were dramatically crippled by the Civil War.

As the eighteenth century unfolded, however, there appeared
clear indications of the great changes to come. Enclosures had
steadily increased during the preceding century, and by 1700
many areas such as the Vale of Glamorgan and much of Pembrokeshire were wholly enclosed. To separate in this way a man's
holding from that of his neighbour was a necessary step before
attempting experiments in improved farming. In Anglesey, Owen
Meyrick (whom we met earlier challenging the political predominance of the Bulkeleys) vastly improved his Bodorgan estate.
At the same time his neighbour, Henry Rowlands, tried out new
scientific methods of farming based on the experiments of Boyle
and the use of the microscope. He investigated the soil structure,
and wrote up his findings in his essay, *Idea Agriculturae* of 1704
(though not printed until 1764). A third Anglesey man, the

scholar-priest, Edward Wynn, applied the improved farming methods used in Herefordshire to his estate at Bodewryd. He, it is said, was the first in the island to cultivate turnips in 1714, even before the great 'Turnip Townshend' of Norfolk. Such enthusiasts were undoubtedly the exception; nevertheless they set the trend for the agrarian revolution of the mid-century heralded by the pioneer Agricultural Society of Brecknock in 1755.

The wind of change blew even more strongly in industry. Great advances in all forms of mining and smelting towards the end of the seventeenth century more than compensated for the severe set-backs of the Civil War. The use of scientific methods brought improvements in blast furnaces and in the specialist working of different ores. Above all, now came the discovery that coked coal could be used in the smelting of iron. Montgomeryshire played a notable part in this. The Quaker squire, Charles Lloyd, whose father had been persecuted after the Restoration, set up forges at his home of Dolobran and elsewhere in the valley of the Vyrnwy and the Severn, using pig-iron brought from the furnaces of Bersham near Wrexham. During the first quarter of the new century he was closely associated with another Quaker family—the Darbys of Coalbrookdale, the reputed pioneers in a process of smelting with coal which was long kept secret.* The Severn served as an artery linking Dolobran with Coalbrookdale and the very active iron centres of the west Midlands, and providing bulk carriage at one-fifth the cost of road transport. Lloyd's work ended in bankruptcy in 1728, but a permanent memorial to his products remains in the fine wrought-iron work made in 1720–40 by the Davies brothers of Groes Foel near Bersham.[3] They were the master-smiths of an area extending from Chester in the north to Bewdley in the south. Examples of their craftsmanship remain in gates at Chirk Castle, at Leeswood (Mold), Eaton (Chester) Erddig (Wrexham) and in screens at Wrexham, Ruthin and Oswestry churches (see p. 258). The Davies brothers not only raised the level of wrought-iron

---

* Tradition has it that it was John Thomas, a former shepherd boy of the Lloyds, who discovered the process while working for Abraham Darby.

54. WELSH ARTISTRY IN IRON
The Davies gates at Chirk.

work to its peak in this country, but in their occasional experiments with cast iron for pillar caps and bases pointed the way
of change. John, the last of the Davies family, died in 1755. Two
years earlier the Bersham furnace was taken over by the Wilkinson
family whose products in cast iron were to begin the New Iron
Age of the Industrial Revolution.

Meantime the Revolution had in many ways already begun in
west Glamorgan around the estuaries of the Neath and Tawe. The
outstanding figure here was Sir Humphrey Mackworth (1657–
1727) an 'adventurer' indeed. The younger son of a Shropshire
family who had fought for Parliament in the Civil War, he had
won repute as a lawyer and been knighted by Charles II before
he was twenty-six. In 1686 he married Mary, heiress to the Evans
family of the Gnoll, Neath, who held a monopoly of coal mining in
the area. Mackworth settled in his wife's home and reorganized
her mines with such success that soon they were accepted as the

best in Wales. The man's dynamic enterprise and ingenuity is shown in his construction of a tramroad with wooden rails, the first in Wales, and nearly the first in Britain, to speed the tubs carrying coal from the mines down to the estuary. Not content with this, he fitted sails to the returning 'empties' so that the prevailing wind would ease their return up to the mines! Mackworth also set up many furnaces for smelting lead and copper at Melin Cryddan nearby with a canal joining them to the river. He now cast about for new sources of ore.

Meantime the story of lead-mining in Cardiganshire had taken a dramatic new turn. It had long been clear that the mining and working of copper and lead could never thrive until the Crown monopoly of the precious metals associated with them had been removed. Then in 1690 a very rich deposit of lead was discovered at Esgair Hir in Cardiganshire and the landowner, Sir Carbery Pryse of Gogerddan, began to work it. At once the Crown claimed the mine because of the high content of silver in the lead. Sir Carbery, however, contested the Crown claim and won his case at Westminster. As a result a new law in 1693 provided that mines remained in the hands of their individual owners; the Crown's only right being that of buying the ore at a fixed price within thirty days of its being mined. This was a death blow to the Mines Royal Company. Suddenly a flood of individual enterprise was released.

The company set up by Pryse to develop the mine, however, met with little success. Then one day William Waller, steward to the Gogerddan estate, met Mackworth by accident at an inn at Llanbadarn where the knight had halted on his way from Swansea to Shropshire—by sea to Aberystwyth, presumably, and then down the Severn valley—and persuaded him of the value of the lead mine. Ample lead ore from Esgair Hir could easily be brought by sea from the Dyfi estuary to the Neath where vast reserves of coal were at hand to smelt it. The result was the establishing of 'The Company of Mine Adventurers of England', with Mackworth in charge. The company flourished for ten years before it ran into financial difficulties and was declared bankrupt in 1709.

Its failure was due partly to technical problems in the mines, partly to the lack of oversight by Waller and other directors, and partly to the continued hostility of some of Mackworth's Whig neighbours. These used their political influence to have Mackworth charged in the House of Commons with 'notorious and scandalous frauds', but he was saved by the fall of the Whigs in 1710. Mackworth had probably been grossly neglectful but hardly deliberately fraudulent. He had certainly been busy, both as an active Tory M.P. and as a philanthropist. Some of the profits and much of his own personal share he allocated to the welfare of his workers in old age, sickness and injury. He was a founder member of the S.P.C.K., as we shall see,* and set up charity schools in both Cardiganshire and Neath. All in all, this 'Adventurer-in-Chief' was a curious mixture of the hard-headed industrialist and the pious philanthropist—a worthy precursor on a smaller scale of the great Robert Owen of Newtown a century later.

There were also growing mines and copper works in the Tawe valley which gave promise of the vast industrial transformation to come. A great Newcomen steam-engine was pumping water from Lord Mansel's collieries at Swansea as early as 1717; here too tramroads were soon employed above and below ground. The value of land rose sharply where it was known to hold minerals. And towards the mid-century immigrant English capitalists were replacing local landlords as ironmasters, and pooling their resources to provide the huge sums required.

The climate for industrial change was also being prepared by the great religious revival of the eighteenth century (Chap. 19), for it encouraged hard work, perseverance and thrift. The point is well borne out in the life and work of William Edwards (1719–89). For 44 years after 1745 he was pastor of the little Methodist/Independent chapel in his native Eglwys Ilan, above the lower Taff Valley. But he is best remembered as the dogged architect who, after three vain attempts (1746–54), finally succeeded in bridging the Taff at Pontypridd. His final magnificent

* See p. 277.

55. THE 'RAINBOW' BRIDGE AT PONTYPRIDD

William Edwards's magnificent 140 ft. arch was said in its day to be the largest in the world. It was certainly the largest in Britain until 1830.

single-arch still stands, but was never of great use. The experience he gained, however, enabled him and his sons to build many bridges at key-points over the swift flowing rivers of South Wales, and so speed travel and transport in the later eighteenth century.

In all, the stage was set for massive industrial change.

MEN OF LETTERS AND OF SCIENCE

In the field of culture too the period produced some notable 'adventurers' whose work would later flower into a general revival of literature and language in Wales. John Jones (of Gelli-lyfdy, Flintshire) had probably died just before the Restoration, but most of the hundreds of valuable manuscripts which he had copied and embellished, many while he was in a debtor's prison, were fortunately preserved for us by his friend Robert Vaughan

of Hengwrt (near Dolgellau). Vaughan (1592?–1667), himself
a copyist and antiquarian, gathered together 'the finest collection
of Welsh manuscripts ever assembled by an individual'. Now
known as the Hengwrt-Peniarth collection, it is safely in the
custody of the National Library of Wales.

The patient work of copyists and collectors in preserving past
treasures was to remain important for a long time yet. There was
need, however, for a more popular, widespread and creative
literature. Welshmen had hitherto been dependent on the printing presses of London and Shrewsbury. But in 1718 the first
permanent press in the Principality was set up at Adpar (Newcastle Emlyn) by Isaac Carter. Others quickly followed and
poured out profitably not only a stream of religious books but
also exciting ballads, love-poems, interludes (moral dramas) and
gossipy almanacs. Sold at markets and fairs and by pedlars, they
were enormously popular. Their literary quality was low, but
they satisfied the hunger of the common folk for reading material
that was entertaining and informative.

Wales also shared in the scientific progress of the end of the
seventeenth century. Its effect on farming and smelting we have
already seen. Wales had its eminent mathematician in William
Jones, a native of Llanfihangel-Tre'r-Beirdd in Anglesey, who
was the friend of Isaac Newton and of Halley, and a fellow of the
Royal Society. The greatest name, however, is that of Edward
Lhuyd (1660–1709) a native of Oswestry. An undoubted genius,
his brilliant scientific studies while he was still a student at
Oxford secured for him the post of assistant-keeper of the great
Ashmolean Museum there at its opening in 1683, and soon he
became keeper-in-chief. A tremendous worker, his enthusiasms
multiplied as he grew older, from Botany to Geology and then
to the scientific study of Antiquities and Philology. In 1696, in
order to compile an authoritative historical-geography of Wales,
he printed 4,000 copies of a questionnaire and distributed them
to well-informed people in every parish. For the next five years
he made exhaustive journeys through all parts of Wales, seeing
for himself and meeting his informants. With him went David

By permission of the Ashmolean Museum   By permission of the
                                             Radio Times Hulton Picture Library

56. THE NOTABLE AND THE NOTORIOUS

(a) Edward Lhuyd;
(b) Sir Henry Morgan.

Parry from Cardigan who directed the Ashmolean after Lhuyd's
death (only to neglect his duties and die at an early age because
of his addiction to drink, the curse of his age). They also made
excursions in search of comparative material to the other Celtic
countries of Ireland, Scotland and Brittany, (where they were
imprisoned for a time as spies!). Then Lhuyd settled back in
Oxford with a team of young scholars, all from Cardiganshire—
David Parry, Moses Williams and Alban Thomas—as his assis-
tants at the Ashmolean. Together they sorted out the vast pile of
documents, drawings and curiosities Lhuyd had collected on his
journeys. The first publication as a result was *The Glossography*
of 1707. It has been called 'the most wonderful book, remem-
bering its period, ever published by a Welshman'.* Poor Lhuyd

* Parry, T.: *A History of Welsh Literature*. Trans. H. Idris Bell, p. 275.

died suddenly in 1709 before he could produce the next volume. He left behind him, however, a great number of books, articles and notes. Many of them, alas, were lost in two disastrous fires, one in a London book-binder's and the other at Hafod, the home of Thomas Johnes, the man who, at the end of the century, transformed a remote Cardiganshire vale into a sylvan centre of culture.

Lhuyd was probably the most cultured Welshman of his day, ranking with the best of contemporary English and continental scholars. He remains the pioneer of Celtic studies. Two other remarkable prose works now appeared: Ellis Wynne's *Gweledigae-thau y Bardd Cwsc* (Visions of the Sleeping Bard) of 1703 took a poetical view of the contemporary scene, while Theophilus Evans' *Drych y Prif Oesoedd* (The Mirror of the Chief Ages) of 1716 gave an entertaining but prejudiced account of early Welsh history. The one was not intended as geography, and the other was certainly not good history, but they remain classics of Welsh prose.

Poetry, as we have seen, had been at low ebb. Now there appeared a school of poets who gave Welsh verse new life and refinement, and one man who gave it an inspiration and a wider appeal than ever before. The school was composed of the poets and critics who followed the lead of Lewis Morris and his brothers; the man was the revivalist Williams Pantycelyn.

Anglesey seems to have been the centre of the new movement. Its followers owed much to the patronage of that Owen Meyrick who improved his Bodorgan estates. The Morris brothers came from Llanfihangel-Tre'r Beirdd and from the next farm to William Jones's home. Lewis Morris (1701–65) was the eldest and most influential of the three brothers. A surveyor and civil servant by profession (he published authoritative 'Plans of the Harbours, Bays and Roads in St. George's and the Bristol Channel' in 1748), he spent the last twenty years of his life in Cardiganshire. Here, in spite of his work as a crown servant and lead prospector, and in spite, too, of his own ill-health and haughtiness, he was able to influence other young men of the neighbourhood, notably Ieuan Fardd, who was to become the outstanding Welsh scholar of the later eighteenth century, and Edward Richard the famous schoolmaster of Ystrad Meurig. A man of many gifts, Lewis Morris was above all a critic who encouraged and schooled others both in the older 'cynghanedd' poetry and in the newer 'free' metres. Richard, his brother, also left Anglesey at an early age and settled for life in London, becoming a chief clerk to the Navy. He shared his brothers' love for Welsh literature, but unlike them he was generous and sociable. Deciding that London Welsh-men needed some sort of literary club, he founded the famous Cymmrodorion Society in 1751. It was destined to become a key-factor in the revival of Welsh culture in the nineteenth century. William, the third brother, remained in Anglesey as a customs officer. More practical than his brothers, his first love was Botany, but he, too, made a great contribution to literature by his prolific letter-writing, which has recorded for us much of his brothers' thinking and some of the social history of the Anglesey of his day. By their patronage, by their collection of Welsh manuscripts, and by their acceptance of the best influences from the Classics and from contemporary English poets, the Morris school nourished Welsh literature and restored to it again discipline, dignity and refinement.

Their greatest protégé was Goronwy Owen (1723–69), a native of an adjacent Anglesey parish. Feckless and unstable, he moved around considerably in his office as curate—he spent his last years in a tobacco and cotton plantation in America. Yet he is undoubtedly the most prolific and gifted classical poet of his day, who valued above all in poetry clear meaning and polished language.

Williams Pantycelyn (1716–91) stands alone. He owned no previous tradition and poured out hymns in the free metres from pure lyrical inspiration in a flood of nearly a hundred books. His was poetry with a purpose, that of saving souls, as we shall see in a later chapter. As such, it had enormous popular appeal. Pantycelyn more than any other man made memorable the poetry of the people.

WELSHMEN ABROAD

Welshmen undoubtedly played their part in enterprises over-seas and in the succession of wars that Britain now fought world-wide. We know, for example, that much of the money given by Sir John Philipps and others to provide schools derived from commerce with the Indies. But on the whole the record of such 'adventurers' is thin. William Bulkeley, the squire of Brynddu, Llanfechell, Anglesey kept a diary from 1734 to his death in 1760, in three books, two of which have fortunately been pre-served for us. They are records of tremendous interest, quaint informative, amusing. In them we find repeated echoes of the wars.

There is ample record, however, of Welshmen as pirates! During the reign of Charles II, Henry Morgan from Monmouth-shire turned buccaneer and scoured the West Indies, capturing Porto Bello and Panama in daring raids and winning an un-enviable reputation for greed and cruelty. But by 1674 he had turned 'respectable', was knighted and made deputy-governor of Jamaica. Howel Davis was such another Welshman. It was he who captured Pembrokeshire-born Bartholomew Roberts in 1718 and compelled him to turn pirate. Soon 'Black Barty' had become the most daring and feared buccaneer of his day, though, by comparison with others of his 'profession', sober and humane. But his career was brief. He was killed in a battle with a ship of the Royal Navy in 1722, and his body, dressed in all the finery which pirate-captains sported, thrown to the sea he loved.

And repeatedly we find Squire Bulkeley, in his remote home at the most northerly tip of Wales, entering his almost daily record of anxiety for his poor foolish daughter Mary, who had married a brewer turned pirate of the colourful name of Fortunatus Wright![5]

ORIGINAL EXTRACTS

1 JACOBITISM REVIVED, 1722:
(John Meller of Erthig, Denbighshire, a Whig, writes—)

Indeed the Jacobites in our parts are strangely animated of late . . . they are so barefaced, as to drink the Pretender's health in public Companys. But tho' we have Incimation of it, yet we cannot prevail with any Company to prove it upon them. It is not long since that the Lord Buckley came hither out of Anglesea to keep up the spirit of the Party, and he and Mr. Watkin Williams audaciously burnt the King's picture and the several pictures of all the Royal Family.

(quoted in P. D. G. Thomas: *Jacobitism in Wales*, Welsh Hist. Rev. 1962)

2 THE YOUNG PRETENDER'S ASSESSMENT OF WELSH JACOBITISM:
I will do as much for my Welsh friends as they have done for me; I will drink their healths.

(*ibid*, p. 298)

3 THE DAVIES BROTHERS ARE PAID FOR THEIR WORK:
1719, Jly. 28: Pd. Robert Davies Smith in full of what he and his brother did at ye Iron Gates from ye Octob. 1717 to ye 21 December following .. £10 – 16s – 9d.

1720 Oct. 7: Pd. Robert Davies, Smith, 10 li (£10) wch my master subscrib'd towards ye Iron Gates at Wrexham Churchyard .. £10 – os – od. 1720 Nov. 2. Pd by Mr. Roberts (the Chirk Agent) to Robert Davies for ye Iron work done at Ruthin Church .. £23 – 18s – 1d.

(Chirk Castle Accounts; from Ifor Edwards: *Robert Davies of Croes Foel.*
Trans. Denbs. Hist. Soc. 1957–8)

4 RURAL SPORTS, EIGHTEENTH CENTURY STYLE:
(William Bulkeley of Brynddu, Anglesey, records in his Diary—)

1734 Ap. 16. A fair clear day. There was a great match at football played today at Maes y Cleifion in Tyddyn Rono betwixt 12 men of Llanbadric parish and 12 men of Llanfairynghornwy and Llanrhwydris: each of the parties won one end and the third was to decide the conquest, but they were so near equal and the play being maintained on both sides with equal courage, skill and resolution such as none of the spectators (who were four to five hundred persons) ever saw the like before . . . and being besides quite spent with three or four hours at such violent exercise, they agreed to desist and so parted as good friends as they came.

1734 June 4. The wind S.W. and very cold all the morning; There was a match of quoiting this morning at Llanfechell betwix three of Caerdegog and three of Llawr y Llan and won by Caerdegog people. I went to the cock fight at Llandyfrydog about ten which was for eight silver spoons . . . I got the first battle and consequently a spoon.

1742 Sep. 21. Paid a Flintshire smuggler that was come to Cemaes from the Isle of Man 25/– for 5 gallons of French brandy, which I think is right good.

(H. Owen: *The Diary of William Bulkeley*, *Trans. Angl. Antiq. Soc.*, 1931, pp. 29, 42, 73)

5   WILLIAM BULKELEY'S ANXIETY FOR HIS DAUGHTER:

1756 Nov. 10. Received a letter from my daughter dated Oct. 13th giving an account of the death of her only son and the dismal situation she and the children are left by her husband who is gone from Leghorn a-privateering.

(*ibid*, p. 83)

CHAPTER XVIII

THE TEACHERS

CHARITY EDUCATION IN BRITAIN

'Charity is doing good to the souls and bodies of men'

Robert Nelson

THE eighteenth century is usually regarded as the age of corruption in politics and of self-seeking and immorality in life in general. By strange contrast it is also the age of charity, and particularly of philanthropic individuals combining in societies to relieve the poor, the sick, the aged, the prisoners, the slaves and especially the children. Providing free schools was the outstanding and most successful feature of this benevolence.

Wales experienced this educational charity in the last quarter of the seventeenth century and ahead of England, Scotland and Ireland with Thomas Gouge's 'Welsh Trust'. The schools died with their founder in 1681 but his idea and the funds that still poured into the Trust created a fashion for similar charities based on London. So it was in the capital that the most comprehensive educational charity was established in 1699, the Society for the Propagation of Christian Knowledge, a society still active today.

Hundreds of schools were established by the S.P.C.K. in the four countries of the British Isles, with considerable success. When the movement declined in the second half of the eighteenth century, the Sunday Schools of Robert Raikes in England and of Thomas Charles in Wales came to rejuvenate it.

The charity school movement was more successful in Wales than anywhere. This was due partly to the flying-start given it by Cromwell and Thomas Gouge. But, in addition, the work was not hampered here by the motives that weighed with its supporters in the other three countries: in England to make children industrious and content with their station in life; in Ireland to resist popery; in Scotland to wipe out Jacobitism. Popery and Jacobitism, as we have seen were spent forces in Wales. It had a long record of non-rebellion. It had no middle class of any size as yet to worry about the industry or behaviour of its workers. The Welsh schools more than any other kept the simple aim of giving charity to children for the glory of God.

It would seem from a well known-book published in 1721, *The State of the Diocese of St. David's*, that Wales offered them plenty of scope. Its author Erasmus Saunders was an active supporter of the S.P.C.K., setting up a school of his own and paying for fifty of the society's new Welsh Bibles. Like Thomas Gouge fifty years before, he found the diocese in a most 'melancholy state': its church buildings in poor repair; its clergy overworked, impoverished and ill-educated; its services especially preaching and catechizing neglected, and the flocks accordingly ignorant and superstitious. And all this, he claimed, because of the poverty of the church, for which he chiefly blamed the sale of the tithes to secular landowners, and the indifference of the bishops in Wales who were English-speaking and largely non-resident. Yet he declared no people in Britain were more eager for religion than the Welsh.

Griffith Jones and the Methodists painted equally gloomy pictures of the immorality of the people and the indolence of the clergy. Whether or not conditions were as bad as these good men tell us is open to doubt. The reformer tends always to exaggerate the conditions which he wishes to reform, both in order to 'panic' his hearers to his support, and to throw his later reforms into brighter contrast. All these men too were Anglicans who did not reckon with the good work being done by the Dissenters. Moreover, their criterion of ignorance was inability to read the Bible or to reply to the Catechism. Nevertheless, there can be little doubt that the religious condition of Wales in the early eighteenth century was poor.

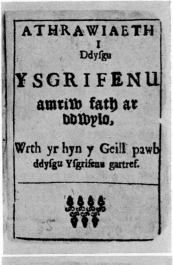

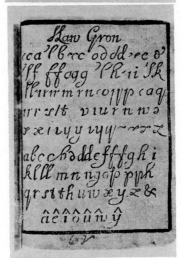

57. THE FIRST WELSH COPY-BOOK

From a little book of 12 leaves, designed to fit a man's waistcoat pocket, published in 1683 by Thomas Jones (1648-1713) printer and bookseller of London and Shrewsbury. It gives not only examples of styles as here, but directions for making ink and quill pens and choosing paper.

This criterion of Bible-reading certainly set the goal for the schools and provided them with a text-book. The education they offered was, by present day standards perhaps, limited; nevertheless it laid the groundwork of literacy.

Finally, the point must be made that the charity school movement in Wales was promoted not by the Anglican Church *as such*, and certainly not by its Welsh-English bishops, nor, surprisingly, by the Methodists (who after all were Anglicans), nor by the Dissenters, who claimed to run their own schools, but by *individual*, broad-minded Anglican clergymen acting in the spirit of the best Puritans.

SCHOOLS FOR CHARITY AND PIETY

It is often said that the character of the Welsh nation today was fashioned in the eighteenth century. It is certainly true that the people as a whole, dead to politics as we have seen, came alive in religion, took on new characteristics and found a new unity and a new means of expression. The common folk of Wales experienced in the Methodist Revival of the mid-century a great wave of emotional fervour, one of the most remarkable outbursts of the human spirit anywhere.

It was accompanied by 'perhaps the most remarkable experiment in mass religious education undertaken anywhere in Great Britain', namely the system of circulatory schools organized throughout Wales by Griffith Jones, Llanddowror. The remarkable feature of this movement again is not Jones's device of the moving school, nor his own shrewd gift for organization, but the overwhelming appetite for learning to read that appeared among ordinary Welsh folk. Griffith Jones's experiment, however, was preceded by three others, two of them peculiar to Wales alone. These—Commonwealth, Trust and Charity schools—had all been initiated and supported from outside Wales itself. Yet for a period of over eighty years they had accustomed the Welsh to the idea of schooling for the ordinary child. Indeed the Methodist Revival is often seen as the reappearance of early Puritanism, another movement that came from England (the first Welsh

Methodists were nicknamed Cradocians, after the Puritan Walter Cradoc). Schools and chapels in fact sprang from the same source. But the Welsh people made them something distinctively their own.

Yet we must remember that of the succession of devout and utterly sincere men who now adventured in education none except the very first were strictly Puritans—Independents, Baptists or Presbyterians. Philipps, Mackworth, Griffith Jones himself and even Thomas Charles later were all loyal Anglicans, as indeed all the Welsh Methodists claimed they were throughout the eighteenth century. Yet they brought to the provision of schools the essential spirit of Puritanism, and their work has been described as 'Puritanism in action'. Their great concern was saving the souls of men; their manual of instruction was the Bible. By their efforts they not merely stemmed the tide of illiteracy and immorality, they prepared the ground for the transformation of a whole nation. The schools and the religious revival go hand in hand.

Nor must we forget that there were other schools whose work has not been recorded. In 1700 there were a good number of grammar schools in Wales teaching the Classics not only to the sons of the rich but to poor boys (schooling was not thought necessary for girls!) We know from the complaints of the bishops that many 'illegal' schools were carried on by Nonconformists during the Restoration years, and these must have increased greatly after 1670 when anyone could keep a school without licence from the bishop. Private schools too were common, and of course some sort of schooling was given in the workhouses. The Dissenters, excluded by law from going to Oxford or Cambridge, provided a form of university education in their popular academies, though those were found almost certainly in south Wales alone. The best known of them was that run by a fine scholar, Samuel Jones, at Brynllywarch in Glamorgan, after he had been ejected from the nearby living of Llangynwyd under the Act of Uniformity in 1662.

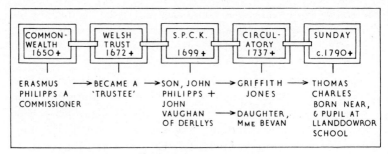

COMMON- WEALTH 1650+	WELSH TRUST 1672+	S.P.C.K. 1699+	CIRCUL- ATORY 1737+	SUNDAY c.1790+
ERASMUS PHILIPPS A COMMISSIONER	BECAME A 'TRUSTEE'	SON, JOHN PHILIPPS + JOHN VAUGHAN OF DERLLYS	GRIFFITH JONES DAUGHTER, MME BEVAN	THOMAS CHARLES BORN NEAR, & PUPIL AT LLANDDOWROR SCHOOL

58. THE CHAIN OF SCHOOLS
Note the 'links' in the chain.

No doubt these individual ventures did good work in their day. Few of them, however, had value for the future; they were temporary in nature and have left little or no records. They lacked a central aim and a common pattern and standard of working. They were neither free nor evenly distributed.

In contrast, the nationwide charitable ventures with which we must now deal had permanent value for our day. Though started by individuals, they quickly became corporations or societies which have left detailed records. Their schools had a set aim and uniform procedure. Moreover, each new venture was grafted on to the previous one by a closely linked chain of individual good men. (See the chart above). They thus had well over a century of continuity, and out of them our present-day system of state education finally evolved in the nineteenth century.

THE WELSH TRUST: THOMAS GOUGE AND STEPHEN HUGHES

The first experiment in charity education was started by two clergymen, one Welsh, the other English. Stephen Hughes was a Carmarthen man who began under the Commonwealth to publish religious books in Welsh and to keep schools. After 1662 he was ejected from his living in Meidrym and gave up his good work. But after 1670, when persecution slackened, he resumed publication with new vigour, recruiting help from gifted Welsh scholars and clergy both Anglican and Non-conformist. In 1672 Hughes

was up in London superintending publication of the verses of
Vicar Prichard, the New Testament, the Psalms and the Catechism. It was now he met Thomas Gouge, a Londoner, who had
also been ejected from his living of St. Sepulchre's in 1662.
Gouge may well have heard of the religious state of Wales from
Vavasor Powell when the latter was on parole from his nearby
prison in 1670. He had certainly read of it in a life of Joseph
Alleine who had vowed to evangelize Wales only to be thwarted
by death. Although well in his sixties Gouge journeyed to Wales
to see for himself. Like Stephen Hughes he realized that preaching
was not enough; the Welsh peasants needed teaching; they must
be given books and taught how to read them with understanding.
He set up some schools at his own charge, but learnt to his own
cost that the problem was beyond his limited means. He appealed
for funds to set up a Welsh Trust and now his friendly, tolerant
disposition won its reward. He got a speedy and generous response
from influential churchmen, Anglican and Non-conformist, from

By permission of the National Library of Wales   *By permission of the National Museum of Wales*

59. PIONEERS IN CHARITY EDUCATION
(a) Thomas Gouge   (b) Sir John Philipps.

the City of London and from the Welsh gentry. Outstanding among these last was Erasmus Philipps of Picton Castle (Pembrokeshire).

The policy of the Welsh Trust remained that of the S.P.C.K. and largely of Griffith Jones also. The aim was to get ordinary Welshmen to read the Bible and other religious books. The children could be taught to do this in English at school. The adults, however, it was thought, were too old and too busy to learn a new language; they must therefore be provided with books in their native Welsh. English schools for the children, Welsh books for the adults—this was the Trust's two-pronged attack on illiteracy. Hughes looked after the publication and distribution of Welsh books, helped among others by Charles Edwards the author of a Welsh classic *Y Ffydd Ddiffuant* (The Genuine Faith) and probably the greatest Welsh writer of the second half of the seventeenth century. A spate of new religious books, originals and translations, soon poured from the presses. The crowning achievement came in 1677–78 with a new impression of the Welsh Bible and the metrical Psalms. This was sold at 4s. 2d. (21p) to those who could afford it, and given freely to those who could not.

Gouge saw to the schools, some 300 of them in all, over the years, paid for partly out of his own pocket, partly by the Trust, and partly by certain Welsh towns. Reading English was the main concern, though the boys were also taught a little writing and simple arithmetic. Unfortunately the schools lasted for only some nine years. The Welsh bishops fearing a Puritan revival had always bitterly opposed them, to their shame, and when in 1681 Charles II gave up tolerating the Dissenters, the opposition had free rein. The Welsh Trust, too, had faults of its own making. The insistence on teaching in English, while it pleased the squires, made both the parents and Hughes and his friends reluctant to co-operate in the work of the schools. Moreover, Gouge had not provided for training teachers in his own methods. When therefore he died in 1681 there was no-one to succeed him, and most

of the schools disappeared. Many must have continued unrecord-
ed, however, ready for the S.P.C.K. to use them as 'going
concerns'.

In any case the work of publication continued unabated till at
least 1688 when Hughes died. Two important issues were: in
1681 a complete edition of Vicar Prichard's popular verses, now
under the title of *Cannwyll y Cymry* by which they have ever since
been known, and in 1688 a Welsh translation of Bunyan's
Pilgrim's Progress.

In its brief life the Welsh Trust had achieved much. By dis-
tributing Welsh books it started the peasantry on the road to
becoming a reading public. The individual Welshman could now,
by reading, lay the foundation of his own personal religious faith.
He became, in so doing, a guardian of the Welsh language.
Thomas Gouge had set the pattern for all the attempts of the
eighteenth century to give the ordinary boy and girl a free ele-
mentary education. When the schools lapsed in Wales, sub-
scriptions to the Trust were used to begin similar charities in
London. The Welsh Trust was a vital link.

THE S.P.C.K.

Four of the five original founders of the S.P.C.K. were con-
nected with Wales, one of them being the remarkable Sir
Humphrey Mackworth, leading industrialist and M.P. for Cardiganshire. Within a week Sir John Philipps of Picton Castle
joined them, and became the outstanding Welsh member, even
more tirelessly active in all sorts of charitable works than his
father Erasmus. His counterpart in North Wales was Dean Jones
of Bangor. At once help poured in: from the landed gentry,
from the few leaders of industry such as Mackworth, from the
Dissenters, even from the Welsh bishops and particularly from
the parish clergy. Success in Wales was immediate.

The S.P.C.K. like the Welsh Trust had two aims: to provide
schools and to publish religious books in Welsh. (At first they
aimed for an overseas mission but this was very soon taken over
by the Society for the Propagation of the Gospel). The second

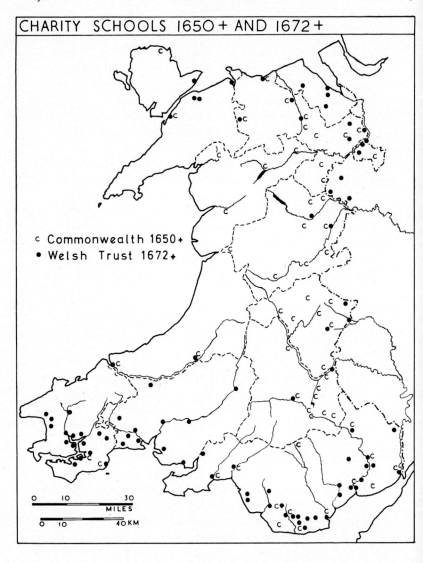

CHARITY SCHOOLS 1650 + AND 1672 +

c Commonwealth 1650+
• Welsh Trust 1672+

0   10   30
      MILES
0   10   40 KM

60. COMMONWEALTH AND TRUST SCHOOLS
(After M. G. Jones: *The Charity School Movement.*)

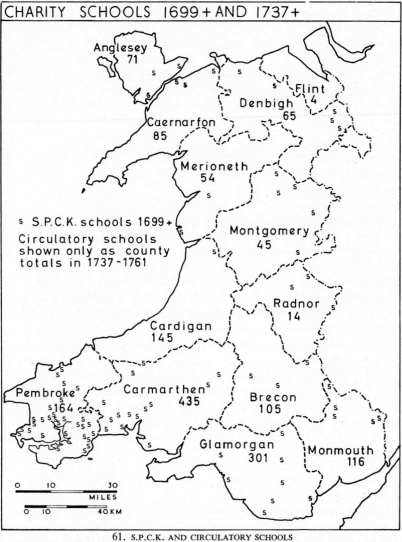

CHARITY SCHOOLS 1699 + AND 1737 +

Anglesey 71

Flint 4

Denbigh 65

Caernarfon 85

Merioneth 54

s S.P.C.K. schools 1699 +
Circulatory schools
shown only as county
totals in 1737-1761

Montgomery 45

Radnor 14

Cardigan 145

Pembroke 164

Carmarthen 435

Brecon 105

Glamorgan 301

Monmouth 116

0 10 30 MILES
0 10 40 KM

61. S.P.C.K. AND CIRCULATORY SCHOOLS
Note that sometimes there was more than one S.P.C.K. school in the place
marked (in Merthyr Tydfil, e.g. there were three). The figure given in the square
for circulatory schools gives the number of *places* in which they were held;
many schools (i.e. a course of 3/6 months) were often held in the same place.

aspect was an unqualified success for which Wales is greatly indebted to the Society. To it do we owe most of the books that
were published at this time, not only two new issues of the
Welsh Bible in 1717 and 1727–8 and a whole spate of Prayer
Books, Catechisms and religious manuals but also other outstanding works such as Ellis Wynne's *Gweledigaethau*, Theophilus
Evans's *Drych* and a host of Welsh translations. It was from the
S.P.C.K. that Griffith Jones obtained books for his circulatory
schools, long after those of the Society itself had waned.

At first the schools of the Society were also a marked success.
They were held where possible in houses adapted for the purpose, but if necessary in the parish church itself. They offered a
four-year course in the Scriptures and the Catechism, and in
reading and writing, with some arithmetic for boys and needle-
work for the girls. Their teachers were generally parish clergymen glad to add £4 or £5 to their meagre average stipend of £10.
Local gentry or clergy acted as inspectors, making regular visita-
tions to the schools. John Vaughan of Derllys served for Carmarthenshire, for example. He was the close friend of Sir John
Philipps and the father of Madame Bevan, Griffith Jones's colleague. His great contribution was providing free libraries, especially for children. The Society was more tolerant than the
Welsh Trust in the matter of language. English was generally
favoured as the medium of instruction, but the vernacular was
used in monoglot Welsh areas and was the majority language in
north Wales, where keen supporters like Dean Jones insisted
on Welsh when endowing schools.

For some fifteen years the schools increased in number. By
1715 there were sixty-eight. Then came a sudden slowing down.
Only twenty-eight were added in the next twelve years. There
is no record of a single new school after 1727. The immediate
reasons for the decline were chiefly political. In 1714 the
society lost the support of Queen Anne by her death, and that of
the Dissenters because of the Schism Act, which tried to make it
impossible for them to teach. And when in 1716 the Archbishop
of Canterbury ordered all teachers and scholars at school to offer

daily prayers for the Hanoverian king George I, all those who had Jacobite leanings took offence. Among them was Sir John Philipps who opened no more new schools, though he continued to support the society. The early patronage of the Welsh bishops too had soon cooled.

In Wales the society had also fundamental difficulties and weaknesses. One was the general level of poverty which compelled supporters like Sir John to spend large sums on feeding and clothing children before they could be got to school. Poverty too compelled the parents to rely on the labour of their children and withhold them from attending school. The society, moreover, had no system of teacher training but relied on the parish priests, a large number of whom were either lazy or themselves unlearned. Language also presented difficulties. Probably the greatest factor limiting the S.P.C.K.'s work was the fact that, like the Commonwealth and Trust schools, the society was energized, initially certainly, from outside, from London, and not from among the Welsh people themselves.

Nevertheless, the achievement of the S.P.C.K. schools was considerable. That it has been underrated is probably due to the enormous success by comparison of the circulatory schools which stemmed naturally from those of the S.P.C.K.

THE CIRCULATORY SCHOOLS OF GRIFFITH JONES

In the summer of 1716 Sir John Philipps made a journey through North Wales to the north of England and the Scottish Border. With him went a man whom he had newly appointed to be rector of Llanddowror, a quiet village on the great road leading westward from Carmarthen. They went, it seems, in order to visit churches and gentry, but much of their conversation must have been about schools: both were members of the S.P.C.K., the rector, when curate of Laugharne, had run the charity-school there, and this journey was undertaken in the very month in which the Archbishop had offended Sir John by ordering all schoolmasters to pray daily for the new Hanoverian king. By their friendship they were forging the link between the charity

schools and the circulatory schools. The rector of course was
Griffith Jones. His is one of the great names of Welsh history.

He was born of humble parents in the parish of Penboyr in the
western corner of Carmarthenshire, where it meets both Cardiganshire and Pembrokeshire. Left fatherless in his infancy, and
troubled by the asthma which never left him, he grew up a
reserved, temperamental, serious-minded youth who is said to
have had visions of heaven and hell. Jones had the conviction
that he was 'wonderfully called to be a shepherd of men', and
early turned to religion. After some education at Carmarthen
grammar school, he was ordained a priest in 1709. About 1712
he first met Sir John Philipps who recommended him to the
S.P.C.K. to be a missionary in Madras. By the next year, however, Griffith had decided he was more immediately required
in his own country, which he dolefully saw to be in a state of
'extremely miserable blindness'. So south-west Wales remained
his headquarters for the rest of his life. But the links with the
S.P.C.K. and Sir John had been forged. In 1720 he married Sir
John's sister.

His whole interest now turned to preaching. Soon he carried
a reputation for his most powerful sermons, but he gave offence
to his superiors by holding services in the adjacent parishes
without the permission of their priests, and frequently in the
open-air. Already he had the idea that his was a roving commission. Gradually, however, he became convinced that preaching was not enough. The peasantry must be taught not merely
to listen but to learn the Catechism with conviction, and to
express themselves. Inevitably he turned to the charity schools
as the vehicles for this. They were now failing and doubtless the
reasons were clear to him; they must provide a quick, cheap
education, flexible and attuned to the Welsh temperament.

His first school was held probably at Llanddowror in 1731.
By 1733 he was satisfied that the 'circulatory' system best met
the need. Notice of holding a school at a place was announced
in advance in the churches around and the inhabitants invited to
take advantage of the teaching and books supplied; the school

was duly held, then, usually after three months, it moved on to a new locality. Probably in deference to Sir John, whose mantle Jones now felt he wore, the schools were known as charity-schools. But when Sir John died in 1737 Griffith gave them the title of 'Circulatory Welsh Charity Schools'.

The schools were an immediate success. By 1761 when Griffith Jones died, 3,325 schools had been held in almost 1,600 different places with 153,835 scholars, a staggering number at a time when the total population of Wales was probably no more than 450,000 in all. There is little doubt too that the schools wrought a 'visible change for the better in the lives of the people' and created an interest in religion that made the schools nurseries for the Methodist movement.

Griffith Jones succeeded where the S.P.C.K. failed fundamentally because he understood the Welsh people: he was one of them and knew their difficulties in a way that no outside charity or local gentry ever could. Firstly, he appreciated the difficulties of the parents and won their co-operation. The schools were held normally in the winter months when the peasantry did not urgently need their children's labour, and frequently in the evening when hired servants and farm labourers were free to come. The simple needs of the tuition given, moreover, made little demands upon the parents' pockets; indeed a great many of them contributed freely to the upkeep of the schools. Above all, Griffith drew the parents themselves into his schools; in fact he claimed that 'two-thirds of his scholars were grown-ups'.[1] The schools thus became a pioneer experiment in adult education, and began a tradition in Welsh education that has lasted, through the Sunday schools, until today. In all, the humble Welsh folk had the idea that the schools were theirs; the essential spirit of the movement was democratic.

Jones similarly handled the clergy, both Anglican and Dissenters, with sympathy and tact. The help of parish priests was sought to find a suitable building—the church, if possible, a barn or such if not—and to find and superintend teachers of the right

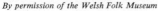

62. PIONEERS OF CIRCULATORY SCHOOLS
(a) Griffith Jones   (b) Madam Bevan.

calibre. If consent was not forthcoming, the school was not held; but increasingly the attitude became one of co-operation and goodwill.

Teachers were largely found from among the peasants themselves, many of them Nonconformists. They were chosen more for their piety and moral worth than for their educational qualifications, which of course were generally meagre.[2] Dedication was their hallmark; otherwise they could not have subsisted on the meagre £3 or £4 per year which was their pay. Their only training was the brief, intensive course of a few weeks that the leader gave them on teaching the Catechism at Llanddowror; then they dispersed to the far corners of Griffith's ever growing empire. They came like the friars and wandering poets of the days of the Welsh princes in their heyday, and the Welsh peasants welcomed them the readier for it.

In fact, the very meagreness of their curriculum was another major reason for the success of the schools. They were simply catechetical schools; reading and the Catechism were to be the only subjects of study. Griffith directed his teachers specifically that they were not to teach writing or arithmetic.[3] 'It is but a cheap education we desire', he declared. The instruction given *was* cheap, mechanical and superficial. Yet it met the immediate need which Jones, with the true instinct of the teacher, had diagnosed.

Griffith Jones too was fortunate in his supporters. He formed no special society for his purpose; indeed he regarded his work as a continuation of that of the S.P.C.K. which was his main supplier, providing him freely with thousands of Bibles, catechisms and other religious books. Like the Welsh Trust and the S.P.C.K., he was financed by charitable Englishmen as well as by collections from the Welsh peasantry. From the outset his unfailing patron was Bridget, wife of wealthy Arthur Bevan, M.P. for Carmarthen, and, more significantly, daughter of John Vaughan of Derllys who had generously supported the S.P.C.K. Charity, it would seem, ran in families. It was in her house that Griffith died in 1761; to her, as trustee for the schools, he left his private fortune of £7,000; and she carried on his work with marked success until her own death in 1779. It was during the period of her trusteeship indeed that the movement reached its peak achievement with the 1773 figures of 242 schools and 13,205 pupils. It was in her time, in 1764, that Catherine the Great of Russia sent emissaries to Britain to inquire into the remarkable success of the circulatory schools.

Moreover, Griffith Jones correctly assessed the situation with regard to language. Undoubtedly, he knew his priorities; religion came before any language, so in English Pembrokeshire and on the border his schools were conducted in English. But otherwise he had no doubt that the language of his movement was Welsh. He was not concerned, he declared, with the presentation of the Welsh language merely for its own sake. To him, nevertheless, it was the vehicle in Wales for serving 'the glory of God, the

interest of religion and the salvation of the poor Welsh people'.
And, as he told his English subscribers, English charity schools
in Wales were as ridiculous as French charity schools in England.
Nor is there any doubt that Griffith Jones held his native language in great affection. 'I was born a Welshman', he declared,
almost defiantly, 'and have not unlearned the simple honesty and
unpoliteness of my mother tongue'. In fact William Morgan in
translating the Bible, and Griffith Jones in disseminating it rescued
the Welsh language.

Griffith Jones was fortunate in his patrons and in being the
'man for the hour'; but when all has been said it remains true
that the circulatory schools succeeded because of him. His genius
does not lie in the originality of his methods; the circulatory
idea was already in use in Scotland for him to see when he
journeyed there with Sir John; it had been long suggested by
the versatile Sir Humphrey Mackworth, who had also advocated
schemes for teacher-training. In any case a fashion had long
grown among the Welsh peasants, especially those who belonged
to Nonconformist 'societies' of holding 'home schools' in each
other's cottages to study the Scriptures. Griffith Jones's genius
lay in his tremendous capacity for large-scale organization; he
could take other people's suggestions, and, with the seriousness
and dedication that marked him, make a successful working
system of them. His gift was matched by an enormous capacity
for hard work in spite of his delicate health; training the teachers
and organizing the schools, persistent travelling, collecting funds,
writing hundreds of letters and compiling reports to his supporters, especially his annual report *Welch Piety*, our best source of
information—all these tasks and many more he took upon himself. Irritable and domineering he could be, but he had the power
to inspire young men, notably those who were to be leaders of
Methodism in Wales.

Like Bell and Lancaster a half century later, with their moni-
torial schools, he may have done education a disservice by im-
plying that it was something superficial, cheap, easily got and
makeshift. But the solid achievements of this man who, like his

contemporary, the musician Handel, began his best work at fifty-two are undeniable; he raised the moral tone of a nation, prepared it for a religious revival which was to change its character, pioneered adult education and saved the Welsh language. 'Wales and the Welsh language' said an official report of 1927, 'are very largely what they are today because of Griffith Jones'.

ORIGINAL EXTRACTS

1   GRANDSIRE AND GRANDSON AT SCHOOL IN TRELECH;
BY THE VICAR:

In a short Time after the School was opened, I went to visit it, & was agreeably surprised to see there an *Old Man*, seventy-one Years of Age, with his Spectacles on his Nose, & the Church Catechism in his Hand, with five other poor People far advanced in Years, who came there with their little Children to be taught to read the Word of God. Some of them were beginning in the A, B, C, others could read a little. . . . The Tears trickling down from their Eyes, when they saw that the little Children had gained more knowledge in three Months at the *Welch* School, than many of them had acquired in hearing Sermons for fifty or threescore Years

(*ibid*, p. 56)

2   RULES OF THE WELSH SCHOOLS:

The masters must be sober, God-fearing, members of the Church of England, loyal to the King and the Government, and such as devote themselves sincerely to their work; not strolling about needlessly and idling about the place; not contending about controversial questions of Religion.

(quoted in F. A. Cavenagh: *Griffith Jones*, p. 51)

3   THE SOLE AIM OF THE CIRCULATORY SCHOOL:

Neither the Poor nor any others, are, at all, to be taught *Writing* or *Cyphering* in these Schools, that the Masters may exert *all* their Endeavours, and lay out *all* their Time, and *all* their Pains, to instruct them in the Catechism . . . for as they are, for the most Part, very Poor, they cannot afford to stay long in School: and besides, it is by no means the Design of this spiritual kind of Charity, to make them *Gentlemen*, but *Christians*, and *Heirs* of eternal Life.

(Gruffydd Jones and Madam Bevan: *Welch Piety*, 1749–50)

APPENDIX

THE SCHOOLS

The following list,* together with the maps on page 278/9 provide material for the exercises suggested for this chapter.

The first three columns show, as accurately as possible, the places (given their present spelling) in which were held all the schools of the Commonwealth (in 1650), the Welsh Trust (1674-5) and the S.P.C.K. (1699-1737). The last column indicates whether a circulatory school was later held at these sites during 1738-61. There were, of course, many more circulatory schools, held in wholly new places.

NORTH WALES

	Com.	W. Tr.	SPCK	Circ		Com.	W. Tr.	SPCK	Circ
Anglesey					**Flintshire**				
Amlwch	x				Hanmer	x			
Beaumaris		x	x		Bangor-on-Dee		x		
Llanfihangel					Flint Town		x		
Ysgeifiog			x		Northop		x		
Llangeinwen			x	x	Caerwys		x		
					Mold		x		
Caernarvon-					Overton		x		
shire					Worthenbury		x		
Caernarfon									
Town	x	x			**Merioneth**				
Conwy		x			Bala	x			x
Llandegai		x		x	Corwen	x			x
Llanllechid		x	x	x	Dolgellau	x		x	x
Bangor			x		Festiniog	x			x
Gyffin			x		Towyn			x	
Denbighshire					**Montgomery-**				
Abergele	x	x			**shire**				
Denbigh Town	x	x	x	x	Llanfair	x			x
Glynceiriog	x				Llanfyllin	x		xx	
Holt	x	x			Llanidloes	x			x
Llandegla	x			x	Llansantffraid	x			
Llanfair D.C.	x			x	Machynlleth	x			
Llangollen	x				Montgomery	x			
Llanrwst	x	x			Newtown	x			
Llansilin	x				Welshpool	x	x	x	
Ruthin	x	x		x	Meifod		x		
Wrexham	x	x	x		Llanfihangel			x	
Marchwiel		x	x		Llangynog			x	
Gresford		x	x		Kerry			x	
Bettws Abergele		x							

* The Commonwealth schools are taken from T. Richards: *The Puritan Movement in Wales*, pp. 226-30, and the others from M. G. Jones: *The Charity School Movement*, Appendix IV.

SOUTH WALES

	Com.	W. Tr.	SPCK	Circ
Breconshire				
Brecon Town	x	x	xxx	x
Builth	x			x
Llanbedr	x			
Llangors	x			x
Llanigon	x			
Llanddeti	x			
Talgarth	x			
Talybont	x			
Tretower	x			
Hay		x		
Llandilo			x	x
Cardiganshire				
Cardigan Town	x	x		x
Lampeter	x	x		x
Esgair-Hir Mines		x		
Llandysul			x	x
Carmarthenshire				
Laugharne		x	x	x
Penboyr		x	x	x
Llanboidy		x	x	
St. Clears		x	x	
Marros		x	x	x
Llanelli		x		x
Llandovery		x	x	
Kidwelly		x		x
Llanarthne		x		x
Llanddowror		x	x	x
Carmarthen Town		x	xx	x
Abergwili			x	x
Llangadog			x	x(?)
Llangain			x	x
Llangynog			x	x
Pembrey			x	x
Glamorgan				
Cardiff	x	x	x	
Cowbridge	x	x	x	
Llantwit Major	x		x	
Merthyr	x		xxx	x
Neath	x	x	x	x
Penmark	x	x		
St. Mary Hill	x	x		x
Swansea	x	x		x
Margam		x	x	x
Kenfig		x		x

	Com.	W. Tr.	SPCK	Circ
Glamorgan— cont.				
St. Nicholas		x		x
Llancarfan		x		
Llantrithyd		x		
St. Hilary		x		
Wenvoe		x		
Llandilotalybont		x		x
Bridgend		x		x
Betws		x		x
Landore (?)			x	
Llantrisant			xx	x
Llanwonno			x	
(unlocated)		xx		
(unlocated)		xx		
Monmouthshire				
Abergavenny	x	x	x	
Chepstow	x	x		
Magor	x			x
Newport	x	x		
Usk	x	x		x
Llantrissent		x		
Caerleon		x		x
Llangybi		x		
Machen		x		x
Basaleg		x		
Monmouth		x	xxx	
Pontypool		x		
Michaelston-y-Vedw		x		
Llanthony			x	x
Mitchel Troy			x	
Llantilio Pertholey			x	
(unlocated)	x			
Pembrokeshire				
Carew	x	x		
Tenby	x	x	x	
Lampeter Velfrey		x	x	x
Uzmaston		x	x	
Pembroke Town		x	xxx	x
Haverfordwest		x	x	
Nolton		x		
Brawdy		x		x
Trefgarn		x		

SOUTH WALES—continued

	Com.	W. Tr.	SPCK	Circ		Com.	W. Tr.	SPCK	Circ
Pembroke-shire— cont.					**Radnorshire**				
					Bleddfa	x			
Freystrop		x			Llangynllo	x			
Llangwm		x(?)		x	Clyro	x			
Martletwy		x			Nantmel	x			x
Slebech		x	x		New Radnor	x	x		
Roch		x		x	Rhayader	x			
Cosheston		x			Llanbister	x			
Narberth		x	x		(unlocated)	x			
Amroth			x	x	Knighton		x		
Begelly			x		Presteigne		x	x	
Boulston			x		Glasbury			xx	
Dinas			x	x	Glasbury			xx	
Haroldston-west			x		Maesgwin			x	
Hasguard			x						
Lambston			x						
Lawrenny			x						
Llanychar			x	x					
Maenclochog			x	x					
Marloes			x						
Mounton			x						
Penally			x						
Prendergast			x						
Puncheston			x						
Rudbaxton			x						
St. Brides			x						
St. Ishmaels			x						
Steynton			x						
Templeton			x						
Walton East			x						
Walton West			x						

CHAPTER XIX

THE PREACHERS

On Palm Sunday 1735 a young schoolmaster named Howell Harris turned into his local church at Talgarth, Brecknockshire to hear the vicar, Pryce Davies, preach. What he heard affected him profoundly (see p. 292). Indeed, the event became a turning point not only in his career but, through him, in the history of Wales in general. Such revelations experienced by a number of remarkable young men began the great Methodist movement, the most powerful, single force operating in the England and Wales of the eighteenth century.

The strange fact is that Welsh Methodism was not an imitation of English Methodism, nor vice-versa. The two movements sprang up quite independently of each other and never joined, though their leaders had friendly associations. Methodism owes its name to England but in point of time Wales led: Howell Harris' move-ment was well on its way before Charles, the first of the Wesley brothers, had had his revelations. Both began as movements within the Anglican church, both finally (England first) formed Nonconformist sects. They differed in their fundamental beliefs however; the Methodists of Wales are Calvinistic, those of England Wesleyan (or Arminian).

The first leaders in both countries formed a triumvirate, each with his distinctive talent to preach, to organize or to sing; and in both their methods were the same: preaching in the open air, discussing in private houses, forming religious societies, singing hymns. Their popular appeal among the neglected industrial classes of England, and especially among the leaderless peasantry of Wales was tremendous.

The three leaders in Wales were Howell Harris (1714–73), Daniel Rowland (1713–90) and William Williams (1716–91)

NEAR the Altar lie the Remains of
HOWELL HARRIS Esquire,
Born at Trevecka January the 23d 1713/14 O. S.
Here where his Body lies, He was convinced of Sin,
Had his Pardon Sealed,
And felt the Power of Christ's precious Blood,
At the Holy Communion.
Having Tasted Grace, He resolved to declare to others
What God had done for his Soul.
He was the first itinerant Preacher of Redemption
In this Period of Revival in *England* and *Wales*.
He Preached the Gospel
For the Space of thirty-nine Years,
Till He was taken to his final rest.
He received all who sought Salvation
Into his House.
Thence sprung up the Family at
Trevecka.
To whom He faithfully Ministered unto his end,
As an indefatigable Servant of GOD,
And faithful Member of the *Church* of *England*.
HIS END
Was more blessed than his Beginning.
Looking to Jesus crucified
He rejoiced to the last, that Death had lost its Sting.
He fell asleep in Jesus at *Trevecka* July 21st 1773.
And now rests blessedly from all his labours.

UNDER the same *Stone* lie also the Remains of his late Wife,
ANN HARRIS
Daughter of *John Williams*, of *Skreen Esquire*;
Who departed this Life March 9th 1770, AGED 58.
She loved the Lord Jesus, Relied on his redeeming
Grace and Blood, and with her last Breath declared her
Confidence in HIM.
They left one beloved Child, who was the constant
Object of their Prayers and Care, and who Honours their
Venerable Memory.

Ar doethion a ddisgleiriant fel disgleirdeb y ffurfafen; ar rhai a
droant lawer i gyfiawnder, a fyddant fel y Ser byth yn dragywydd.
Dan. Pen. XII. Adn. 3.

GAMEL fecit.

By permission of the Howell Harris Museum, Trefecca

63. A RECORD OF REVELATION
The Plaque in Talgarth church.

though we must not forget the father-figure of Griffith Jones
(1683–1761) who remained a sort of confessor, consultant and
moderator for the three young men. Harris was probably the
most remarkable of them; to many he is the greatest Welshman
of the eighteenth century as John Wesley is the greatest Englishman.

Harris was a born organizer, as indeed were his two elder
brothers, Joseph, who became assay-master at the Mint, and
Thomas, who won less reputable fame and fortune as an army
contractor. After his spiritual experience in Talgarth, Howell
immediately started to evangelize in the surrounding districts,
preaching and forming his converts into family groups or societies
(*seiadau*) after the fashion of the Nonconformists. By so doing he
gave offence to his vicar who refused to recommend him for
ordination as a priest. Now he thought of going to university. He
went up to Oxford, but left after a week, probably impatient to
evangelize. In 1736 he went to see Griffith Jones who advised
him to be more moderate, to keep to his schoolmastering and
not to get over-involved with the Nonconformists. A few weeks
earlier, Daniel Rowland, a young curate from Llangeitho had
heard Griffith preach and experienced a similar revelation to
Harris's. He too began to travel in west Wales preaching most
powerfully to large congregations about sin and salvation. In 1737
Harris and Rowland met and joined forces. Harris's personal
and local venture was shaping into an altogether wider movement.

The following year, 1738, was an all-important one.
Firstly young William Williams, a native of Llanfair-ar-y-bryn,
Carmarthenshire, out from his school, Llwyn-llwyd Academy
nearby, chanced to hear Harris preach in Talgarth churchyard
and was 'convinced'. Soon he was showing his tremendous talent
for hymn-writing, the element in the Methodist armoury that
was the most popular in its appeal. Secondly, Harris, with the
help of Nonconformist sympathizers, took the revival into Glamorgan and Monmouthshire and even into North Wales. Thirdly,
in this year a similar movement began in England and almost

immediately made friendly contact with the Welsh pioneers.[1]
The leaders in England were the Wesley brothers and George
Whitfield, all three, unlike the Welsh trio, university men. Sons
of a country rector at Epworth in Lincolnshire, John and Charles
Wesley had set up, while at Oxford, a 'Holy Club' dedicated to
a frugal life and good works. It was here that the rigour of the
programme they set themselves won them the nickname of
'Methodists'. But neither their self-denial at Oxford nor missionary work later in America brought the two brothers either the
satisfaction or the success which inwardly they craved. Then on
24 May 1738, John (1703–91) went, as he had often done, to a
meeting of a Moravian 'society' at Aldersgate in London. There
suddenly the mystical revelation came to him:

> I felt my heart strangely warmed. I felt that I did trust in Christ, Christ
> alone for salvation; and an assurance was given me that He had taken my
> sins, even *mine* and had saved me from the law of sin and death

A similar experience had come to Charles (1707–88) a little
earlier. With their friend George Whitfield they determined to
bring their revelation to others. For the remaining fifty-three
years of his life John Wesley alone tavelled some 224,000 miles
and preached 40,000 sermons! Charles, in the half-century left
to him, journeyed rather less, but he surely holds the all-time
record with his 6,000 hymns, many composed on horseback,
often with his Welsh wife Sally Gwynne riding side-saddle and
singing behind him.[2]

George Whitfield and Howell Harris quickly became firm
friends. The Wesleys too met Harris and Griffith Jones at
Bristol, which had become the headquarters of English Methodism
outside London, and were invited to Wales. In October 1739
John came, preaching his way as far as Cardiff. The extract from
his diary on p. 304[3] reveals how long and fatiguing was his day.
His routine at Abergavenny was typical:

> 'About a thousand people stood patiently (though the frost was sharp,
> it being after sunset) while, from Acts XXVIII, 22, I simply described the
> plain old religion of the Church of England which is now almost everywhere

64. JOHN WESLEY AT WORK

Preaching in the open air. Note the dress and the expressions of the congregation.

spoken against under the new name of Methodism. An hour after, I explained
it a little more fully in a neighbouring house'.

In the next four years the Wesleys journeyed frequently in
south Glamorgan and Monmouthshire, establishing many societies
and working in friendly co-operation with Howell Harris. Cardiff
was apparently their centre of work, but the favourite 'base' of
all these men was Fonmon Castle with Robert Jones, great-
grandson of that Colonel Philip Jones who had prospered with
Cromwell. This devout country gentleman, however, died suddenly in 1742. But in the next year the brothers found a new
friend, and Charles a father-in-law, in Marmaduke Gwynne of
Garth near Builth, an equally sincere Anglican converted by
Howell Harris. His home became their accustomed stopping
place in all their unwearied riding. In his lifetime John Wesley
visited Wales fifty-three times, eighteen of them on his way to or
from Ireland via Holyhead, and Garth was conveniently central
on the Bristol road.

Serious difficulties faced the early Methodists. One was the
hardship of constant journeying, often in bad weather and always
on bad roads. Another was the frequent violence the travellers
faced when they preached to large crowds. The movement co-
incided with a period of almost constant war, and the preachers
were often accused of being in the pay of England's enemies,
though in fact the Methodists, both Welsh and English, were
staunch Tories and firmly on the side of law and order. The main
stumbling block, however, was the Anglican Church which dis-
approved of the itinerant ministry, the private societies, the
services in the open air, and the use of laymen as preachers. But
without the approval of vicar and bishop the lay 'exhorters'
could not be ordained, and certainly could not administer the
sacraments. Howell Harris himself was repeatedly refused
ordination, and both Rowland and Williams although curates
were never promoted to full priests; Rowland in fact served as
curate at Llangeitho first to his brother and later to his own son
until 1763 when he lost even his curacy. Yet all three, like
Griffith Jones, remained devoted Anglicans throughout their

lives, urging their listeners always to attend the sacraments at their parish churches.

In spite of difficulties Methodism spread 'like flame on the flax' and more so in Wales than in England. Reasons are not hard to find. The ground had been well tilled. First by the Noncon-formists since way back with the Commonwealth preachers and during the Restoration persecution. Both Harris and Williams received their education at the dissenting academy of Llwyn-llwyd near Hay; Rowland, although son of an Anglican priest, was brought up in an area of strong Nonconformity. In the first days all three sought and received ready help from the Noncon-formists, whose activities in almost all things were identical. Indeed, even within the established church the practice had grown since about 1680 for like-minded people to meet in societies, to pray, read the Bible, and sing psalms or religious songs (called *cwndidau* or *halsingod* in Wales) rather like Negro spirituals. Harris and Wesley were able to take immediate advantage of these and work through them.

Now too the work of the charity schools was having its effect. This was especially true of Wales with its extra bonus of circula-tory schools. The instruction that was given in them to adults as well as children whetted that appetite for religion which Erasmus Saunders in 1721 claimed was evident among the common folk of Wales. Though now in his mature years, Griffith Jones counselled moderation to the young triumvirate; he himself had practised all their methods at the outset of his career and been reprimanded for them. Nor could he prevent his teachers—these 'South Wales, Enthusiastic Itinerants', as a Bangor cleric bitterly described them—from exhorting as well as teaching. It was no accident that Methodism in the eighteenth century was strongest where the circulatory schools had been most numerous. After his first meeting with Griffith Jones at Bath in 1739 young George Whitfield wrote:

'You ask me if I have seen Mr. Jones? Yes; bless'd be God I have seen him, to my great comfort. He is an old soldier of Jesus Christ. O that I may follow him as he has Christ'.

Little wonder that a critic wrote that it was Gruffydd who had 'put a windmill into Whitfield's head and sent him Don Quixoting up and down the world'.

By 1742 Harris had master-minded for the movement an ordered democratic constitution rather like Presbyterianism, with authority passing upwards from 'exhorters' through 'super-intendents' and 'moderators' to the Association or *Sasiwn*. A sort of 'gentleman's agreement' had been arrived at with the English Methodists that they should evangelize in the English-speaking areas of Wales, and especially the south-east, leaving the Welsh remainder to Harris's men. And in January 1743 a joint Associa-tion of Welsh Methodists and Whitfield's followers was held at Watford, near Caerphilly. The event is important. Firstly it marks the official birth of Welsh Methodism as an institution. Secondly, the meeting, though held in a Nonconformist chapel, decided not to break away from the Anglican church, a decision incomprehensible to the Nonconformists, who thereafter lost sympathy with the Methodists. Thirdly, the absence of Wesley's followers underlined the growing rift between him and Whit-field. Their major dispute was over a matter of fundamental belief; Whitfield believed with the austere Calvin that salvation was pre-ordained for a selected number only, while Wesley held the more hopeful Arminian doctrine that all could be saved. Harris now lined up with Whitfield; a fateful choice which determined that Welsh Methodism thereafter would in the main be Calvinistic and not Wesleyan.

A rift too was appearing in the Welsh movement itself between Harris on the one hand, and Rowland on the other. The two men differed markedly in temperament and talent. Harris was an enterprising, often flamboyant personality; a man who moved from one bursting enthusiasm to another, a born organizer, plan-ner and publicist. Scholars are still wading through the enormous mass of his writings—280 exercise books of his diaries, 400 books of his letters to others, over a 1,000 sent by correspondents to him, apart from a great file of records from societies and associa-tion meetings. Rowland was essentially conservative. To him the

65. A WELSH METHODIST GALLERY

Howell Harris (*top left*)
Daniel Rowland (*top right*)
William Williams (*below*)

preaching, for which he had an enormous gift, was everything. He alone of the revivalists did not itinerate, but stayed put at Llangeitho, thundering out sermons to the thousands of Welshmen who flocked there as if to Mecca from all parts of Wales to hear him. Unlike his colleagues also he wrote very little, and he had no gift for administration. So in 1744 William Williams was appointed to help him and more than made up for Rowland's deficiencies. For fifty years the 'Sweet Singer' covered an annual average of 3,000 miles over Wales, and his literary output apart from his hymns, in both prose and poetry, was so great and so good that he is accepted as the first Romantic poet of Wales. But his hymn writing is his fame; in this he far outshone his two colleagues, both of whom recognized the value of this medium. After his marriage in 1748 Williams—when not travelling—settled in his mother's old home of Pantycelyn. Thereafter he is remembered with affection as 'Williams, Pantycelyn' or just 'Pantycelyn'. Now in the thousands of hymns that flowed from his pen, over a hundred of them in English, he displayed an individual quality of lyric poetry that owed nothing to tradition except a little *cynghanedd*, and everything to his own burning religious fervour. There can be little doubt that Pantycelyn in the long run did more than anyone to endear Methodism to the Welsh people. For it must be remembered that the revival was not *primarily* a protest against the inefficiency of the Anglican clergy, nor a statement of doctrine. It was essentially an appeal to the emotions, to the heart. Read this first verse of one of his better known hymns:

Rwy'n ofni'm nerth yn ddim
   Pan elwy'i rym y don:
Mae terfysg yma cyn ei ddod,
   A syndod dan fy mron.
Mae ofnau o bob rhyw,
   Oll fel y diluw'n nghyd,
Yn bygwth i fy nhorri lawr,
   Pan ddeloi'u hawr rywbryd

I fear my strength is naught
   When in the clutch of the Wave.
There is turmoil here before it comes
   And amazement in my heart.
Fears of every kind,
   All gathered like the deluge,
Threaten wholly to o'erwhelm me,
   When at times their hour comes.

It has no suggestion of religion, it is all emotion, the emotion almost of nervous derangement. But such lines were to be recalled by Welsh folk in times of sorrow and of joy long after the sermons of Rowland and the rules of Harris had been forgotten. Pantycelyn's hymns were the essential cement of the Revival.

Harris and Rowland gradually drifted apart. They disagreed for one thing over the style of their preaching. Harris too was becoming almost impossible to work with. From 1745 to 1748, while Whitfield was in America, he was left in charge of the Calvinistic societies of both England and Wales and perhaps grew to regard himself as indispensable. In 1748 too began Harris's association with Madame Sidney Griffith who, estranged from her boorish husband, William Griffith of Cefn Amwlch in Llŷn, attached herself to the Methodist leaders and claimed prophetic powers. Harris—and his wife—took care of her, and Rowland and Williams in fairness accepted the relationship as the innocent and compassionate act that it surely was. But tongues wagged, especially among 'Rowland's people', and by 1752— the year in which Madame Griffith died—the rift between the two camps was open and complete. It could only do harm to the movement; Rowland and Pantycelyn more than held the cause in south-west Wales, but much of the south-east was lost to Methodism.

Harris had to admit ruefully that the revival which he had fathered prospered without him. But meantime his genius for enterprise had found new expression. He set up at Trefeca, his mother's old home, a 'Family' or self-supporting community of earnest men and women who desired to live apart from the outside world; they pooled their resources on entry, and supported themselves thereafter by their labours in farming, weaving and other trades. By 1754 they numbered 120, living in a new building erected for the purpose or in nearby farmhouses. The routine that Harris imposed on them was rigorous; three times a day the Family came together to pray and hear Harris, after the manner of a father, expounding the Bible. The following time-schedule,

taken from one of his diaries, reads like the 'daily-routine orders'
of a monastery.

> 4 a.m.—rise to breakfast and sermon: 6 a.m.—go to work and call children
> for breakfast and work; 10 a.m.—children's meal; 12 noon—call the men
> to dinner from the fields; before 2 p.m.—expound the Word then all to
> work again; 8 p.m. supper for the children; 8.30 p.m.—evening service,
> after 9 p.m.—supper and questioning (by Harris) on the state of their
> souls; 10 p.m. bed.

Many of course could not live up to this strict code and left. But
others replaced them, and until Harris's death in 1773 the Family
at Trefeca was a material and spiritual success.

The Family might live and work apart from the world, but
Harris apparently did not wish them to forget their duty to the
wider community. He himself led the way. He was a keen farmer
and in 1755 became a founder member of the Brecknockshire
Agricultural Society, the first of its kind in Wales. And in 1760
when the country, then fighting the Seven Years' War, was
threatened with invasion, he formed a company of militia from
among the Family with himself as captain. He continued to preach
of course, and for the next three years took advantage of his
scarlet uniform to quell mobs who tried to break up his meetings
with violence.

By this time much of the bitterness had gone out of the 'split'
between 'Rowland's People' and Harris's. In 1762 Harris again
joined his old friends at society and 'sasiwn' meetings. He was
able to restore to the movement some of the good order that
Rowland, by his own confession, had lost in Harris's absence.
But never again was he to be the unquestioned, indomitable leader,
as little John ('Pope') Wesley continued to be in England until
his death. Harris's movement had grown much greater than the
man.

The story of Methodism in our period is only a beginning;
tremendous developments were to follow, such as the growth of
the movement in north Wales to even greater popularity than the
south, the Sunday Schools which effectively carried on the work
of the circulatory schools as 'nurseries' of the movement, and

the fateful decision in 1811 finally to break with the Anglican church. But a number of events make it fitting that we should end this part of the story at about 1760: the death of Griffith Jones in 1761, Harris's reconciliation in 1762, and the dismissal of Rowland from his curacy in 1763.

Harris died in 1773, but Rowland (d. 1790), Pantycelyn (1791) John (1791) and Charles (1788) Wesley continued to serve the cause unweariedly for almost another generation. These leaders of the great religious Revival lived long enough to witness two other vast upheavals that were to change the economic and political life of Britain as they had changed its religion—the Industrial Revolution and the French Revolution. Nor was the work of the Methodists unrelated to these; by preaching thrift in daily life they energized the first, by fixedly supporting the established order, they brought stability to counter the second.

But one effect was evident even by 1760. The religious schools and societies had taken hold of the Welsh people and shaken them to their depths. Suddenly, the people of Wales became alive and articulate, and found in the preachers, most of them sprung from the peasantry a new aristocracy to replace the leaders they had gradually lost since Tudor days. With the Methodists the story of Wales graduates from the Adventurers to the People.

ORIGINAL EXTRACTS

1 HOWELL HARRIS WRITES TO JOHN WESLEY:

May 27 – 1743.

My Dr Dr Br

I have been just now readg your earnest appeal to men of reason and religion and I think I was never so knit to you before. . . . My Soul was made thankfull to God for you and all the graces & gifts he has conferred upon you & may yr God & my God strengthen yr hands and Make you the Spiritual father of thousands!

(G. M. Roberts: *Selected Trevecka Letters* (1742–47), p. 96)

2 COURTSHIP AND MARRIAGE BY CHARLES WESLEY:

April 5th (1748) I took horse at three. Mr. Gwynne and Miss Sally accompanied me the first hour.

April 19th. . . . It was then a distant first thought, not likely ever to come to a proposal; as I had not given the least hint, either to Miss Gwynne or the family. . . . "How know I, whether it is best for me to marry or no?" . . . It should be now or not at all.

June 28th Quite spent with examining the classes, I was much revived in singing with Miss Burdock and Sally.

July 19th. . . . I set out at four (a.m.) with Mr. Gwynne and Sally. At eleven, in Windsor, my horse threw me with violence over his head. My companion fell upon me. The guardian angels bore us in their hands, so that neither was hurt . . . By seven we came to Reading, and I preached in great bodily weakness.

April 7th (1749) I rose at four, and got an hour for prayer and the Scripture. . . . I came to Garth by nine. . . . We read over the (marriage) settlement . . . We crowded as much prayer as we could into the day.

April 8th. Not a cloud was to be seen from morning till night. I rose at four; spent three hours and an half in prayer, or singing, with my brother, with Sally, with Beck. At eight I led MY SALLY to church. . . . Mr. Gwynne gave her to me (under God): my brother joined our hands. It was a most solemn season of love! Never had I more of the divine presence at the sacrament. . . .

A stranger, that intermeddleth not with our joy, said, "It looked more like a funeral than a wedding".

My brother seemed the happiest person among us.

(*Selected from The Journal of Charles Wesley*)

3 JOHN WESLEY'S FIRST DAY IN WALES, 15 OCTOBER, 1739:

$4\frac{1}{2}$ (i.e. rose 4.30 a.m.), Writ to Fish, on business; 7, at Mr. Deschamps', tea, conversed, many tarried, singing, prayer; 8, set out with Deschamps, Williams; 10, at the New Passage, wind high; 1, Chepstow; 2 set out, Devauden, Wr. Edwards's, singing, dinner, conversed; 3.45, upon the Green, I Cor. i, 30, 400 (i.e. no. in congregation); 5.30 at Mr. Nexey's; 5.45 Matt. v. 3, singing, etc; 7.45, conversed; 8.45, supper, conversed; 11.

(Wesley's Diary: from A. H. Williams: J. Wesley in Wales, p.1)

EXERCISES

THE following suggestions for exercises, based on the text, the illustrations and the extracts from contemporary documents, have in mind work not only for individuals but also for co-operative groups and classes as a whole. An attempt has been made to involve a variety of talents—imaginative description, map and chart making, drama, debate, illustration, etc.

Four approaches, it is assumed, can be employed with every chapter, namely

(a) keeping a cumulative time-chart, on an individual or class basis.

(b) compiling brief biographies of outstanding 'adventurers' as they occur in the several chapters. Many—e.g. Sir John Price—feature in more than one chapter, and compel the use of the Index and of *The Dictionary of Welsh Biography*,

(c) collecting illustrations for a scrap book.

(d) rewriting many of the original extracts in modern English.

The need to use local sources and materials wherever possible is, of course, imperative. The Index has been structured to help.

CHAPTER 2: THE MODERN PERIOD, RENAISSANCE AND REFORMATION

1. Find more about the early printing-press in (a) Europe (b) Britain.

2. You are a radio-announcer. Compile a news-bulletin on Luther's nailing his 95 theses to the door of Wittenberg church on 31 October, 1517. Include interviews with bystanders.

3. Using extract 4 on page 18, either imagine a conversation between Erasmus, Luther, Calvin and Loyola, all beginning 'I believe . . .', *or* debate your opinions about their declarations.

4. On a map of the world complete the routes of the voyages shown on page 4. Add those of Magellan and Drake.

CHAPTER 3: THE LAST MEDIEVALS

1. In four groups, find further material about Erasmus, Wolsey, More and Thomas Cromwell, and compile a paragraph on each for class reading.

2. Enquire if there is any new work of building or decoration in a local church ascribed to the period of *c.* 1450–1530. If so, pay a visit and attempt a pencil drawing of a part or the whole of it.

3. Draw a 'spoke' chart to show the chief factors in the decline of the medieval church in Wales.

4. Find information about the nearest monastery to your school. (Department of the Environment leaflets and county volumes of the Royal Commission on Ancient Monuments are two good sources).

CHAPTER 4: MAKERS OF MODERN WALES I: THE POLITICIANS

1. Describe dramatically *either* an incident in which Rowland Lee successfully pursues a band of cattle rustlers *or* the subsequent trial in court.

2. You are a Welsh gentleman of 1535. Write a letter to King Henry VIII setting out reasons why you wish him to unite Wales with England.

3. On the map on page 46 identify the areas which are in different counties since 1974; attempt to explain the changes. Find out how, if at all, the Acts of 1536, 1543 and 1972 affected your own county.

4. Complete the chart 'Tudor Policy in the Balance' on page 52.

CHAPTER 5: MAKERS OF MODERN WALES II: EARLY REFORMERS

1. Draw a 'step' chart to show the main events in the Reformation in England and Wales up to 1559 (Step down in Mary's reign).

2. List the Christian churches and chapels in your town or part of it, or, if you live in the country, within a radius of ten miles. Give their denomination (Anglican, Baptist, Catholic, etc.), their date of origin, and any fact of interest you can find about them.

3. Here's a table showing the state of Welsh monasteries at the dissolution.[1]

Order/Monastery[2]	No. of Houses	No. of Inmates	Net Income in 1535	When dissolved
			£	
Benedictine	8	23	487	1536–39
Cistercian	?	?	?	
Basingwerk		8	150	1535
Conway		8	162	1536
Cwm-hir		3	24	1536
Cymer		4	51	1536
Grace Dieu		2	19	1536
Llantarnam		6	71	1536
Margam		8	181	1536
Neath		8	130	1539
Strata Florida		8	118	1539
Strata Marcella		4	64	1536
Tintern		13	192	1536
Valle Crucis		7	188	1536
Whitland		5	135	1539
Others	12	53	867	1536–39
Nunneries	3	13	134	1536
Friaries	10	69		1538
Hospitallers	1	4	184	1540
	?	?	?	

First complete the totals (marked '?') for (a) the Cistercian monasteries: (b) all the religious houses. Then calculate which order had (1) the highest average number of inmates per house; (2) the highest average value per house.

4. You are a monk/nun whose monastery has recently been dissolved. Tell dramatically the story of what happened and what the future holds.

CHAPTER 6: THE PROGRESS OF THE REFORMATION

1. You are the boy who ran with Sir Roger Williams to catch the assassin in the extract on page 82. Describe the incident in a three-act drama: (a) In the palace, (b) In the garden, (c) In the torture-chamber.

[1] I am indebted to Professor Glanmor Williams for these statistics taken from his *Welsh Church from Conquest to Reformation*, Appendix B, pp. 559–661.

[2] For the sites of these monasteries see *The Defenders* pp. 20, 37 and 83.

2. Write one sentence on each of six of the places marked on the map of Europe on page 80. Use the Index to help you—some of the names figure in later chapters.

CHAPTER 7: THE PROTESTANTS

1. Make a chart entitled: 'Main steps in the making of the Welsh Bible'.

2. Mark on a suitable time-chart the life-spans of Bishop Richard Davies, William Salesbury and Bishop Morgan. Include major events (e.g. the Armada) below.

3. Describe the scene in a church where an old man/woman hears the Psalms in his/her native Welsh for the first time.

4. 'How I took my Bible to the Printers', by Bishop Morgan (Include a drover, a highwayman, the difficulties at the printers, the Armada scare).

CHAPTER 8: CATHOLICS AND PURITANS

1. Make a sketch-map of Wales showing the Catholic centres named in the chapter.

2. Write a dramatic story on one of the following titles:
   (a) What the fisher-boy of Rhiwledyn saw.
   (b) The Priest-hole of Plas Cilfach (an imaginary mansion).
   (c) The search of Plas-Du.

3. Compile a radio news-bulletin describing the death of Richard Gwyn.

4. Draw a pencil sketch of the Rhiwledyn cave as you picture it; add an imagined plan of the interior, marking probable items found there.

CHAPTER 9: ELIZABETHAN AND JACOBEAN ADVENTURERS

1. Read more about Sir Philip Sidney.

2. Write a three-act play entitled 'Brown Gold'.
   Act 1: (on deck) Waiting for the Spanish galleon.
   Act 2: (in the hold) No gold but tobacco.
   Act 3: (an inn in London) Smoking 'cigars' (illustration on page 120).

3. Compare Humphrey Llwyd's map (page 129) with a present-day map; list differences.

4. You are a radio commentator watching prominent people arriving for the Thanksgiving Service in St. Paul's Cathedral after the defeat of the Armada. Among them are Sir Roger Williams, Sir Thomas Morgan, Thomas Prys, Bishop Morgan, Gabriel Goodman. Describe each one and his achievement briefly . . . 'Ah, now here comes . . .', etc.

CHAPTER 10: SOCIETY AND POLITICS

1. Write a dialogue between an Elizabethan town boy/girl and a country boy/girl comparing their lives.

2. Make a model of an Elizabethan house in strip-wood and plasticine.

3. Describe three games played in Elizabethan times.

4. Draw a sketch-map of your town, or the nearest one, on the lines of Speed's map of Denbigh on page 131. Mark on it places of interest.

CHAPTER 11: MEN AT WORK

1. Find a map of the Drovers' Roads in Wales. Make an enlarged strip-map of the one nearest your home and mark on it the places, points of interest, etc. through which it passes.

2. Comment on the picture on page 152.

3. You are *either* a boy stowaway on a pirate vessel *or* a boy-apprentice at the Tintern wire-works. Describe a day in your life.

4. Make a model of *either* a horse-whimsy at a coal shaft *or* a water-wheel at a lead mine. (See pictures in William Rees: *Industry before the Industrial Revolution*).

CHAPTER 12: THE FIRST STUARTS

1. With the aid of the Index, gather up all references to the Council of Wales and the Marches and write a brief history, including a list of outstanding presidents.

2. Enquire more about Shakespeare and the Herberts.

3. Make a 'scales-diagram' (as on page 52) to weigh up the advantages of the two sides, King and Parliament, in the Civil War.

4. Hold a debate on the motion: That responsibility for the Civil War rests with Parliament rather than King.

CHAPTER 13: ADVENTURERS AT WAR

1. Dramatize any one of the original extracts on pages 198/9.

2. Use a 'spoke-chart' to summarize reasons for the defeat of the royalists in Wales.

3. You are beseiged *either* in Chester during the First War *or* in Pembroke during the Second. Describe the situation dramatically.

4. Write a newspaper report of the final session of the trial of Laugharne, Poyer and Powell.

CHAPTER 14: PURITANS IN POWER

1. Why was September 3rd a 'fateful date' in the career of Oliver Cromwell? Check from a general history.

2. List the facts that prove that 'Puritanism in Wales was an English import'.

3. On a map of Wales mark the places that feature in the growth of Puritanism. Write one sentence on the importance of each.

4. Find some verses from Vicar Prichard's *Cannwyll y Cymry* (The Welshman's Candle) and have them translated.

CHAPTER 15: THE AGE OF LOUIS XIV AND LOUIS XV

1. On a suitable time-chart show the wars of Louis XIV. Relate to them the significant events in Britain.

2. Draw a map of Europe in the Age of Louis XIV.

CHAPTER 16: CAVALIERS IN CONTROL

1. Make a time-strip of the ministries of Charles II.

2. Refer to *The Dictionary of Welsh Biography* for details of the six politicians mentioned on pages 227–8.

3. Dramatize any incident of persecution described in the text.

4. Find out more about (*a*) the places in North America to which Welshmen emigrated, (*b*) the Quakers, (*c*) the Lloyds of Dolobran and Birmingham.

CHAPTER 17: LIFE IN WALES 1688–1760

1. Write a story based on one of the following:

    (*a*) Lady Nithsdale rescues her husband.

    (*b*) Sir W. W. Wynn's wife burns his papers after the '45 or, at his death in 1749 (refer Cymmrodorion Transactions, 1948 and Welsh History Review 1962, vol. i, no. 3).

    (*c*) A burglar trapped behind the curtains of the library in a great house witnesses a meeting of either the Cycle of the White Rose or the Society of Sea Sergeants. Describe what he sees.

    (*d*) The custom among Welsh Jacobites of planting groves of Scotch firs near their mansions as a sign to Jacobite agents from the continent of their sympathy.

2. Make a map like Ogilby's of ten miles of main road near your home.

3. Construct a simple model of Humphrey Mackworth's tramroad at Neath. Fit your tubs with 'sails'.

4. Find more about Sir Henry Morgan and Black Barty Roberts.

CHAPTER 18: THE TEACHERS

1. How many of the Commonwealth, Trust and S.P.C.K. schools shown on the map on pages 278–9 can you identify from the lists on pages 288–90.

2. Make a map of your own showing the counties. Draw suitably on each county a small frame of four sections and write in the number of the four types of school in that county.

i.e.

COM.	TRUST
SPCK.	CIRC.

e.g. Pembrokeshire

2	16
31	164

3. Find the grammar-schools in Wales in 1760 and mark them on the above or a separate map. *Or* make a detailed map of the different types of schools in your own county.

4. Use a spoke-chart to summarize briefly the reasons for the success of the circulatory schools.

CHAPTER 19: THE PREACHERS

1. Account for the fact that Howell Harris for Wales and John Wesley for England are said to be the outstanding individuals of the eighteenth century.

2. Find six English hymns by William Williams. Copy two verses that appeal to you.

3. Charles Wesley was on at least one occasion accosted by a highwayman. Imagine the conversation that followed. Assume that Charles's Welsh wife Sally was riding behind him on his horse.

4. Look through either A. H. Williams: *John Wesley in Wales* or Gomer M. Roberts: *Selected Trevecka Letters* and copy two short extracts that strike you.

REFERENCES

THE period covered here is well documented, and the following is a select list only of the main available sources. For a complete catalogue the student will of course turn to:

A Bibliography of the History of Wales : Univ. of Wales Press, 1962 and Supplements 1963 and 1966.

A wealth of original material in both English and Welsh is now available in the series *Llygad y Ffynnon* (ed. Hugh Thomas) Univ. of Wales Press especially:

THOMAS, HUGH: *Cyfnod y Tuduriaid*, 1973.

THOMAS, HUGH: *Cyfnod y Rhyfel Cartref*, 1975.

BEDDOE, DEIRDRE: *Bywyd Cymdeithasol yng Nghymru yn yr Ail Ganrif ar Bymtheg*, 1975.

EVANS, MURIEL BOWEN: *Diwygiadau'r Ddeunawfed Ganrif*, 1972.

(A) GENERAL SURVEYS OF WELSH HISTORY

SOCIETY OF CYMMRODORION: *The Dictionary of Welsh Biography to 1940*, 1959. The essential work of reference.

WILLIAMS, DAVID: *A History of Modern Wales*, Murray, 1950. The standard general history of the period.

RODERICK, A. J. (ed.): *Wales through the Ages*, vol 2, Davies, 1960.

PARRY, THOMAS: *A History of Welsh Literature* (trans. H. Idris Bell) Oxford, 1955.

THOMAS, HUGH: *A History of Wales 1485-1660*, Univ. Wales Press, 1972.

THOMAS, Sir B. B.: *Braslun o Hanes Economaidd Cymru*, Univ. Wales Press, 1941.

(B) PARTICULAR TOPICS (in roughly chronological order)

JONES, R. BRINLEY: *The Old British Tongue*, Avalon Books, 1970.

WILLIAMS, GLANMOR: *Dadeni, Diwygiad a Diwylliant Cymru*, Univ. Wales Press, 1964.

WILLIAMS, GLANMOR: *The Welsh Church from Conquest to Reformation*, Univ. Wales Press, 1962.

CROSSLEY, F. H. & RIDGEWAY, M. H.: *Screens. Lofts and Stalls in Wales and Monmouthshire*, Archaeologia Cambrensis 1943-52, 1957.

LELAND, JOHN: *The Itinerary in Wales*, ed. L. T. Smith, London, 1906.

REES, WILLIAM: *The Union of England and Wales*, U.W.P., 1948.

EDWARDS, J. G.: *The Principality of Wales*, Caerns. Hist. Soc., 1969.

WILLIAMS, W. OGWEN: *Tudor Gwynedd*, Caerns. Hist. Soc., 1958.

REES, J. F.: *Tudor Policy in Wales*, Hist. Assoc., 1935.

PUGH, T. B.: *The Ending of the Middle Ages*, Glamorgan County History vol. III, Chapter XI, U.W.P., 1971.

WILLIAMS, GLANMOR: *Welsh Reformation Essays*, U.W.P., 1967.

SEABORNE, M. V. J.: *The Reformation in Wales*, S.P.C.K., 1952.

BOWEN, GERAINT (ed.): *Y Traddodiad Rhyddiaith*, Gwasg Gomer, 1970.

THOMAS, D. A.: *The Welsh Elizabethan Catholic Martyrs*, UWP., 1971.

JONES, EMYR G.: *Cymru a'r Hen Ffydd*, U.W.P., 1951.

GRUFFYDD, R. GERAINT: *Argraffwyr Cyntaf Cymru*, U.W.P., 1972.

WILLIAMS, DAVID: *John Penry; Three Treatises*, U.W.P., 1960.

WILLIAMS, E. R.: *Elizabethan Wales*, Welsh Outlook Press, (1924?).

EVANS, JOHN X.: *The Works of Sir Roger Williams*, Oxford, 1972.

OWEN, G. DYFNALLT: *Elizabethan Wales*, U.W.P., 1962.

JONES, R. GWYNDAF: *Richard Clough*, Trans. Denbs. Hist. Soc., 1970-73.

NORTH, F. J.: *The Map of Wales*, U.W.P., 1935.

NORTH, F. J.: *Humphrey Lhuyd's Maps*, U.W.P., 1937.

WILLIAMS, PENRY: *The Council in the Marches of Wales*, U.W.P., 1958.

BALLINGER, J.: *Katheryn of Berain*, Y Cymmrodor, 1929.

ROBERTS, ENID: *Priodasau Catrin o Ferain*, Trans. Denbs. Hist. Soc., 1971.

REES, WILLIAM: *Industry before the Industrial Revolution*, 2 vols., U.W.P., 1968.

DAVIES, D. J.: *The Economic History of South Wales to 1800*, U.W.P., 1933.

LEWIS, W. J.: *Lead Mining in Wales*, U.W.P., 1967.

DODD, A. H.: *The Pattern of Politics in Stuart Wales*, Trans. Cymmrodorion, 1948.

DODD, A. H.: *Studies in Stuart Wales*, U.W.P., 1952.

REES, J. F.: *Studies in Welsh History*, U.W.P., 1947.

PHILLIPS, J. R.: *The Civil War in Wales*, Longmans, 1878.

LEACH, A. L.: *The Civil War in Pembrokeshire*, London, 1937.

TUCKER, NORMAN: *North Wales in the Civil War*, Gee, 1958.

RICHARDS, THOMAS: *The Puritan Movement in Wales, to 1653*, Nat. Eist. Assoc. 1920.

RICHARDS, THOMAS: *Religious Developments in Wales (1654-1662)*, Nat. Eist. Assoc., 1923.

RICHARDS, THOMAS: *Wales under the Penal Code (1662-1687)*, Nat. Eist. Assoc., 1925.

RICHARDS, THOMAS: *Wales under the Indulgence (1672-1675)*, Nat. Eist. Assoc. 1928.

O'KEEFFE, M. C.: *Four Martyrs of South Wales and Monmouthshire*, Cardiff 1970.

DODD, A. H.: *The Character of Welsh Emigration to the United States*, U.W.P., 1953.

VAUGHAN, H. M.: *Welsh Jacobitism*, Trans. Cymmorodorion, 1920-21.

NICHOLAS, DAVID: *The Welsh Jacobites*, Trans. Cymmorodorion, 1948.

THOMAS, P. D. G.: *Jacobitism in Wales*, Welsh History Review, 1962.

OWEN, HUGH: *The Diary of William Bulkeley of Brynddu*, Trans. Ang. Antiq. Soc., 1931.

AYRTON, M. & SILCOCK, A.: *Wrought Iron and its Decorative Use* (Chap. on the Welsh smiths), Country Life, 1929.

JONES, M. G.: *The Charity School Movement in the Eighteenth Century*, Camb. Univ. Press, 1938.

CLEMENT, MARY: *The S.P.C.K. and Wales, 1669-1740*, London, 1954.

CAVENAGH, F. A.: *The Life and Work of Griffith Jones*, U.W.P., 1930.

KELLY, THOMAS: *Griffith Jones Llanddowror*, U.W.P., 1950.

WILLIAMS, GLANMOR: *Welsh Circulating Schools*, Church Quarterly Review, clxii, 1961.

JENKINS, R. T.: *Hanes Cymru yn y Ddeunawfed Ganrif*, U.W.P., 1928.

ROBERTS, GOMER M.: *Selected Trevecka Letters*, Calvinistic Methodist Bookroom, 1956.

ROBERTS, GOMER M.: *Hanes Methodistiaeth Galfinaidd Cymru*, vol. i, Calvanistic Methodist Bookroom, 1973

WILLIAMS, A. H.: *John Wesley in Wales*, U.W.P., 1971.

ROBERTS, GOMER M.: *Y Pêr Ganiedydd*, Gwasg Aberystwyth, 1949.

Useful short biographies are given in *Famous Welshmen* (University of Wales Press, Reprint 1974) and fuller biographies are to be found in the bilingual St. David's Day Series of the University of Wales Press, including:

THOMAS, ISAAC: *William Salesbury*, 1972.

JONES, J. LLOYD: *The Welsh Bible*, 1938.

WILLIAMS, SAMUEL: *John Penry*, 1956.

ROWLAND, WILLIAM: *Tomos Prys o Blas Iolyn*, 1964.

EMERY, F. V.: *Edward Lhuyd*, 1971.

JENKINS, R. T.: *Gruffydd Jones Llanddowror*, 1930.

JONES, J. GWILYM: *William Williams, Pantycelyn*, 1969.

GRUFFYDD, W. J.: *The Morris Brothers*, 1939.

WILLIAMS, W. D.: *Goronwy Owen*, 1951.

INDEX

As in the two previous books, the entries here have been made as full as possible in order to promote local studies. Place-names in Wales and the Border are followed, in brackets, with the county in which they occur. The old pre-1974 divisions are used in order to facilitate the locating of villages, houses, etc.

A number of general topics, mainly of a social and economic nature, are printed in heavy type to enable them to be picked out easily for project work, e.g. **Agriculture, Literature.** Certain items such as Anglican, Catholic, England, Europe, Nonconformist, and Protestant, occur too frequently in the text to be usefully indexed.

Abbreviations

Taff (R.) — River Taff
55—illustrated on p. 55.

Ang.	Anglesey	Mer.	Merioneth
Brecs.	Brecknockshire	Mons.	Monmouthshire
Cards.	Cardiganshire	Monts.	Montgomeryshire
Caerns.	Caernarfonshire	Pems.	Pembrokeshire
Carms.	Carmarthenshire	Rads.	Radnorshire
Denbs.	Denbighshire	Ches.	Cheshire
Flints.	Flintshire	Hers.	Herefordshire
Glam.	Glamorgan	Salop	Shropshire

Versailles, 216, 219.
Vikings, 14, 65.
Virginia, 174.
Virginia Coy., 125.
Voltaire, 219–20.
Vyrnwy (R.), 257.

Wallenstein, Albert von, 77–81, **78**.
Waller, William, 259–60.
Walpole, Sir Robert, 218, 220, 245–50.
Walsingham, Sir Francis, 85, 103–6.
Walter, Lucy, 223.
Ward, Luke, 161.
War of the League of Augsburg, 217.
War of Spanish Succession, 218.
Wars of the Roses, 19, 67, 149, 182.
Watford (Caerphilly, Glam.), 298.
Welch Piety (G. Jones), 286.
Welsh Language, 30, 40, 34, 54, 87–98, 115-6, 146, 205, 210, 237, 242, 275–81, 285–7.
Welsh Newton (Hers.), 236.
Welshpool (Monts.), 165, 169, 229, 237.
Welsh Tract, 242.
Welsh Trust, The, 269–80.
Wem (Salop), 186.
Wentworth, Thomas (Earl of Strafford), 177–8.
Wesley, John (1703-91), 220, 293–6, **295**, 298, 303–4.
Wesley, Charles (1707-1788), 220, 291–6, 303–4.
Wesleyan Methodists, 291, 298.
West Indies, 5, 115, 215, 218, 266.
Westminster, 47, 50–51, 92, 97, 167, 225, 245–6, 259.
Westminster (school), 145.
Westphalia, Peace of, 81, 216.
Whigs, 223–4 *et seq.*
White, Rawlins, (d. 1555) 69.
White Sea, 16.

Whitfield, George, (1714-70), 294–8.
Whitford, Richard (d. 1542?), 28–30, 37.
Whitgift, John (Archbishop), 97, 111, 113.
Whitland (Abbey) (Carms.), 35, 62.
Wiliam Llŷn, 115.
Wiliems, Thomas (1545?-1622?), 116, 139, 169.
Wilkinson (family, of Bersham, Denbs.), 258.
William of Orange ('the Silent') (d. 1584), 73–75, **74**, 82, 100, 105, 117–8, 217.
William III (of Orange, and England 1689-1702), 217–8, 228, 245, 248.
Williams, Henry (Ysgafell), 231.
Williams, John (1500?-1559) (Keeper of the Jewels to Henry VIII), 146.
Williams, John (Archbishop) (1582-1650), **172**, 173, 177–8, 182–3, 187–93, 197.
Williams, John (1584-1627?) (goldsmith), 146.
Williams, John (of Tremeirchion, Flints.), 101.
Williams, Moses, 263.
Williams, Richard, 122.
Williams, Sir Roger (c. 1537-95), 74, 82, 117–9, 133.
Williams, William (1634-1700,) 227–8.
Williams, William (Pantycelyn, 1716-91), 220, 253, 264–5, 291–3, 297, **299**, 300–3.
Williams-Wynn (family, of Wynnstay, Ruabon), 245.
Williams-Wynn, Sir Watkin (d. 1749) 246–7, **251**, 251–3, 267.
Willoughby, Sir Hugh, 16, 122.
Wilton (Wilts.), 139, 165.
Winchester (school), 145.
Wittenberg, 10.

Wogan, Col. Thomas, **198**, 198.
Wolsey, Thomas (Cardinal), 8, 25–6, 37–9.
Worcester, 183.
Worcester (Earl of), 49, 63–64, 134. *see* Somerset (family).
Worcestershire, 51, 86, 168.
Wren, Sir Christopher, 219.
Wrexham (Denbs.), 105, 111, 182, 186, 204, 207, 210, 212–3, 223, 248–50, 255–8.
Wright, Fortunatus, 266.
Wroth, William (1576-1641), 204.
Wybrnant (Penmachno, Caerns.), 96.
Wynn (family, of Gwydir, Caerns.), 135, 146, 155, 124, 173.
Wynn, John (Wyn) ap Maredudd (d. 1559), 166.
Wynn, Sir John (1553-1627), 95, 146–7, **160**, 166–7, 169–71, 180.

Wynn, Maurice (d. 1580), 96, 136, 147, 166.
Wynn, Sir Richard (d. 1649), 173.
Wynn, Edward, 257.
Wynne, Elis (1670-1734), 264, 280.

Y Dalar Hir (Caerns., battle), 195.
Yeomen of the Guard, 21.
Yn y Llyfr Hwn (Sir J. Price), **57**, 58, 67.
York, 86.
Young, Thomas (Archbishop) (1507-68), 58, 68, 86.
Young Pretender, 247–52, 267.
Y Ffydd Ddiffuant (C. Edwards), **276**.
Ysbyty Ifan (Denbs.), 135.

Zouche, Lord, 167.
Zutphen, 118.
Zwingli, Ulrich (1484-1531), 9, 12.